Other Books by Jack Harpster

Lumber Baron of the Comstock Lode – The Life and Times of Duane L. Bliss

The Curious Life of Nevada's LaVere Redfield: The Silver Dollar King

Captive! The Story of David Ogden and the Iroquois (With Ken Stalter)

King of the Slots: William "Si" Redd

The Railroad Tycoon Who Built Chicago: A Biography of William B. Ogden

100 Years in the Nevada Governor's Mansion

Helping Hands, Helping Hearts: The Story of Opportunity Village

John Ogden,
The Pilgrim (1609–1682)

John Ogden

The Pilgrim

(1609-1682)

A Man of More than Ordinary Mark

Jack Harpster

AHP
American History Press

Staunton Virginia

AHP

American History Press

Staunton, Virginia

(888) 521-1789

Visit us on the Internet at:

www.Americanhistorypress.com

ISBN 13: 978-1-939995-13-1

Library of Congress Control Number: 2015959011

Manufactured in the United States of America on acid-free paper.

This book meets all ANSI standards for archival quality.

Dedication

For Cathy

(1952 – 2015)

My wife, best friend, inspiration,

and fellow researcher

Contents

Illustrations

Preface

WHY A BOOK ON JOHN OGDEN?

John Ogden, the Pilgrim,* my great (8) grandfather, emigrated from England to the New World in late 1641. He died in East New Jersey, a colony he fathered, forty-one years later. In that span of time, he left a significant footprint in early colonial America.

With the exception of the Jamestown and Plymouth colonists, history has not been kind to our earliest colonial ancestors, those who arrived on these virgin shores in the early to mid-seventeenth century. Most Americans, indeed even many historians, know very little about the deeds of these earliest pioneers. But it is these men, men like John Ogden, who are the true fathers of our country, the ones who planted the first seeds of the freedom and democracy we enjoy today.

This book, and the research behind it, is not a genealogical study. However, it makes a significant contribution to the genealogy of one extended American family by debunking many commonly held beliefs about its root ancestor, his background, and forefathers. The Church of Jesus Christ of Latter Day Saints (LDS) genealogical collection in Salt Lake City, Utah, is massive, by far the largest in the world. Within their library they receive and electronically store data on more than eighty million names. The library does not vouch for the accuracy of the information they house. They are a repository only, and leave it to the user to decide what to believe and what to reject. I would posit the same warning for any of the genealogical information you find within

---

*The appellation "The Pilgrim" that is often appended to John Ogden's name in twentieth-century Ogden genealogies came originally from the Rev. Edwin Hatfield's 1868 *The History of Elizabeth, New Jersey.* In his panagyric to Ogden, he wrote: "And now 'Good Old John Ogden,' whose wandering for forty years had justly entitled him to rank with the 'Pilgrim Fathers,'. . . ." In all my readings, the next place I found the appellation is in the title of William Ogden Wheeler's book, *The Ogden Family in America* . . . , from whence, I believe, it has spread.

this book. It is accurate in every case, to the very best of my knowledge; but with the exceptions noted, I have made no attempt to personally verify it.

The foundation for much of our knowledge about John Ogden is a privately published 1907 book by William Ogden Wheeler, *The Ogden Family in America, Elizabethtown Branch, and Their English Ancestry: John Ogden, the Pilgrim and his Descendants, 1640–1906, Their History, Biography & Genealogy*. The extensive Ogden genealogy from this book is the basis for most present-day Ogden history and family trees. From December 7, 1641, the date Ogden was voted into the settlement of Rippowam (present-day Stamford, Connecticut) until his death in 1682, the information from those pages appears to be accurate. But copy on John Ogden's family history and genealogy prior to that date, including his birth and earliest years in England, is another story. It's based largely on fraud.

In his text, Wheeler says, "To discover the immediate family connection in England of John Ogden, of Elizabethtown, N.J., has long been a perplexing problem. The name appears on the parish records of several different localities in England, and all efforts to clearly trace these families to a common ancestor have failed."[1]

Wheeler died in 1900, seven years before his book was published. His sisters entrusted the work of finishing the book to Lawrence Van Alstyne of Sharon, Connecticut, and Charles Burr Ogden of Woodstown, New Jersey. Failing on their own to find the family connection in the British Isles, the two editors made an innocent but disastrous error: they hired a well-known genealogist, Gustave Anjou, to dig up the truth in England. That it was the two editors, not Wheeler, who hired Anjou is clearly stated in a publisher's offering letter written by the two men prior to the book's publication.[2]

Gustave Anjou (1863–1942) is well known in professional genealogy circles. He was born Gustaf Ludvig Ljungberg in Sweden, the illegitimate son of a writer of language and travel books. Prior to his emigration, he served a six-month prison term for forgery. In about 1890 he and his wife Anna, probably using forged documents, left Sweden for the United States. By this time, he had begun using his wife's maiden name, Anjou.

Beginning around 1900, he made his living inventing European pedigrees and their supporting documentation for wealthy American clients, who paid up to $9,000 for his "expertise." A dapper man with gray hair and a waxed gray mustache with turned up ends, Anjou was not a genealogist but a forger of genealogical records. His work, sold through his company, American Consumers Society of New York City, is estimated to have polluted over 300 surnames; and in the intervening years, this faulty information has been republished thousands of times over by unsuspecting family historians and genealogists.[3]

Milton Rubicam, an eminent member of the American Society of Genealogists and a founder of the Board of Genealogical Certification in Washington D.C., wrote of the Anjou fraud perpetuated on the Ogden name in a 1973 article in *The Connecticut Nutmegger:*

> He [Anjou] didn't make any fanciful claim—no royalty, no nobility, just good old English yeoman stock. He gave dates apparently derived from parish registers as far back as 1539. He cited deeds and other documents back to 1453. When I searched to find the exact location of this wealth of documentation, I hit a stone wall . . . I finally appealed to my friend, the late Charles Carroll Gardner, the noted expert on New Jersey families, for advice and assistance . . . he told me the whole thing was a pure and outright forgery. Bradley Plain does not exist now and did not exist at any time in the history of Hampshire. The parish records do not exist, nothing exists . . . the whole English lineage was made up by a clever forger . . .[4]

Wheeler's book also cites another source for Ogden's English genealogy, *Berry's Visitation of Hants, (1634).* This, I believe, was the source of the problem. So, what is a visitation?

During the sixteenth- and seventeenth-century reign of the Tudor and Stuart families in England, most of the country's wealth was in the hands of the nobility and gentry. If such a family died without heirs, the crown would attach the family's wealth. Even if there was an heir, the crown would collect a hefty fee, like an estate tax. So it was in the crown's best interest to keep track of family inheritances. To handle this task the king (or queen) had a corps of heralds, descendants of the olden knights-in-armor. Every so often, a herald would visit a village, and call in everyone who had a claim to nobility or gentry, instructing them to bring documents to prove their claim. The herald would record these documents as a family pedigree. The herald's visit was called a Visitation, and the resulting documentation a Visitation Pedigree. In theory, it was a good idea; but the people often falsified their records to avoid having to pay the levy, or they would bribe the herald to falsify his records. So depending solely upon this kind of genealogical information is fraught with peril.

The evidence supports that Wheeler discovered the Ogden (or Oakeden) Visitation of Hants pedigree during one of his research visits to England. After his death, the editors hired Anjou to verify the visitation findings, ensure that it represented the correct Ogden family line, and flesh out the family tree. Anjou was more than willing to help. He simply extended the known family back in time to tie into the record from the visitation pedigree. Then he invented a hometown—Bradley Plain in Hampshire—and some parish records and wills and deeds to document his work.

So it would seem that the visitation pedigree would at least give us a starting point for John Ogden's English lineage. Unfortunately, however, there exists no proof whatsoever that this Oakeden family (the name used in the visitation pedigree, and one of the older versions of the surname Ogden) is the same family line as John Ogden, the Pilgrim. It is but one of a number of Ogden lines that can be found throughout England, and to this day there seems to be no way to link them.

How then would I tell the story of John Ogden, the Pilgrim, when I knew nothing of his life prior to 1641? This was work that had to be accomplished in England. Since I did not have the expertise to conduct my own research "across the pond," I contacted an esteemed member of the United Kingdom's Independent Specialist Researchers Association to conduct the research for me. In Mrs. Kay Priestley I found the perfect person. She has been active in family history work since the early '60s; and has been a professional historical researcher for more than two decades. In addition to extensive experience, she has deep contacts within the research community. Perhaps most importantly, she was able to keep me focused on the correct way to get the job done, usually with a velvet glove, but occasionally with a hammer when necessary.

After six months of research, we were not able to identify with 100 percent certainty where and exactly when John Ogden was born, nor his ancestral line. There are Ogdens throughout the British Isles, and today, 400 years later, there is no way to tie them to a common ancestor. What I have developed, however,

through Mrs. Priestley's efforts, my own research, and information supplied by a number of serious Ogden genealogists, is the
most plausible theory on the ancestral strain of John Ogden, the
Pilgrim. This theory is not invented from thin air, but is based
upon a number of verifiable facts coupled with a common-sense
conclusion. I have 95 percent confidence that this theory is correct.

Ogden historians and genealogists have been misled with false
information about the America stem ancestor of this important
family line for the past one hundred years. Dozens, perhaps hundreds, of history books have incorrect information about John
Ogden; and literally thousands of Ogden family trees are polluted
as well. Given this background, I decided not to simply state my
own theory about John Ogden's roots, but to include as well information about the other two most likely locations from where
he might have descended, based upon our research.

In chapter 1 and the beginning of chapter 2, my theory will unfold. Then, let the reader decide. From that point on, the remainder of the book is based upon verifiable facts about the life and
times of John Ogden, the Pilgrim.

Finally, although the exact date of John Ogden's emigration to
America has not been discovered with certainty, he could not possibly have landed at Southampton in early 1640, as Wheeler indicates.[5] I'm sure that information was based on Anjou's falsified
report that Ogden sold his property in Bradley Plain on October
18, 1639. However, Southampton was not even settled until June
1640, by a group from Lynn in the Massachusetts Bay Colony.

Wheeler states that Ogden ". . . was granted, April 17, 1640,
the tract known as Shinnecock Hill, which adjoined Southampton
on the west;" and that ". . . he was a leader among the settlers in
founding the town."[6]

Both of these statements are wrong, according to Southampton
Town Records.

April 17, 1640, was indeed the date the Lynn settlers' deed to
Southampton from the Indians was recorded; but there is no
mention of John Ogden or Shinnecock Hill, nor is their a second
record on that day that indicates any Ogden purchase. The records with the names of all the Lynn founders are extant, but
John Ogden is not among them.

Finally, although John Ogden would become a leader in South-

ampton, that did not happen until the early 1650s when he first
moved there from Hempstead, Long Island.

I sincerely hope the foregoing information does not reflect
badly on William Ogden Wheeler's landmark genealogy book.
The man and his successors spend nearly a quarter-century and
a considerable amount of their own money researching and writing *The Ogden Family in America. . . .* Working with the tools
that were available over a hundred years ago, they did an incredi-
ble job of telling the story of this amazing man, John Ogden. For
Wheeler, there were few telephones to help search for information, no Internet to scour for leads, no e-mail for quick communication, few historical societies to hound for answers, no faxes or
computers or printers. Worse, there was a greatly diminished
supply of credible books to pore over for words of Ogden's deeds.

The con man Anjou's slippery ways were not even suspected
until seventy years or so later, so they had no reason to suspect
he was not the professional European genealogist he claimed to
be.

Each time I have debunked a commonly held myth about John
Ogden and his family, I have made a sincere effort to replace it
with accurate, verifiable information. Unfortunately, I have not
always been successful. The passage of so much time, plus the de-
terioration of many very early records, make many things about
this man unknown and unknowable. To the best of my knowledge, he left behind no letters or journals that might have shed a
little light on his character or his wanderings. Even the extant
colonial records of the day can be stingy in what they offer: often
damaged, occasionally missing entire pages, and sometimes even
undecipherable in their seventeenth-century English spelling
and vernacular.

As the author, I was faced with two choices because of this di-
lemma. First, I could simply begin the story on December 7, 1641,
the first verifiable record of John Ogden in America, and move it
forward. Or second, I could deduce certain things, based upon
solid facts I did know, and write that portion of the story as I *believe* it happened. In the end, I decided on the latter. To do otherwise would be to strip some of the illumination from the life of
this man. John Ogden *was* born in England; he *did* spend the first
thirty-two years of his life there; and he *did* sail across the ocean
to the New World. This cannot be denied, so I decided not to deny
it.

Still, this is not a work of fiction. In parts of chapters 1 and 2, where I have made conjectures, I've carefully identified them. When, in chapter 1, I discuss some "coming to America" activities, I clearly labeled them as representational only. All the facts in these pages are an accurate representation of time and place. I just cannot say with 100 percent certainty that John Ogden was in those places, and during those times, and doing those things. From Ogden's December 7, 1641, appearance in Rippowam, until his death in 1682, the story is based completely upon verifiable facts.

Nineteenth-century writer J. D'Israeli said, "The popular historian composes a plausible rather than an accurate tale." I know my tale is plausible, and I pray it is accurate as well.

So, why a book on John Ogden? My hopes for this story are threefold. First, that it will re-introduce John Ogden to history, and help secure his spot as an important early colonial American. Second, that it will instill a sense of pride in the descendants of all very early colonial Americans, most of whom have been abandoned on the scrap heap of American history. And finally, that it will provide a starting point for pruning the rotten roots from all those faulty Ogden genealogies.

—Jack Harpster

Acknowledgments

THREE GENTLEMEN, ONLY ONE OF WHOM I HAVE EVER HAD THE PLEA-
sure of meeting, were instrumental in helping me research the
life and times of John Ogden. These three men, who are undoubtedly very, very distant cousins of mine, are Oliver Ogden of Lan-
caster, Pennsylvania, Robert Ogden of Sunnyvale, California, and
Henry Ogden of Wichita Falls, Texas.

Oliver and Robert have extensive libraries on Ogden genealogy,
and local histories of places where the Ogdens resided in colonial
times. Oliver, like me, is a descendant of John Ogden, the Pilgrim; while Robert is descended from John Ogden of Rye. Each
of them generously and without hesitation made available to me
material from their collections that helped me paint an honest
and accurate portrait of John Ogden. Without their help, I don't
believe I could have written the book.

Henry Ogden is also a committed student of the Ogden line.
For twelve years, from 1979 through 1990, he was the progenitor
and editor of "The Ogden Newsletter," a quarterly genealogical
publication that dealt with all things Ogden. Over the years, and
from his hundreds of Ogden subscribers around the world, he
amassed an enviable cache of irreplaceable Ogden genealogical
material. When he learned of my project, he spent untold hours
copying appropriate pages from past newsletters, which he
shared generously with me.

Finally, the true inspiration for the book came from my
mother, Lurene Meyer Harpster, and my maternal grandmother,
Lubelle Ogden Meyer, through whom I trace my ancestry to John
Ogden. "Grandma Lu," as she was known to all of us, was well
aware of her distinguished ancestry. For fifty-nine years, until
her death in 1982, she was a proud and active member of the
Daughters of the American Revolution, through the Ogden line.

My mom too was very proud of the Ogden name, though I don't
believe she or Grandma Lu were aware of the historical importance of John Ogden, the Pilgrim. As a child, I recall asking my

17

dad about his family. A reticent man, his only response was, "They were a bunch of horse thieves!" Of course this statement only spurred my interest in his side of the family, while ignoring mom's more distinguished lineage. Thus, it wasn't until I retired in 2002 and began studying my roots that I discovered John Ogden for myself.

So Mom, this one's for you!

Introduction

DECEMBER 7, 1641, HAD BEEN A BITTERLY COLD DAY IN RIPPOWAM. FOR many of the men in the tiny settlement, it had been one of the coldest days of their entire lives. Their previous winters in other New World colonies, or in the mother country, had never reached such temperature extremes. It had snowed almost all day long, and as evening approached the temperature had dropped to a bone-chilling low. In each crude log hut strung around the common, the man of the family began to layer his clothing, piece upon piece, before going out into the bitter wind and snow to make the short trek to the meetinghouse. Each man knew it would be a long meeting as there was much community business to be considered in a village that had not even existed nine months earlier.

The first few men arrived at the heavy wooden door. They were unrecognizable with coarse woolen scarves wrapped tightly around their entire faces, only their eyes visible through narrow slits in the rough cloth. The meetinghouse sat in the middle of a clearing, only a few of the stumps from the recently felled trees tall enough to peek through the huge drifts of snow. At the edge of the clearing, the ice-caked branches on the naked trees sparkled in the moonlight like diamond tiaras. As the men listened, they could hear the sharp snaps and cracks as the branches bowed, then broke, under the weight.

The snow had already been shoveled away from the door, indicating somebody had arrived early. Chances were it was Rev. Richard Denton. As the minister and one of the town leaders, Denton also used the meetinghouse as his church, so he was usually the first one there.

As the men entered, they saw Rev. Denton in the front of the room, chatting amiably with one of the town's newcomers, a tall, sharp-featured man who had come to build the dam and gristmill. The men silently took their assigned seats on the roughly hewn benches that lined the middle and both side of the room. They watched the two men as they talked, each spoken word punctu-

19

ated by a small burst of frosty air. Finally the stranger walked to
the back of the room and took his seat.

A wooden table, coarsely made of tree limbs and planks, sat at
the front of the room, with five simple chairs behind it. A lantern
sat in the middle of the table and three others were strategically
hung from pegs in various spots throughout the room. The four
lanterns cast an eerie glow across the hard-packed dirt floor and
onto the faces of the men as they hunched over in their seats.

Soon the room began to fill as other men filed in. Most kept all
of their heavy coats and gloves on. The temperature in the room
was frigid. At least the mud-and-wattle that filled all the cracks
between the logs kept the icy wind out. After a little while, when
the door was closed for good and the room was full, body heat
would raise the temperature quite a few degrees, and many of the
men would shed their outer garments. They shifted around to
find comfortable positions on the hard benches, and muttered
tired greetings to one another. The chairs in the front filled, and
soon Rev. Denton rose to offer a short prayer before the town
meeting could begin.

Rippowam, or Toquams, as the Indians who had only recently
sold it to some New Haven investors called it, sat along the northern shore of an inlet of the ocean, today known as Long Island
Sound. Stamford, as the settlement would be renamed in 1643,
was toward the western end of the inlet, near the Dutch New Amsterdam settlement, and just across the inlet from Long Island. It
had been settled in the spring of that same year by a group of
twenty-nine men and their families from Wethersfield, seventy-
five long and dangerous miles north through the thickly wooded
forest, on the Connecticut River.

Most of these Wethersfield men had also known each other in
Watertown, near Boston, before heading for the Connecticut
River valley in 1635. For many of them, the friendships went
back even further, to their homes, farms, and parishes in England. These men knew deprivation and hardship; even in the
dim glow of the lanterns, it could be seen in the rugged, lined
faces of even the youngest among them.

Seated now in the front of the room were the men who had
been chosen as the leaders of Rippowam. Rev. Denton sat beside
his longtime friend, Matthew Mitchell, the wealthiest man in the
settlement. Both men had come to America at the same time from
their homes near Halifax in northern England. At least three of
the other men in the room had come from the same vicinity.

Oddly, two of the three bore the same name, Jonas Wood; but they were from different parishes and we don't know if they were related. The third man, the one who had earlier been exchanging pleasantries with Rev. Denton, sat quietly in the back row. He was not one of the original twenty-nine settlers, but had come some months later; so he was not a member of the inner group who had traveled together from Watertown to Wethersfield to Rippowan, always seeking a better life for themselves and their families. Tonight, the twenty-nine would vote on whether or not to accept this man, and the other twelve newcomers, into the village. If accepted, they would become freemen, official citizens of the town; and more importantly, they would be given land upon which to build their lives and their futures in America.

In addition to Denton and Mitchell, the honored seats in front were filled by Andrew Ward, Richard Crab, and Thurston Raynor. Raynor had also been elected constable at the October town meeting.

The election of new townsmen was just one of the important decisions that had to be reached. Two important town positions also had to be filled: fence viewers. Richard Gildersleeve and Robert Bates would be chosen for this important task. Building and maintaining strong fences was one of the most important jobs in the entire community. Fences controlled the livestock and kept it secure; protected the individual and communal planting fields and gardens from wild animals; and occasionally acted as a barrier to impede the progress of marauding Indians while the settlers could seek the shelter of the meetinghouse. Any man found neglectful in keeping up his fences would be fined.

By the time the meeting was over, all thirteen newcomers had been accepted. Each man was granted a house lot, and additional woodland acreage for his own planting and pasturing. Most received three acres for their house lot, but two were given ten acres: Thomas Armitage and the silent man at the rear of the meetinghouse, a man known to the settlers as John Ogden.

Ogden had arrived at the settlement with his wife Jane and young son John Jr. at some point after May 16, 1641, when the first settlers arrived from Wethersfield. They had arrived directly from their home in Lancashire County, England, following the rigors of a two-month ocean voyage. To most of the men in the settlement, John Ogden was a stranger when he arrived; but to a few, including two of the most influential leaders of the group, he was an old and trusted friend.

John Ogden,
The Pilgrim (1609–1682)

1

Coming to the New World

THE SURNAME OGDEN HAS A LONG HISTORY IN ENGLAND. THE MOST satisfactory treatment of the surname is by William Arthur in *An Etymological Dictionary of Family and Christian Names*: "*Ogden*. Local (Sax). From *ock*, oak-tree, and *den*, a valley; the oak vale, or shady valley."[1]

A *Dictionary of Surnames* agrees: "*Ogden*, English: habitation name for some minor place, probably the one in West Yorkshire, so called from . . . *OAK + Denu*, valley."[2] From *American Surnames*: "Names combining two or more different landscape features are quite common . . . many English names consist of a landscape word coupled with a word referring to a wood or clump of trees: *OGDEN* "oak valley."[3]

Getting more county-specific, *Surnames of Lancashire* (England) says, ". . . Ogden, a very widespread surname in parts of SE Lancashire over a long period, probably derives from one of two places so named in Salford Hundred;" and ". . . Ogden listed with several other common surnames of Rochdale which originate from local place names."[4]

When searching for the earliest Ogden surnames, we encounter a number of early variations of the name from which "Ogden" finally descended. These include Okton, Okeden, de Oketon (one who lived near a thickly wooded valley), de Hoghton, de Hoton, Oakden, and finally Ogden. The earliest date of the present spelling of the surname is circa 1500, while some the earlier spellings, especially Okeden, are found as late as 1738.

Surnames first began to appear in England in the thirteenth and fourteenth centuries, so it's a safe bet that the Ogden ancestral line predates the use of surnames.

✎

25

The Pennine Hills are an extensive range of hills in northern England that, in 1600, extended from the southern border of Scotland to Derbyshire. From north to south, they transverse or touch parts of the counties of Northumberland, Cumberland, Westmoreland, Durham, Lancashire, Yorkshire, and Derbyshire. The range is often referred to as the spine of England, reaching nearly 3,000 feet above sea level at its highest point.

Sheep farming is, and has been for centuries, the dominant land use. In 1965, the Pennine Way, a 250-mile footpath, was established along the length of the hills, making it a very popular destination for both serious and weekend hikers.

The Pennines form a good portion of the eastern edge of the county of Lancashire. In its southeastern corner was an area known as the Hundred of Salford. A "hundred" is an ancient administrative and judicial division of a county, perhaps originally containing one hundred parishes; but the term is now meaningless. Today, the area once known as the Hundred of Salford is part of Greater Manchester Metropolitan County.

In 1600, its largest town was Rochdale, originally called Recedham. It is one of very few of today's English industrial towns to be recorded in the Domesday Book of 1086, a book commissioned by William the Conqueror to record all the tax-liable units of settlements in England over which he had become master twenty years earlier. The town has ancient roots as a crossroads for trade; and in the thirteenth century was the hub of one of the largest parishes in the country. The medieval St. Chad's Parish Church still serves the city and surrounding countryside.

The Pennine foothills of Rochdale and nearby Oldham, in the Salford Hundred, is almost certainly the area where the family known as Ogden first lived. Then, as now, it was a gritty, rough land of craggy outcrops, vaulting meadowlands, and oak-studded valleys that might have produced a tough, resilient emigrant like John Ogden, the Pilgrim.

The terrain throughout the area is non-arable, stony soil that would have provided a wealth of raw materials for apprentice stonemasons like John and Richard Ogden. In the narrow valleys and clefts between the hills lie the oak trees that are featured so prominently in all Oketon/Ogden coats of arms. Tradition says that the hamlet of Ogden was once known for its fine, large oaks; but today they are smaller and stunted. On the rivers and streams rushing madly down the hillsides one can still see sturdily-built stone water mills, used for centuries to process and spin the fine wool that was a chief commodity of the Hundred of Salford. Also visible all around are drystone walls, those made by skilled masons without mortar, which have stood for hundreds of years.

In the first half of the seventeenth century, Lancashire would not have been considered the jewel of the English realm. It was among the poorest counties in the land. Although its southeastern Salford Hundred area, through its textile industry, was to become the cradle of the world's first industrial revolution, this growing industry was only in its infancy. Wool, linen, and recently cotton, had given rise to a growing home-based business of carding, spinning, and weaving textiles. These businesses augmented the stingy income of the small-scale pastoral farms that dotted the countryside. Most of the county, outside of Manchester and Liverpool, was decidedly rural.[5]

In a private written report, historical researcher Priestley wrote of the Ogdens of this area:

> In Lancashire, there is no shortage of candidates. I soon found that I had Ogdens everywhere I looked. When I examined the surname studies, I found that the earliest references to people called Ogden, albeit in some earlier spellings, were men of Lancashire. The origin of the name was probably one of two possible locations in South Eastern Lancashire.[6]

In *Lancashire Life* magazine we're asked, "Is Your Name Ogden? If so, it seems probable that your ancestors acquired their name from a township in the south east of Rochdale and spread across the southern part of the county. In 1296 Reginald de Ogden released his rights in Ogden to the monks of the Monk Bretton Priory."[7]

Both references are to a number of small villages or hamlets called Ogden, all of which were within a fifteen-mile radius of Rochdale, some in Lancashire and some just across the border in Yorkshire. All of the hamlets were in the hills, but only one remains today.

A nineteenth-century British gazetteer lists two hamlets called Ogden. One is four miles east of Rochdale in Lancashire; the other is five miles north of Halifax in Yorkshire. There are also three Ogden reservoirs in the immediate area. Drowning a village or hamlet by the same name in an earlier time could be the reason for the reservoirs to be called Ogden. So we have probably five hamlets within a small radius that were at one time named Ogden.[8]

Here's an important fact to remember. In our American experience, a town is often named after its founder. However, in England, when surnames were just beginning to come into usage, just the opposite was the case. The town name came first, often some descriptive name of its physical character or surroundings, and the earliest settlers would take their surname from the place where they lived. So a man moving into the village of Ogden would become Reginald de Ogden, or Reginald of the village of Ogden. Thus, there could be many unrelated families in the same village named "de Ogden." So if you're attempting to trace a family by its surname back to the thirteenth or fourteenth century, it's virtually impossible to tell which "de Ogden" is a particular family line.

Here is another indication of how ancient the name "Ogden" is in the Lancashire/Yorkshire area of the early 1600s. There are two large volumes printed in 1812 and 1818 called the Rotuli Hundredorum, which are transcripts of documents held in the Special Collection of Hundred Rolls at the National Archives in Kew. The original Hundred Rolls date from the thirteenth century, their aim "to distinguish Tenants holding in Desmesne or as Villeins, Bondmen, Cottagers & Freeholders." In other words, who owned the land, and what fees did they pay. Volume I contains details of all the counties at that time, and there are fifteen references to Okedon and Oketon in the county of Yorkshire. Of these references, two are to families—both headed by a man named Richard—that had sons named Richard and John. All four of the boys were born in the 1606 to 1614 time frame, although in both families the son Richard was born before the son John. In our John, the Pilgrim family, we believe John was born before Richard; but it's entirely possible that we derive that information from records invented by the genealogy con man Gustave Anjou.

It's doubtful that anything can be made of this information except to acknowledge the fact that Ogdens, in their earlier spellings, have been around in Lancashire/Yorkshire for a very, very long time.

The International Genealogical Index (IGI) is a worldwide index, organized by country, of more than 200 million names. It is maintained by the Church of Jesus Christ of Latter Day Saints (LDS) and can be accessed at no charge through their Web site at www.familysearch.org. For Lancashire, it contains parish records of births, christenings, and marriages. For portions of the seventeenth century alone, there are hundreds of Ogden names included, which gives one indication of the prevalence of the surname in the county.

When we searched IGI for a "John Ogden" born or christened in County Lancashire between the years 1605 and 1615, IGI returned eighty-nine possibilities. Narrowing the search to the years 1607 through 1611 returned fifty-three male possibilities. From this bewildering number of choices, I've shown just five as examples, any one of whom could be John Ogden, the Pilgrim:

14. John Ogden—Birth: about 1608 of Oldham, Lancashire, Eng.
31. John Ogden—Christening: about Dec.1609 of Rochdale, Lancashire, Eng.
35. John Ogden—Birth: about 1609 of Hollins, Oldham, Lancashire, Eng.
41. John Ogden—Birth: about 1610 of Rochdale, Lancashire, Eng.
49. John Ogden—Birth: about 1610 of Rochdale, Lancashire Eng.[9]

Unfortunately, none of these parish records—which are not in all cases complete—give us a John Ogden who we can conclusively identify as John Ogden, the Pilgrim. I searched thoroughly through two volumes of the reprinted parish records of Rochdale for the years 1597 through 1643; and again, although there were hundreds of Ogdens who appeared for christenings, weddings, and funerals, none could conclusively be identified as John Ogden, the Pilgrim, or a member of his immediate family.

Mrs. Priestley, in having a friend search the actual parish records of Rochdale and nearby Middleton, may have come closer. There they found two Ogden families that included both a John and a Richard in the correct time period. While neither family could positively be identified as our Ogden family, it did add more relevance to our searches in Lancashire.

From all the evidence I've seen, I favor this place above all others as having been the ancestral home of John Ogden, the Pilgrim. It is here, in the Pennine foothills of Lancashire and Yorkshire, where I believe he was born, and where his ancestral roots are.

In addition to the sheer number of Ogdens living in the area during the early seventeenth century, there is another convincing piece of evidence that points in this direction. Two men you will read of later in the book, who were very close friends with John Ogden in America, are Rev. Richard Denton and Matthew Mitchell. Both men were from Yorkshire, near Halifax, only a stone's thrown from Rochdale. Mitchell, another stonemason with whom Ogden built a dam and mill in Stamford in 1641, was from the village and parish of Southowram. He left Halifax and voyaged to Charlestown, near Boston, aboard the *James of Bristol* in June 1635, arriving on August 17th. Remarks about the final leg of his voyage, off the coast of New Hampshire, speak of the terrifying end to the journey:

> . . . having one hundred honest people of Yorkshire, being put into the Isles of Shoals, lost three anchors: and setting sail, no canvas nor ropes would hold, but she was driven within a cable's length of the rocks at Pascataquack, when suddenly the wind, coming to N. W., put them back to the Isle of Shoals, and, being there ready to strike upon the rocks, they let out a piece of their mainsail, and weathered the rocks.

Perhaps Mitchell should have read this near-disaster as an omen, and headed straight back to England. As we'll see in the next chapter, he was dogged with bad luck in America ever after the foreboding incident aboard ship.

Aboard the *James* with Mitchell were his wife and son, and Rev. Richard Mather and his family. Mather was the father of Increase Mather, and the grandfather of Cotton Mather, the most famous clergymen of early New England.[10]

Matthew Mitchell was about twenty years older than John Ogden, so it's probable he was also a friend of John's father. Because of their age difference, Mitchell may also have been the one who interested John and his brother Richard in following in his footsteps as stonemasons, perhaps even standing as their sponsor for the seven-year apprenticeship.

The Rev. Richard Denton and his family also traveled to America in 1635. Some sources say he traveled with Matthew Mitchell on the *James*; other sources do not list his ship. So we cannot be certain.

Richard Denton, it is said, was born in 1586, making him Og-

den's elder by twenty-five years. His activities were closely inter-
twined with those of John Ogden in a number of New World
settlements. He was apparently born in Warley, Yorkshire, about
a mile west of Halifax. He received his divinity degree from Cambridge University; and was minister first at Turton then at Bol-
ton, two small villages to the west of Rochdale. It appears he then
became the curate at Coley's Chapel in Halifax.[11] Denton's decision to emigrate was probably influenced, at least in part, by his
economic situation. Clergy wages in Lancashire during the mid-
to late-1630s were the lowest in England. The county has been
called a "last resort" for ministers unable to obtain better positions elsewhere. Denton and his family were of the parish of North-
owram at the time of their sailing.

All of these English towns, villages, and hamlets were within a
tight radius, and economically supported in part by the immense
stone quarries located nearby, quarries that John and Richard
Ogden and Matthew Mitchell would have depended upon for the
raw materials of their trade. A few of Mitchell and Denton's children were of the same age as John and Richard Ogden, and perhaps attended the same schools.

There would have been many opportunities for the three men
and their families to spend time together. In fact, one of the oldest roads crossing the Pennines runs from Halifax to Littlebor-
ough, which is just a stone's throw from Rochdale.

Villagers from far and near would gather at one of the market
towns to visit and shop. Only those towns anointed by the king
with a market charter could be a market town. Of the market at
Rochdale, I have read nothing. But Preston, about twenty-five
miles northwest, was probably not very different.

In Preston, the markets were held on Wednesday, Friday, and
Saturday. Local inhabitants were given exclusive access to the
stalls from 8 a.m. until 9 a.m. Hucksters, country people, and
strangers were kept at bay until their turn came at 9. The market
closed at 1 p.m. Almost anything could be had at the market:

Grain, butter, eggs, poultry, crockery, toys, fish, cheese, sweet-
breads, &c., were sold in the Market-place, and linen and flannel
goods in the north-eastern and north-western parts thereof, in cel-
lars. Vegetable sellers were in Cheapside, and people with fruit stood
at the north-west corner of the Market-place. The cattle market was
in Church Street; butchers had also their stalls on the south side of

that thoroughfare; and "under the church wall" the goose and pork market was held.[12]

The markets were always crowded, as market day was not only a chance to buy or sell, but also an event of supreme civic importance unto itself:

> The noise was tremendous as the market people shouted the price and merit of their wares above the din of rumbling carts, bellowing cattle, haggling, laughing, quarrelling and banter . . . coaches and wagons were driven along without regard to the convenience of pedestrians who were forced into doorways, splashed with mud or covered with dust.[13]

Like the markets, annual fairs too required a charter from the crown, and gave people from miles around a chance to gather together for commerce and companionship. Here too local farmers and craftsmen sold their wares to all comers. But unlike the market, where buying and selling was the main goal, the fairs stressed fun and frivolity. There were minstrel shows, ale tastings and favorite sports of the day: bearbaiting, bullbaiting, and cockfighting. A fair could last several days, and few of the men went home sober.[14]

English alehouses of the day were also very popular gathering places. Lancashire historian Walton called them, "the hub of a convivial, tolerant popular culture." They were the main focus for communal festivities as well; and the yeomen of the villages and towns, as well as some of the gentlemen class, gathered together regularly in their favorite spots.[15]

Finally, the parish churches provided a gathering spot. Almost all life, religious and secular, centered at the parish church. It could also be a place of refuge against storms and civil unrest, particularly suitable because of its thick walls and narrow windows.[16]

I believe the facts support that the Ogden, Mitchell, and Denton families were well acquainted in the towns and villages around the Pennine hills before any of them came to America. Certainly both the opportunity and their proximity was present.

Another Lancashire Ogden line, well known in Quaker genealogical circles, is the line of David Ogden, who came to the New World in 1682 with William Penn aboard the *Welcome*. With

Penn, he was among the founders of Pennsylvania. Of David Ogden's ancestry, we find:

> JOHN OGDEN, weaver, of Lancashire, England, had a son JONATHAN or DAVID, who was father of DAVID OGDEN of *ye goode ship Welcome*. That the latter's grandfather was given contracts for cloth by King Charles I for use in the royal army of England, shows that John Ogden was a man of means and prominence, as well as the fact that the indebtedness of the crown was so great it was partially discharged in granting to him of a coat of arms.[17]

There exists no proof of direct relationship between this branch of Ogdens and that of John Ogden, the Pilgrim, as far as can be ascertained.

In my collection of Ogden memorabilia is a small snippet of yellowing paper, two facing pages from an early nineteenth-century book called *The History of Oldham* by Edwin Butterworth. It includes a poem by an unknown author that offers a nostalgic picture of the barren hills that constitute the hamlet of Ogden. As I read it, I could sense John, the Pilgrim, in this place nearly 400 years ago.

> O'er these rugged hills I go,
> Beil and Roche I leave below,
> Ogden's Edge so dark I pass,
> Piles of peat, and wither'd grass,
> Thro' these rugged roads explore,
> Where man's voice is heard no more;
> Cawing fowl, and bleating sheep,
> Here incessant clamour keep;
> Nature in her undress here,
> Frolics wild, devoid of fear;
> Pass another step, and then,
> Buxom Dame, she smiles again,
> Lovelier still we must confess,
> Trim and fair, in neatest dress,
> Yes to her, *the palm we will*,
> When she laughs at *Denshaw* Vil.[18]

About 200 miles due south of the hamlet of Ogden, yet light years apart topographically, is the County of Hampshire, often referred to in its abbreviated form as Hants. With an extremely diversified landscape, Hants ranges from the busy waterfront city

MAP OF SEVENTEENTH-CENTURY ENGLAND
This 1600-era map indicates the three most likely areas for the ancestral home of John Ogden, the Pilgrim.

of Portsmouth to the famed cathedral city of Winchester; and from the enchanted little village of Wherwell with its thickly thatched, half-timbered cottages to the country's newest national park, the wooded wonderland of The New Forest.

The New Forest was once the sole domain of kings and nobility. Created by William the Conqueror in 1079 on the site of a spartan Saxon hunting ground, today its 93,000 acres of mixed woodland, open heaths, and grassy lawns welcomes everyone.

Lying on the western cusp of The New Forest is the town of Ringwood, through which River Avon slowly meanders seaward. Ringwood holds a weekly market in the center of town in the Market Place, a tradition that goes back more than 770 years when it first received its market charter. Just to the north, also enjoying its location on the fringe of New Forest, is Ellingham, part of the parish of Ellingham, Harbridge, and Ibsley.

Known as Adelingham in the eleventh century, the hamlet gained brief fame in the seventeenth century when Lady Alice Lisle, a contemporary of John Ogden, the Pilgrim, was beheaded for supposedly harboring fugitives from the Battle of Sedgemoor. Her husband, Lord Lisle, had earlier been assassinated for his role in the execution of King Charles I, an event that plummeted England into her twenty years of off-and-on civil strife. Lady Lisle is interred in the burying ground of the enchanting thirteenth-century St. Mary's and All Saints church.

"A Church without a village is rather rare," says Ralph Dutton, in his book, *Hampshire*, "but this is the case at Ellingham, where there is not so much as a hamlet to account for its presence. But there it stands, charmingly secluded at the end of a cul-de-sac near the entrance to Somerly Park."[19]

On the same grounds is the Ellingham Priory, cell of St. Sauveur-le-Vicomte Priory. Since the thirteenth century, the small priory has peacefully perched in a thicket of trees beside River Avon, beside the medieval church.

In the preface, I referred to the Okeden family pedigree from the Visitation of Hants in 1634. We now return to that document and its family pedigree of Okeden. The document itself is completely without dates as to the generations listed. However, another volume has added dates to that document. This volume is *The History of Antiquities of the County of Dorset,* published in 1868. (Ellingham is very close to the border of the County of Dorset to the west, so as we examine Ogden family history in this part of Hampshire, some of it spills over into the adjoining county, with Ogdens on both sides of the county line.)

Inside St. Mary's and All Saints Church, in the far northeast corner of the chancel, is a small brass plaque that reads, "Hic jacet Ricardus Puncheidon Cujus ane propitiertur dues. Amen." It recognizes Richard Punchardon who died in 1465, from whom the manor of Ellingham descended to the Okeden family.[20]

The Okeden pedigree begins with William Okeden of Ellingham, whose last will was dated 1517; and his wife Agnes, daughter and heir of John Hamlyn. William was also mentioned in the Visitation of Hants, 1531.[21] Bolstered by administrative and parish records of the area, we see that for well over a century the Okedens bought and sold, squabbled and inherited, until in the early seventeenth century a different Sir William Okeden sold the family's home, Ellingham Manor. Of particular interest in following these transactions are the Inquisitions Post Mortem (IPM), which are the official investigations of the estates of tenants-in-chief, who hold their land directly from the king. They are extant, original documents and can be examined at the National Archives at Kew.

This latest Sir William had three siblings, brothers Philip and John and sister Dorothy. All four were alive when the estate passed to Sir William in 1597 and were of an age that any of them could have been the parents of John Ogden, the Pilgrim. Unfortunately, as has often been the case, the parish records that would prove or disprove this fact are badly damaged. That, and the laxity of recording in some years, makes it clear that complete records of the births, marriages, and deaths in the Ellingham parish at the beginning of the seventeenth century simply do not exist.[22]

The third most likely prospect for the ancestral home of John Ogden is the County of Essex. Tucked neatly into the southeastern coast of England, Essex is encircled by five other counties, with the North Sea to her east coast. Only thirty miles to her southwest is Greater London, the hub of the British Isles and one of the world's great cities. Essex and the counties to her north are known as East Anglia.

Though not one of England's better-known towns, Chelmsford does have her own special appeal. It was the site where "the father of radio" Guglielmo Marconi opened the world's first wireless factory; and it is the home of the smallest cathedral in the entire country. The town was named for the River Chelmer that flows through it.

The East Anglia area is flat farmland, with wheat and barley crops dominating much of the landscape. There are few hills and little building stone, making the area somewhat unlikely for a seventeenth-century local lad to choose stonemasonry as a life's vocation. Pulitzer Prize-winning historian Sumner Chilton Powell wrote extensively of the East Anglican farmers in his book on early American colonizers in *Puritan Village:*

> . . . there were at least three distinct types of English experience in the seventeenth century which had molded these settlers: the open-field manorial village; the incorporated borough; and the enclosed-farm East Anglian village. All of these entities, of course, had some relation to the English parish, but there were many types of intricate social structure.[23]

During her work in Essex, Mrs. Priestley was able to uncover little of substance that assists in finding the ancestral home of John Ogden. Administrative records revealed nothing significant. Research in one book, which explores the relationships between the West Indies and Essex created by the sugar trade in the seventeenth century, reported a total absence of any emigration records for Essex people at the time. The author believes any records have been destroyed, or not properly preserved, due to the preoccupation and ravages of England's civil wars.[24]

The IGI, mentioned earlier, only offers nine entries for Ogden in Essex, and five of them refer to the bogus Bradley Plain. Originally, the IGI only contained data transcribed from the old bound parish registers, so it was an accurate tool. Then the international index, like the American surname index also maintained by the LDS church, began accepting submissions from everybody; so while it is still a valuable resource, much of the information tends to be inaccurate. It is best used to guide you to other primary sources, where the data may still be pristine.

The Rotuli Hundredorum transcriptions, mentioned in the discussion of Lancashire, also contain one listing for an "Octon" in Essex. He was Hugo, and lived about ten miles east of Chelmsford.

The information that pointed me toward Essex is perhaps the

most compelling; but like many leads, it offers as much riddle as result.

Charles Edward Banks (1854–1931) is one of the most eminent genealogical researchers and writers about the period of the Great Migration. His landmark book is *Topographical Dictionary of 2885 English Emigrants to New England, 1620–1650*. The book is comprised of records on nearly three thousand emigrants that lists their English homes, where they originally settled in New England, and in some cases the ship upon which they sailed. He gleaned the information during seven visits to England where he searched the records of nearly two thousand parishes, where information about leaving the country was gathered and stored. Unfortunately, the information is not specifically dated; we know only that the timeframe in which this information was recorded in the parish record was 1620–1650. This provides only a generalized idea of when the émigré left England, as it would have been sometime after his name was noted in the parish record.

The name "John Ogden" is included in Banks's book. It tells us that he was from Chelmsford parish, County of Essex; and that his intended place of settlement was Hartford.[25] Hartford was next door to Wethersfield on the Connecticut River, where both Matthew Mitchell and Daniel Denton lived prior to settling Stamford. As with all very early records, there is no guarantee that this John Ogden is John Ogden the Pilgrim; but he could have been.

❧

Lancashire. Hampshire. Essex. Three possibilities. It is of course impossible to completely eliminate all the other counties of England; in fact, the name Ogden has arisen during our research in a number of the other counties. But one of these three—with Lancashire easily atop the list—appears to be the most likely ancestral home of John Ogden.

❧

Author's Note: As the foregoing information indicates, we do not know with certainty where in England the Ogdens came from; nor from which port they sailed for the New World; nor what ship they sailed on; nor exactly where they landed in America. In a few instances that follow, I have referred directly to John Ogden and his family. But other than those referrals, the following brief account of life in England during the early seventeenth century, and the voyage to America aboard the Charter Oak, *is only representative of the average life and ocean crossing during the time. It is historically accurate in every way.*

To assist the reader in understanding the voyage itself, and what shipboard life was really like, I've interspersed several comments (in boldface) from a remarkable journal published in 1675 by John Josselyn, An Account of Two Voyages to New England Made During the Years 1638 and 1663. *All the other references used for the material in this chapter can be found in the endnotes.*

∝

Life was not easy in England in the early seventeenth century. Religious intolerance, suppression of rights, economic blight, and a host of other social, religious, and economic problems plagued all but the most privileged classes. During the seventeenth century, wages in England grew by two hundred percent; but the cost of living swelled by six hundred percent. Many people could not afford to support themselves and their families. This unrest caused many to dream of a better life.

The earliest impressions these people would have of the New World were usually muddled and erroneous bits of information. English fishermen had visited and written glowingly about the North American coast in the late sixteenth century. Then the establishment and then mysterious disappearance of the Roanoke settlement on the North Carolina coast in the mid-1580s excited the imagination of the English people.

Letters and journals drifting back to the homeland following the1609 Jamestown and 1620 Plymouth settlements fanned these early sparks of interest and enthusiasm. By this time publications became available, most of which reinforced the rosy impressions of a land ideal for exploration and settlement.

One of the major promoters of the New World was Captain John Smith. He had traveled to North America in 1614, and upon his returned published his enthusiastic *Description of New England* in 1616. He crisscrossed England on a promotional tour, giving away thousands of copies of his book that touted the new land with flowery phrases that would have done justice to his contemporary, William Shakespeare: ". . . What pleasure can be more . . . than to recreate themselves before their owne doore, in their owne boates upon the Sea, where man, women and child, with a small hooke and line, by angling, may take diverse sorts of excellent fish at their pleasures.''[26]

It's very possible that one of these books found its way into the hands of a young and impressionable John Ogden, who, like many of his countrymen, yearned for a better life. The promotional literature would have been especially encouraging for young Ogden. Stonemasons, like carpenters and other craftsmen, were highly sought after in the New World; their skills were desperately needed, and opportunities abounded for such craftsmen. Ogden had served a seven-year apprenticeship, beginning at age

A
DESCRIPTION
of *New England:*

OR

THE OBSERVATIONS, AND discoueries, of Captain *Iohn Smith* (Admirall of that Country) in the North of *America*, in the year *of our Lord* 1614: *with the successe of sixe Ships, that went the next yeare* 1615 *; and the* accidents befell him among the *French men of warre:*

With the proofe of the present benefit this Countrey affoords: whither this present yeare, 1616, *eight voluntary Ships are gone to make further tryall.*

At *LONDON* Printed by *Humfrey Lownes*, for *Robert Clerke*; and are to be fould at his houfe called the Lodge, in Chancery lane, ouer againft Lincolnes Inne. 1616.

John Smith's 1616 booklet, distributed throughout the British Isles, featured the first use of the term "New England" in print. In it, Smith, leader of the original Plymouth Plantation, encouraged his countrymen to emigrate to the New World.

fourteen, to become a journeyman stonemason; and he was probably looking for the best opportunity he could find.

Most of these early promotional writings spoke of New England, but that term was very unfocused. The average Englishman thought of New England as everything north of the Jamestown Colony, and Jamestown or Virginia as everything south of there. However, a pool of information was beginning to reach critical mass. Phrases like ". . . wholesome air and brimming larders" caught the attention and the imagination of a suppressed citizenry hungry for change.

"Communication was the seed as well as the spore of migration, and the Great Migration of the 1630s was the final fruit."[27]

One of the major factors in deciding to seek a new life overseas for many young Englishmen was the English Civil War. It was a devastating time. The country was torn in two. Those who supported King Charles I were known as Royalists, while those who opposed the king were called Parliamentarians or Roundheads. The conflict between the king and Parliament, and between the two factions within the citizenry, permeated the land. Many friends, and even families, were split apart and became bitter enemies.

The argument was not a simple one. It revolved around loyalty to one's king or to one's God; politics and religion became entwined. For many, the prospect of a new home in a new land, away from the hatred and strife, was very attractive.

Once an English family made the life-changing decision to try their luck in a distant wilderness, the hard work really began. Property had to be disposed of; any land the family may have been fortunate enough to purchase or inherit was the first to go, followed by most of their personal belongings. They kept only their clothing, tools, a few of their household goods, and their most treasured personal possessions, the things they could easily transport with them to the new home.

Then came the task of purchasing all the things they'd need to take along. Virginia Anderson, in *New England Generations . . . ,* quotes one traveler of the day, the Rev. Francis Higginson:

Before you come be carefull to be strongly instructed what things are fittest to bring with you for your more comfortable passage at sea, as also for your husbandry occasions when you come to the land. For when you are once parted with England you shall meete neither with taverns nor alehouse, nor butchers, nor grosers, nor apothecaries shops to helpp what things you need, in the midst of the great ocean nor when you are come to land here are yet neither markets nor fayres to buy what you want. Therefore be sure to furnish yourselves with things fitting to be had before you come.

Higginson went on to describe some specifics: "Victuals for a whole yeere for a man," which included eight bushels of meal, two bushels each of peas and oatmeal, two gallons of vinegar, one gallon each of oil and aquavitae and a firkin of butter. He also advised a variety of spices, such as sugar, pepper, cloves, mace, cinnamon, and nutmeg; dried fruit; and cheese and bacon.[28]

Once all the preparations had been made, it was just a matter of waiting. Families usually lived with relatives or with friends for their last few months in England, having sold off their home and most of their possessions. When the time neared, they would make the trip to the nearest port of debarkation, all their worldly possessions now looking very meager in a borrowed or rented ox-cart. The sights and sounds and smells of London, the busiest port, would not have gladdened the hearts of the rural people entering its confines:

... a city dirty, with ill-paved streets unlighted at night, no sidewalks, foul gutters, wooden houses ... with small windows from which slops and refuse were at any moment of the day or night liable to be emptied upon the heads of the passers by; petty little shops in which were beginning to be displayed the silks and luxuries of the continent; a city crowded and growing rapidly, subject to pestilence and liable to sweeping conflagrations.

The Thames had no bridges [except the London Bridge] . . . Southwark, where were most of the theatres, the bull-baitings, the bear-fighting, the public gardens, the residences of the hussies, and other amusements . . . the town swarmed with idlers, and with gallants . . . there was much lounging in apothecaries' shops to smoke tobacco, gossip and hear the news . . .[29]

The streets, many too narrow for the emigrants' heavily loaded oxcarts, were filled with garbage, and with human and animal waste. The smell was overwhelming. But even stronger was the omnipresence of smoke, whose eye-burning, throat-choking gray curtain overhung everything. Every house stayed warm, and cooked by burning wood or coal; and what passed for industry in seventeenth-century London—brewers, lime-burners, dyers, soap-boilers, and dozens of others fire-fueled businesses—added to the extreme discomfort that assaulted every one of the emigrants' senses.

The Thames, itself described as "a sour soup of filth and waste," snaked its way through the town, most of the buildings being north of the great river. As an emigrant family finally made their way to the docks, they would have gotten their first look at the ship that would take them to their new home. For landlocked people, these ships would have looked so small and frail, bobbing up and down in their moorage. The *Charter Oak* was among the many ships awaiting cargo and passengers.

The emigrants joined the queue waiting to meet with the king's searchers. The searchers administered the oath of allegiance to all the adults, and checked the approvals to travel they had been required to secure from their parishes. A cursory search was made of the goods they had carefully packed for the voyage. Most of the food they had brought along was intended to see them through the first year in the New World, so it would be packed away in the hold where it could not be accessed once on the ocean. They carefully separated the small bundles and chests that were to remain by their sides during the voyage, providing what small amount of necessities and creature comforts they might require. The emigrants watched as the remainder of their goods were hoisted from the oxcart and carried into the hold of the *Charter Oak*.

Finally, they joined the other travelers as they jostled their way up the gangplank to the deck of the ship. It was only a few hours later that they stood quietly on the deck, shoulder-to-shoulder with their new shipmates, and watched as the land of their birth, and the birth of their ancestors and of their ancestors' ancestors, disappeared slowly into the horizon.

୯୫

"Land ho!"

It was an exuberant shout from the crow's nest, and it reflected the crewman's personal excitement as much as his professional duty.

The trip had been long, and difficult, as most voyages from England to New England were in 1641. It was just over two months—sixty-three days to be exact—since the *Charter Oak* had left her home port of London on the Thames. The crew, many of them first-timers, was as excited about setting foot on solid, dry land as the passengers.

There were seventy passengers on board, not counting the unfortunate Mr. Taylor who had simply vanished from the ship three weeks earlier.

. . . a Servant of one of the passengers sickened of the small pox.
[and later] . . . the partie that was sick of the small pox now dyed, whom we buried at sea, tying a bullet (as the manner is) to his neck, and another to his leggs, turned him out at a Porthole, giving fire to a great Gun.[30]

It was a relatively small group compared to many that were making the trip on other, larger ships. The crew numbered twenty-three, including the master, Jonathan Chittenden, a thirty-two-year-old bachelor from Gloucester.

The seventy passengers who now crowded along the rail, craning to get a first look at their new home, were a mixed lot. It was not entirely a Puritan crowd, a disappointment to Captain Chittenden, because most Puritans had more material wealth, and extra rewards for a speedy and comfortable voyage were one of the perks of his job.

There were forty-five adults over sixteen years of age, and twenty-five children. At only two months old, little Rebecca Hosmer was the youngest passenger. At fifty-three, Edward Sparks was the oldest. The average age of all adult passengers was just over twenty-nine. In general terms, it was the younger men who made the difficult decision to uproot their families and try their luck in an unknown, faraway place.

The average head-of-household man to make the voyage was in his mid-thirties, which was about mid-career for men of the time. Most working families had to save for years just to make such a journey, so younger families, unless they were people of means, simply could not afford the voyage. A family of four would pay about twenty-five pounds for their passage and a nominal amount of goods, a very considerable sum in its day.

The passenger list included a number of craftsmen and tradesmen: four tanners (all from one family), three carpenters, and one each: tailor, baker, husbandman, linen weaver, plowrite, and butcher. There were two wealthy merchants on board too, with their families, and each had two house servants accompanying him. But crowded along the rail, elbowing for space, each man, woman, and child was equal. Each harbored similar hopes and fears, dreams and nightmares, about the decision they had made, and the future that awaited them.

One of the female passengers was the first to smell it . . . a slightly sweet fragrance that smelled of the ocean, but more strongly of pine and of spruce and of the fragrant aroma of the resinous balsam firs. It was the smell that many seventeenth-century diaries called "the sweet perfume" of the American forests. It was generally the first sensory perception most people would have of their new homeland.

For Captain Chittenden, still seated comfortably at his small desk in the great cabin, it was just another day at the office. He was reviewing the one-hundred-pound bond he had signed just prior to sailing, a bond that was posted as surety that he would ". . . observe, or cause to be observed, and put into execution . . ." the stated requirements.

The bond and its requirements were standard for all masters before they were allowed to leave an English port for a "foreign plantation." Their money would be returned if they saw to strict adherence of the requirements from all their passengers. The surety bond, in a nutshell, gives evidence of why so many people were leaving England:

1) Each and every person [including the crew] aboard the ship that shall blaspheme or profane the Holy name of God be severely punish't.

2) That they [the ship's masters] cause the Prayers contained in the Book of Common Prayers Establish't in the Church of England to be said daily at the usual hours for Morning & Evening Prayers & that they shall cause all Persons aboard their said Ships to be present at the same.

3) That they do not receive aboard or transport any Person that hath not certificate from the Officers of the Port where he is to imbarke that he hath taken both the Oathes of Allegiance & Supremacy.

4) That upon their return to this Kingdom they Certify to the Board the names of all such Persons as they shall transport together with their Proceedings in the Execuc'on of the aforesaid Articles . . . .

The *Charter Oak* was not Chittenden's first commission, but he considered it one of his best. At 102 feet long and twenty-three feet wide, she was a relatively small vessel for her day. But she was a sturdy ship, built of well-aged English oak, and she rode the water well.

She carried three masts and a full complement of sails, and was rated for 180 tons of cargo. Due to a series of unfortunate circumstances just prior to her departure, she was carrying neither cargo nor passengers to her full capacity. This was a setback for Chittenden and the *Charter Oak*'s owners; but a blessing for the seventy passengers, who would enjoy more personal space as a result.

The seventy passengers—seventy-one counting Mr. Taylor—made their home aft, in bunks and rude cabins, in an area known as "'tween decks." They were allowed to go on deck and enjoy the crisp, clean air only in fair weather. During rough seas and storms, which were plentiful in the spring, they had to stay below where it was safe and where they would not interfere with the crew's labors.

A few of the more well-to-do families were fortunate. They had one of the few smaller cabins, normally meant to hold eight passengers; but since the passenger load was less than anticipated, some smaller families had the space to themselves.

Shipboard life had quickly developed into a routine. The weather for the first few weeks out of London had been mild, so the passengers spent a lot of time on the deck.

Two mighty whales we now saw, the one spouted water through two great holes in her head into the Air a great height, and making a great noise with puffing and blowing . . . the other was further off, about a league from the Ship, fighting with the Sword-fish . . .[31]

The changing from day to night was the only thing that marked the passage of time for the passengers. The great cabin, the master, or captain's, quarters, was in the stern of the ship, and was off limits to all the passengers and most of the crew, unless invited. In the bow of the vessel, just aft of the forward mast, were the crews' living spaces. The passengers' 'tween decks living space was toward the middle of the ship just forward of the main mast, and it was on the main deck that they now sat or strolled, exchanging pleasantries.

A few of the children were huddled around the first mate, who had taken a few minutes to show them the quadrant and cross staff, instruments that measured the ship's north and south positions, or latitude. Navigational instruments were still crude, and the ship groped its way across the ocean, rather than following a set course.

The women took turns cooking food for their families on the brazier, set in a large box of sand in the middle of the deck to catch any wayward sparks. Today's hot meal would be a treat. When the passengers had to stay 'tween decks, there would be no hot food. At such times they subsisted on biscuits, salted meat, dried fish, hard cheese, a few pieces of dried fruit and perhaps a handful of dried beans and peas, all washed down with warm beer. Some of the food would become filled with maggots as the voyage progressed, but they soon learned to drop such food in a bucket of water and the maggots would rise to the top and could be discarded.

Here we had a good store of Flounders from the Fishermen now taken out of the Sea and living, which being readily gutted were fry'd while they were warm; me thoughts I had never tasted of a delicater Fish in all my life before.[32]

From the first day on, many of the passengers had no interest in eating anyway. Seasickness, even in calm waters, was normal for the many of the emigrants.

For private fresh provisions, you may carry with you (in case you, or any Yours should be sick at sea) Conserve of Roses, Clove-Gilliflowers, Wormwood, Green-Ginger, Burnt-Wine, English Spirits, Prunes to stew . . . to prevent or take Away Sea sickness, Conserve of Wormwood is very proper . . .[33]

There were no labors, nor activities save the prayer sessions, to keep the travelers busy; so time passed slowly. Occasionally *The Courage* would come into view, and all the passengers would line up along the rails and wave frantically, hoping for some sign in return that would prove that they were not alone on the vast ocean. *The Courage* was their sister ship on this voyage, but rarely seen as the two kept their distance from one another. Most

ships of the day crossed the ocean in small squadrons of two or
three vessels to provide safety backup for each other.

**In the afternoon one Martin Ivy a stripling, servant to Cap-
tain Cammock was whipt naked at the Cap-stern, with a Cat
with Nine tails, for filching 9 great Lemmons out of the . . .
Cabbin, which he eat rinds and all in less than an hours
time.**[34]

On the twenty-third day out, the weather changed. The North
Atlantic was known for its violent weather, and this year would
be no different. For the next month all the passengers would be
imprisoned in the tight 'tween decks living spaces, with nothing
to break the monotony of the rolling, pitching waves.

Rev. Francis Higginson colorfully described such a storm encountered during his 1629 voyage:

> . . . there arose a South wind, which encreases more and more, so that
> it seemed to us that are land men a sore & terrible storme; for the
> wind blew mightily, the rayne fell vehemently, the sea roared & the
> waves tossed us horribly; besides it was fearfull darke & the mariners
> maid was afraid; & noyse on the other side with their running here &
> there, lowd crying one to another to pull at this and that rope. The
> waves powred themselves over the shippe that the 2 boats were filled
> with water, that they were fayne to strike holes in the midst of them
> to let the water out. Yea by the violence of the waves the long boate
> coard which held it was broken, & it had like to have bene washed
> overboard, had not the mariners with much payne & daunger recov-
> ered the same.[35]

In the 'tween decks area there was almost no ventilation and
the only sanitary facilities were buckets. The air below deck grew
stale, fetid, and vitiated. Attempts to relieve the stench and to
drive out the stale air by opening the scuttles and hatches were
frustrated by the rush of seawater that soaked the bedding, the
clothing, and the bodies of the passengers.

Above them, gale force winds blew up and the sea rose until the
Charter Oak found herself in the middle of a series of fierce
storms. Under the strain of the foul weather, the ships would
groan, creak, and crack, adding to the near panic among the passengers. Knowing that some bad weather during the crossing was
inevitable, one Pilgrim had predicted to a friend that they would
all soon be "meat for ye fishes."

The One and Twentieth day, the wind S. by W. great Seas and Wind, in'd our courses, and tryed from 5 of the clock afternoon, till 4 in the morning, the night being very stormie and dark . . . the Eight and twentieth day, all this while a very great grown Sea and mighty winds.[36]

Just as the good weather had passed, so did the foul weather. About a week before reaching land, the voyagers dragged their wet bedding and belongings topside to dry them out. And finally, the big day was nigh. The captain, with his trained eye, was the first to see it: the water perceptively changed color, and bits of wood rode and bobbed on the waves.

. . . we Anchored in the Bay of Massachusetts before Boston . . . I went ashore . . . to Mr. Samuel Maverick (for my passage) the only hospitable man in all the Countrey, giving entertainment to all Comers, gratis.[37]

Soon, the joyous passengers saw the first sea birds high overhead and everyone knew they were close to their final destination. And then the final proof . . .

"Land ho!"

2

A New Home in the Wilderness

IT'S IMPORTANT TO UNDERSTAND THE TOPOGRAPHY AND THE INSTI-
tutions of New England and the middle colonies in the early
1640s, when the Ogdens arrived.

These were not the well-defined thirteen colonies from the mid-
to late-eighteenth-century Revolutionary period, nearly 150
years later, that we were taught about in school. Instead, these
early to mid-seventeenth-century colonies were struggling little
independent settlements, or ragged strings of small settlements
aligned with a nearby nucleus town that would provide religious
or politically founded oversight. To understand the concept of the
day, we can think of these settlements, or plantations[1] as they
were called, like today's towns or villages, while a colony was
more like today's state.

In what is today considered New England, there were already
a number of English plantations in various stages of development
by the early 1640s.

Present-day Maine was one of the first places to be settled, even
before Plymouth; but the brutal winters along the rugged coast
were too much and none of these communities endured into the
late 1640s. Vermont too remained unsettled by white men.

The genesis colony in present-day Massachusetts was the
Plymouth Colony, from 1620. Up the coast, north of Boston,
Salem had begun as the Dorchester Company, an English-
chartered group that had failed as a commercial farming and
fishing plantation planted in 1625. When the company pulled out,
many of the settlers remained. In 1629 the Massachusetts Bay
Colony was chartered by the crown; and the land it encompassed
included the Salem settlement as well. The Plymouth Colony
would remain independent of the Massachusetts Bay Colony
until England combined them in 1691.

Present-day Massachusetts was the most populous area of the

late 1630s, with eighteen individual settlements flourishing by
1638.

John Winthrop Sr. is considered the father of the Great Migration. During the ten-year period from 1630 to 1640, it is estimated that between ten and fifteen thousand English men,
women, and children made the voyage to New England. Winthrop's Puritans were a group of wealthy men who were challenging the Church of England for reform. When he obtained a royal
charter as the Massachusetts Bay Colony from King Charles I, he
and his group of dissenters and entrepreneurs lost little time in
bringing over a thousand of their number to the New World in
1630–31. Many of them settled on the Shawmut Peninsula, a spit
of land that featured three large hills. They called their settlement Boston. Unlike many other groups of early settlers, the Puritans were well financed and supplied, which ensured they would
get off to a running start.

Many from the remnants of the Dorchester Company had already claimed the best open meadowlands in the area, so the remaining Puritans scrambled inland in small groups, seeking
tillable soil for their plantations. Within three months, three to
four hundred families had scattered themselves around the bay,
principally along the Charles River, establishing the towns of
Charlestown and Watertown.

In present-day New Hampshire, a number of small isolated
fishing settlements had been established in the mid-1620s, and
they endured. By the 1640s the four plantations had aligned
themselves with the Massachusetts Bay Colony, until they
formed a separate colony in 1680.

Roger Williams was a Cambridge-educated minister who firmly
believed in religious freedom. He came to America in 1631, ministered in Salem and Plymouth, and was on the verge of being sent
back to England because of his differences with the Puritan
clergy. Instead, in 1634 he fled to present-day Rhode Island, purchased land from the Indians and established a settlement that
he called Providence, where all were free to follow their own religious consciences. He eventually obtained a royal charter for his
colony, which included three additional nearby plantations, in
1643.

The tillable lands nearest to the sea and the navigable rivers
filled quickly as the Great Migration picked up steam in 1632–33.
Already groups from the Massachusetts Bay Colony were begin-

ning to dream of the uncrowded lands to the south. In 1633 a group from Watertown received permission from Winthrop to try their luck, and established the first settlement in present-day Connecticut at Wethersfield in the rich Connecticut River valley. They were followed by a group from Cambridge, an outgrowth of the Watertown settlement. In June 1636, under John Winthrop Jr., they founded Hartford, which was to become the nucleus settlement in the Connecticut Colony. Windsor followed shortly thereafter, the three settlements becoming known as the River Towns.

Puritans settled on the coast of Connecticut, creating the beginnings of the New Haven Colony, which would eventually include a string of towns along the Connecticut coast and the northern coast of Long Island.

Throughout the aforementioned settlements and colonies in New England, the soil was generally thin and stony, with relatively little level land and long, hard winters. It was difficult for the early settlers to make a living from farming. Overcrowding only made it worse. For these reasons, New England colonists began to look south for new lands.

The area that was to become known as the middle colonies is made up of present-day New York, New Jersey, Pennsylvania, and Delaware. New Jersey would be founded in 1665 by John Ogden and others, while Pennsylvania would not accept its first white settlers until William Penn established his Quaker Colony in 1681. Today's Delaware was first settled in 1638 when Peter Minuet established the small colony of New Sweden, under Dutch sponsorship.

The Dutch had founded their New Netherland holdings about the same time as the English were founding Plymouth. These holdings, a commercially based enterprise of the Dutch West India Company, were vast. They stretched from Albany, New York, in the north to Delaware in the south, and encompassed parts of what are now New York, New Jersey, Pennsylvania, Maryland, Connecticut, and Delaware. Much of this land overlapped with lands that were to also be claimed by the English over the next forty years.

Peter Minuet, an early Dutch colonist and director general of the company, purchased the island of Manhattan for 60 guilders (about $24) in 1626 from the Native Americans. Interestingly, the island was not purchased for its own intrinsic value, but to provide a safeguard at the mouth of the Hudson River for the company's fur trading settlements upriver at Fort Orange and Beverwyck, now Albany. At the very southernmost tip of Manhattan Island, the Dutch constructed Fort Amsterdam, around which grew the town of New Amsterdam (now New York City) which would become the New World headquarters of their holdings.

By virtue of the establishment of Fort Amsterdam, the Dutch had to contend with two major Indian groups. The Iroquois Five Nations, including the fierce and powerful Mohawks, occupied the upper valleys of the Hudson. They were vital to the fur trade, as well as being dangerous, so the undermanned Dutch maintained a none-too-comfortable peace with this group. In the lower Hudson valley, including the land that was to become New Jersey, lived the Algonquian tribes, fewer in numbers, less hostile and less important to Dutch commercial interests. The Dutch

PETER MINUET BUYS MANHATTAN ISLAND
Peter Minuet, then Director General of the Dutch West India Company, buys Manhattan Island from the Indians in the summer of 1626. The purchase, one of history's greatest bargains, cost the company sixty guilders, about $24 in today's currency.

treatment of these tribes was inhumane at best, brutal at worst; and would have a far-reaching effect on colonization of those lands.

North Carolina came close to being the first permanent English colony in America with the planting of the Roanoke Island settlement, first in 1585 then again in 1587. In the second settlement, under the auspices of the Raleigh charter of 1584, ninety-four men, women, and children settled on the island, off the coast of North Carolina. Within three years, however, when a ship returned to supply them, the entire colony had vanished without a trace. It would be nearly a century before the English returned to that land; so in the early 1640s it was still a wilderness.

To the south, the Chesapeake colonies included Virginia and Maryland. The Maryland Colony was founded in 1634 by Lord Baltimore, with a royal charter in hand. His goals in founding the colony were twofold. First, he was motivated by the desire for profit; and second, he wanted to create a refuge for Roman Catholics who were being persecuted in Protestant England.

Finally, Jamestown, the first permanent English settlement in the New World, had been founded in 1609. King James I had granted a royal charter to a group of English entrepreneurs, the Virginia Company, to establish a satellite English settlement in the Chesapeake region of North America. Their Virginia Colony had gotten off to a rocky start, but the able leadership of Captain John Smith had saved the colony from going under.

The English would grow and prosper in this new land, while the Dutch would not. The difference between the two countries is what would ultimately decide who would prevail. The English people were hungry to leave their homeland where religious and economic freedoms were restricted; the Dutch people had the best of everything in their flourishing little country, and only a small handful of adventurers had the desire to relocate to a wilderness area thousands of miles away.

At this time in American history, there were only about twenty-five thousand Europeans stretched across the entire eastern seaboard.

With distances so great, and with so few white settlements along the way, travel was difficult and dangerous. Moving from one plantation to another, as many families did, including our Ogdens, was challenging. Colonists used navigable waterways whenever possible. Single-masted pinnaces or schooners were often used, as were canoes, barges, and rafts. The second choice would be horses or oxen, usually expensive and scarce, with which they could traverse well-worn Indian trails. The final choice, and the only one available to many early travelers, was to walk.

Politically, there were three types of colonies in early English and Dutch America: royal, proprietary, and corporate. In royal colonies, like the Massachusetts Bay Colony, the crown granted a charter and appointed a governor who ruled nearly absolutely in the king's name. In proprietary colonies, like New York following Dutch rule, the crown gave the land to one or more proprietors, generally friends of the royal court, who were permitted to rule as they saw fit. In corporate colonies, like New Netherland, it was the board of directors of a company that was given the land and allowed to rule it themselves.

One of the most important factors in establishing this new country was actually taking place thousands of miles away, back in the mother country. England was involved in her own civil wars from 1639 until 1660, and during that span they virtually ignored their foreign plantations. In fact, the impending war was one of the chief factors in enticing so many English yeomen to flee the country during the Great Migration period. Because of this absence of oversight, the colonies developed their own forms of government and their own social and religious institutions. Despite their freedom, however, they often clung tenaciously to all they had ever known: that the church was the foundation upon which the civil institutions were built. So though they may have dreamed of democracy, they were usually not capable of building the foundation of their town based upon democratic principles, simply because the concept was too alien to them.

When the crown was restored to power in 1660, and Oliver Cromwell's Protectorate dissolved, England began tightening its grip on its foreign plantations, including those in America. Of all the colonies affected by this change, none was more affected than New Jersey, which in its infancy straddled the two time periods of this epic upheaval. This fact would have a life-altering effect on John Ogden, who was to become the leading founder in establishing New Jersey.

❧

One final distinction should be made, a religious, not a geographic or political, one: the difference between Puritans and Pilgrims. The two groups had more similarities than differences.

Both groups were Protestant, primarily Congregationalists, followers of the stern Swiss theologian John Calvin. They believed that every person was predestined for either salvation or damnation, but that only God knew who fell into which group. Thus, every person must strive relentlessly against sin so as not to hurt his chances if he was one of the chosen. Naturally, each individual congregation of men fell somewhere on a scale from extreme belief to more tolerant belief in these principles.

The two groups had one more very important belief in common: that the Church of England was badly in need of reform. They felt the church needed to be further purified (thus, the name Puritans) from the lingering effects of its Catholic roots. Puritans wanted to completely purge the church of its elaborate rituals and structured hierarchy. Congregational churches, on the other hand, were self-governing bodies, answerable to no higher authority. It was from this belief that the differences between Puritans and Pilgrims sprung.

Puritans were mainly wealthy, well-educated Englishmen, often the leaders in their cities, towns, villages, and parishes. They wanted to remain as part of the English establishment, working for biblical reform in the Church of England from within. Even as they emigrated to the New World, they maintained their loyalty to the mother country. They saw, in their new colonies, a great purpose: to establish godly settlements in this new place and to reinforce the marriage of church and state.

Pilgrims, on the other hand, wanted to achieve reformation on a fast track, and without compromise. If it meant separation from the Church of England, or even from the mother country itself, that was an acceptable risk. While they continued to think of themselves as English, their emphasis was on their new political and spiritual identity. They especially emphasized individual righteousness before God.

※

No physical description of John Ogden exists, as far as I can tell. Looking at portraits of men in the earliest direct line of descent does offer a few clues. Abraham Ogden (1743–1798), Reverend Uzal Ogden (1744–1822), Nathaniel Ogden (?–1826), and Governor Aaron Ogden (1756–1839) are the four earliest I've seen. All four men shared two physical traits that may have also been present in John Ogden, the Pilgrim. Each man had a prominent or aqualine nose, and each had a high receding forehead, tending to partial baldness in the front. Though we don't know if John Ogden was tall or short, there can be no doubt that he was a hard, muscular man, owing to his primary vocation as a stonemason. One clue to his stature may come from a description of Gov. Aaron Ogden, who was said to be tall, broad-shouldered, and muscular. Whether or not you wish to form a mental picture of John the Pilgrim based upon this information is solely a personal decision.

From my numerous readings, I have formed a much stronger image of the character of the man, however: what kind of person he was. First and foremost, John Ogden was a good man, a man of strong moral character. He was a pious man, but not as rigorous in his beliefs as the extreme Puritans of the day. There are numerous accounts of his having taken the high road when confronted with moral choices, and I believe you'll recognize those instances as they occur.

He was also a conscientious leader. In most towns in which he lived—and in many of those he was an original founder, or patentee—he assumed leadership roles. These roles ranged from the most important—virtual Governor of the English colonies of New Jersey—to the most trivial—fence viewer, to watch for errant oxen in the town's pastures. If Ogden was asked to serve, he always acquiesced, regardless of the status of the job.

He was often appointed to lead delegations to work with the Indians with whom the settlers dealt. The Indians trusted him completely, a mark of the fairness he always sought to achieve in any dealing.

As the foregoing paragraphs indicate, he was also a superb leader of men. From the time of his arrival in this country, he was always looked up to as a man who could be believed and trusted, one who could be depended upon to act in the best interest of his community. His advice was often solicited, and his words usually heeded.

He was a hard worker, and one of America's first true entrepreneurs. By trade, he was a highly skilled stonemason; but he was also a real estate investor, owner of a commercial whaling enter-

PORTRAITS OF MALE DESCENDANTS
Portraits of Abraham Ogden (1743–1798) (above), Nathaniel Ogden (c.1750–1826), and Gov. Aaron Ogden (1756–1839), are the three oldest of which I am aware in the male line of descent from John Ogden, the Pilgrim. The three have some physical characteristics in common that may give clues as to what John Ogden looked like.

prise, a trader, and owner of a number of gristmills, which he built himself from the ground up. He also built and ran a sawmill, and established a tanyard and leatherworks business that endured in the family for nearly two hundred years.

That he was brave and resourceful is without question. Otherwise he would never have forsaken the home of his ancestors, regardless of how difficult the times may have seemed. He also showed a wandering spirit, one that not only brought him to this

Nathaniel Ogden

Aaron Ogden

country in the first place but also led him from one wilderness to another in search of a better life.

Finally, and perhaps most importantly from a historical perspective, John Ogden was a staunch defender of democracy. He was opposed to arbitrary government; and he often stood as the last man against foreign intervention into local affairs. He was a true patriot.

There is some confusion in many early colonial records because there were two John Ogdens living in America at the same time. Historians refer to the second Ogden as John Ogden of Rye, because he eventually took up residence at Rye, near the western end of Long Island Sound. However, since both men probably earned their appellations after they arrived in America, and as they were not normally used in early records, these appellations offer no help in distinguishing between the two men. Both men moved around a great deal, as was customary at the time; and both earned reputations as leaders of their communities. On occasion, they also lived in the same settlements at the same time. (For more on John Ogden of Rye, see chapter 9, "Ogden Family Notes.")

ℰ

In the spring of 1640, there was unrest in Wethersfield, in the Connecticut River valley. The town was split into two camps, with no sign of compromise by either side. There are no records of exactly what caused the schism, but it was undoubtedly something to do with the church. And it was contentious.

Already, a peace commission had been sent down from Hartford, and a church committee from faraway Watertown, to intervene and bring the two factions together. But harmony could not be restored.

The Wethersfield Church had only seven voting members. Four were on one side of the controversy, and three on the other. But to confuse the issue, the three represented the opinion of the majority of the entire community, while the four represented the minority.

As a peace measure, the majority of the voting members agreed to emigrate from the settlement with the minority of the community. And so, the accord was made; but a new decision loomed: where would they go?[2]

A string of English church settlements were just beginning to spring up along the coast of present-day Connecticut, on Long Island Sound. There was New Haven, the nucleus and "capital" of the Puritan New Haven Colony, Guilford, Milford, Stratford, Fairfield, and Norwalk.

In the summer of 1640, Captain Nathaniel Turner had set out to explore the coast in more detail. On July 1, on behalf of a group of men in New Haven, he bought most of the lands belonging to the Toquam and Shippen Indian tribes. Twenty acres were set aside within the purchase that were to remain the home of some of the Toquams. The Turner Purchase stretched eight miles from east to west, and sixteen miles inland. For the land, he agreed to immediately pay twelve glasses, twelve knives, and four coats. He further agreed to pay within a month an additional twelve each of coats, hoes, hatchets, glasses, and knives, four kettles, and four fathoms of white wampum. It was within this purchase that the settlement of Toquam, or Rippowan, would be planted.[3]

The Reverend Mr. Davenport from New Haven had visited Wethersfield to see if he could help mend the rift. His New Haven Colony, in its zeal to maintain an equal footing with the Hartford-based Connecticut Colony, had just concluded the Turner Purchase. Now he offered this new land to the separatists, and they gratefully accepted. On September 4, 1640, the General Court of New Haven formally ratified the agreement.[4] Thirty men, with their families, originally pledged to emigrate. The actual number to eventually make the move was twenty-nine. They agreed to raise one hundred bushels of corn, at three shillings the bushel, to be sent to New Haven toward the purchase of the plantation, which they decided to call Rippowam, after the Indian name for the river that ran through it.[5] The men also agreed to begin their settlement by May 16, 1641, and to have their families join them by November.

One final caveat that New Haven insisted upon was that the proposed new settlement should join New Haven "in the form of government" in the same manner as had been agreed upon by its earlier settlements.[6] This may have seemed like a small concession at the time; but it would ultimately lead many of the Rippowam founders to seek another home in the years to come.

So the twenty-nine men and their able-bodied sons bid goodbye to their wives and began the journey to their new home. Rippowan was about seventy-five miles southwest of Wethersfield, along the northern shore of Long Island Sound. To arrive at the place would take a number of days of dangerous travel. They could have traveled along well-worn Indian paths, or perhaps taken the Connecticut River due south to Fort Saybrook, at the mouth of the river on Long Island Sound, then west to Rippowam.

When they arrived, there was unanimous approval that the journey had been worthwhile. The virginal tract of land was beautiful. Much of it was rolling land descending to the sea, which allowed for harbors for their boats. There were three large rivers and a series of ridges and valleys with smaller streams within them, and the land was fertile for farming. The river estuaries and salt marshes were rich in herring, oysters, fish, and shellfish, and the salt meadows and numerous necks held cord grass and salt hay for the cattle. It was easy to overlook the area's shortcomings: rock-strewn land that would be difficult to clear; and the proximity to the Dutch of New Netherland, whose rough treatment of the local Indians would cause constant problems.

A little hill between two swamps was chosen as an ideal spot for the meetinghouse. It could be fortified to serve as protection against any unfriendly Indians. A nearby Indian trail would serve as the main road running east and west, and other roads were planned to go north and south, all ending at the meetinghouse. As was the English custom, a liberal amount of land was allocated for the meetinghouse, those lands known as the commons. Nearby would be located the burying grounds, and close at hand, the parsonage and land for its support.

The meetinghouse was square and low. Its posts were twelve feet high, and the thatched roof pointed, the four sides coming together about thirty feet above ground. There was only one entrance, with plain windows.

One of the roads led to the swift-flowing Rippowam River, a location that would serve well for the building of a dam and gristmill the town would require.

Level land was set aside for the communal pastures and the planting fields. House lots of one to two-and-a-half acres were laid out by two of the men, and the early arrivers began clearing land and building cabins for their families.

Housing in the earliest English settlements was crude. Simple shelters of the type built by the English peasant class prevailed in most settlements. Tree branches were used to frame a small one-room cabin, with wattle (walls of woven twigs) covered by daub, or mud. Thatched roofs had a hole to let out smoke from a stone hearth in the center of the earth floor. Sometimes such a cabin would have a mud-and-stick chimney.

In some cases, early dwellings were even cruder. Dugouts were made in banks or hillsides, with roofs and walls made of brush and sod.

Generally the first more permanent house in each community

STAMFORD TOWN RECORDS PAGE FRAGMENT

A page from the original Rippowam (Stamford) Town Records, 1641. These irreplaceable original records, which are now available in a modern-day transcribed form, are held in a vault in the City Clerk's office at the Stamford City Hall. Stamford is fortunate; the original records from many early settlements have been lost or destroyed.

would be the parsonage, built for the minister. Modeled after the half-timbered thatched-roof houses of England, walls were formed of heavy oak timbers and filled in with wattle-and-daub or sun-dried mud bricks. The following year, the settlers would also approve building, at community expense, a house for a man to be hired to head their defense against the Indians.

Once all the necessary building was done for the community's day-to-day living, the settlers would go back and improve their houses and outbuildings as time allowed. Exterior walls would be covered with weatherboards, thatched roofs would be replaced with wood shingles, and interior spaces would be refined and improved. Large stone fireplaces would be installed, with chimneys, and perhaps a sleeping loft built for larger families.

In Rippowam, spring and summer passed in hard work. An itinerant traveler and diarist, David DeVries, happened by and noted in his journal that there were ". . . Englishmen at the mouth of the Rippowam building houses."

Soon the men returned to Wethersfield to gather their families. The women had packed their few valuable possessions into chests and bundles—homemade clothes, essential bedding, spinning wheel parts, a few pots, kettles and skillets, and wooden ware. They also took along the tools of the men's various trades. A few animals would have made the trip as well—cows and horses, pigs, chickens, and sheep. Finally, any remaining supplies of food would be packed away with care, as were seeds for future crops.[7]

A list of the original thirty patentees, as reflected in the first town records of Stamford, does not include John Ogden. But in a town meeting held on December 7, 1641, an additional thirteen settlers were accepted into the community, including Ogden, who was granted a house lot and ten acres with woodlands:

> . . . and in town meeting, December 7th, was there granted, besides house lotts as the other men had, Tho. Armitag, ten acres; Jo. Ogden, ten acres; Wm. Mayd, five acres; and 3 acres woodland, in the fields now to be inclosed. . . .[8]

So Ogden arrived in Rippowam at some time during the seven-month period between May 16, 1641, when the first settlers arrived, and December 7, 1641, when he was voted into the community.

There are two possible explanations for Ogden's sudden appearance in Rippowam during the second half of 1641. In order to understand his movements in America, it's important to examine both possibilities.

The first possibility is that Ogden had arrived in America at some earlier time, and at some other place. Wheeler said he arrived in early 1640 in Southampton; but I explained in the preface why Southampton was impossible. Between my personal research, and the research of a contracted professional historical researcher in New England, we have been unable to turn up any reference to Ogden prior to December 1641, in any of the town records in Connecticut. Some, though by far not all, of the records of New York and Massachusetts were also searched, with the same result. We did not cover every town and village in the New World, but those where his appearance seemed likely. This included Hartford, Wethersfield, Windsor, Fairfield, and New Haven, Conn., Watertown, Mass. (where the Wethersfield people came from), and New Amsterdam.

Thousands of people came to the early colonies during the period, and only a small percentage of their names made it into the town records that existed then, or are extant today. Thus, absence of any town record notations of John Ogden does not positively mean he was not in any of those places.

There is another factor that suggests an earlier arrival. A few months after his appearance in Stamford—twelve months at most—John Ogden and his brother Richard received the contract to build the stone church in New Amsterdam, discussed more fully in the next chapter. This was a very sizable contract for its time. It seems unlikely on the surface that they would have been offered such a significant contract without a body of work in the colonies to recommend them, work that would have taken a longer amount of time to accomplish.

So, for these reasons, it is not impossible that John Ogden was in America somewhere prior to his appearance in Rippowam in the latter half of 1641. Not impossible, but I believe unlikely, which is the reason I think the weight of evidence supports the second possibility.

Two of the original twenty-nine men who, with their families traveled from Wethersfield and founded Rippowam, were Matthew Mitchell, a stonemason from the Pennine hill country of Yorkshire County; and Rev. Richard Denton, born in the same area, and the minister in a number of Lancashire villages. These are the same two men who came earlier to America, and were, I believe, friends of John Ogden in the small villages, market towns, and stone quarries around Rochdale.

Here's the scenario of Ogden's arrival in Rippowam as I believe it happened. All three Lancashire/Yorkshire men yearned for a better life, and were intrigued with the idea of coming to the New World. Mitchell and Denton were able to come first, both in 1635 and probably on the same ship, either through good fortune, expedient timing, or some other positive set of circumstances. Both men were considerably older than John Ogden, so perhaps it was just a matter of being in a better financial position. Ogden stayed behind and saved his money; and the others promised to stay in touch if a fortuitous opportunity presented itself.

Communication was slow, a letter taking perhaps three or four months to get from one to the other. But the two friends, and perhaps their wives, kept the Ogdens abreast of their new lives in America.

For Mitchell, the move from Yorkshire had proven to be a disaster. He had been dogged by misfortune ever since his arrival in America. He was, it is said, a man of some wealth and social standing, and of eminent character; and he was described as worthy, energetic, and able. But he was truly a "son of misfortune," as Wethersfield historian Sherman Adams called him. At Concord, Mass. he lost much property by fire. At Saybrook, at the mouth of the Connecticut River, he was often a target of the Indians. The Pequots killed his son-in-law by torture, a number of his farmhands, and most of his herd of cattle.[9]

In 1637, he sought peace by moving to Wethersfield. It was said that John Strickland ". . . assisted Mitchell, who was wealthy, in getting his cattle to Wethersfield."[10] But things still didn't work out. Mitchell seems to have incurred the wrath of the General Court when his fellow citizens elected him Town Recorder, to the displeasure of Clement Chaplin, the ruling elder of the Wethersfield church. It was this event that so embittered him that he joined the others in relocating to Rippowam after only two years. And even there, misfortune would follow. Once more his home, farm, and goods burned to the ground, and he was overtaken by a debilitating disease (described by Cotton Mather as "the Stone").[11]

Rev. Denton appears to have come directly to Wethersfield in 1635 when he first arrived in America, though he may have spent a little time in Watertown first. He did not suffer the same deprivations as Mitchell, and seemed reasonably content until the fight-of-faith struggle within the church.

Having made the decision to depart, the group of thirty Rippowam patentees, including Mitchell and Rev. Denton, began making plans for their new community. Vital to any new community was building a dam and gristmill, upon which the settlers depended for their food staples. Stamford historian E. B. Huntington says, "Probably the measures for doing this were taken before they left Wethersfield."[12] Early Wethersfield town records are not extant, so later historians have had to make educated guesses on some matters relating to the move. However, the trouble within the church had been brewing for quite a while, allowing plenty of time for Mitchell to have anticipated the move and contacted Ogden.

It was at this point, I believe, that Mitchell sent word back to John Ogden in Lancashire, telling him of the new settlement and offering him a piece of the Rippowam dam and mill contract. Ogden had been biding his time, waiting for just such an opportunity—and it seems to have come at just the right time.

The first of the English civil wars, the Bishops' War between the English and Scots, had ended just the prior year. Charles I and Parliament were still battling, and it appeared that another war could be on the horizon.

England in the early seventeenth century was more country than city, more rural than urban. Even today's largest cities—London excepted—had only a few thousand people. So the impact of war would be felt throughout the countryside, not just in the urban centers. As it would turn out, many areas in the north were not touched by the civil wars. Armies were not very large, and most of the "battles" were little more than small skirmishes. But these wars were more than just military struggles: they were political and religious struggles at their core.[13]

We cannot know for certain what John Ogden's political leanings were at the time. Judging from his later acts of dissent in the colonies, his loyalties, it can be guessed, may well have been with Oliver Cromwell and the parliamentarians. Lancashire itself, however, was a county traditionally loyal to the crown. So John Ogden could have been a young man in political conflict.

Religious pressures would certainly have been in play too. Lancashire was England's strongest bastion of Roman Catholic holdovers, and polarization between Catholic and Puritan was a fact of life in the county.

Civil war, political and religious schisms, economic hardship: how many reasons did a young man need to decide to seek a better life? For Ogden, the timing of Mitchell's letter was probably perfect. It would have taken only a short time for him and his wife to settle their remaining affairs, say goodbye to family and friends, and set out on their voyage to the New World.

Despite his run-ins with the Wethersfield church leaders, Mitchell certainly held enough power within the departing group to have arranged such a thing for Ogden. In a meeting held a few months before the move, the Rippowam patentees chose Mitchell and four others of their number as the provincial government for their new home in Rippowam. The following month, November 1641, they held a second election of men "to order town occasions;" and again Mitchell was selected.[14]

Since we know for a fact that Mitchell and Ogden were jointly awarded the dam contract, and probably part of the mill contract as well, it's impossible to believe that the two men, who lived only a stone's throw from each other in the Pennine foothills of England, would have happened into this shared contract a half-a-world away by a simple coincidence.

This also easily explains how John Ogden and his brother Richard could have received the sizable New Amsterdam contract after only a few months in America. I believe Mitchell was aware of that contract—perhaps had even been offered it himself—but recommended his friends for it. Mitchell certainly didn't need the money; and had been beaten down by bad fortune to the point he probably didn't want to extend himself as the New Amsterdam job would have required. The Rippowam job was much easier: he may even have agreed to work the job with Ogden just to ensure the Rippowam settlers that this unknown stonemason was well-qualified for the work.

The prior friendship between Ogden and the other two also explains how Ogden, not even an original Rippowam patentee, would have been granted upon his arrival one of the most sizable landholdings in the community. His ten-acre home lot, plus wooded area, placed him in the top twenty percent of all the fifty-nine landowners at the end of 1641.

Finally, there's the case of Richard Webb, who offers evidence of a nature contemporary to the time. In 1664, the Stamford gristmill was in need of repair. A man named Richard Webb had lived in the house next door for thirteen years, and he was offered ownership of the property in return for making the needed repairs. Three years later, the mill now in good working order, Webb certified in a court proceeding that John Ogden, the well-known builder, had had considerable expense in moving to Rippowam to build the dam and mill.[15]

"Considerable expense" certainly didn't mean moving from Wethersfield or Hartford to Rippowam in order to take on the task. But a move from Lancashire County, England, to Rippowam would easily qualify as a "considerable expense." I'm confident that is what he meant.

So, when you look at all the interconnecting evidence, this scenario proves two of my theories with a comfortable degree of certainty. First, it proves that these three men knew each other before coming to America; and second, since we know for certain that Mitchell and Denton hailed from the same Pennine foothills area, it's certain that Ogden too was from that place.

Let me summarize my theory: John Ogden left his ancestral home in Lancashire County England, in early to mid-1641, sailed with his wife Jane across the Atlantic Ocean, and landed at or near Rippowam on the coast of Connecticut two to three months later. There, a job awaited him, to help his old friend (perhaps earlier, a friend of his father) Matthew Mitchell build a dam and mill to serve the new plantation. His friend Rev. Richard Denton was also there, he too probably an earlier friend of John's father.

John's brother Richard also showed up at Rippowam, either at the same time or shortly thereafter, also from Lancashire. Mitchell had arranged for the two men to meet William Kieft, the governor of New Netherland. The three probably took a shallop belonging to Mitchell, crossed Long Island Sound, then went down today's East River to the tip of Manhattan Island, where they tied up their boat. Entering Fort Amsterdam, they went immediately to the home of Governor Kieft, and in so doing walked right past the empty lot that had been earmarked for the new church.

Mitchell may have known Kieft. Who talked, we'll never know. What persuasive words were used, I can't say. But when the three men left Governor Kieft's house, they must have left with the promise that John and Richard Ogden would build his church. And in May of the following year, a contract was signed by all the parties; and shortly thereafter, the first stone church in New Amsterdam was built by the Ogdens.

Weathersfield and Rippowam town records would have greatly aided in proving or disproving this theory. However, as Wethersfield historian Adams said, ". . . the Wethersfield records are even more faulty in this respect . . . indeed, the records of the votes . . . as well as of its church, are entirely lost, as to all transactions prior to 1648, and its land records only begin at 1640."[16] Likewise, Rippowam's (Stamford's) earliest records have been only partially preserved. These two facts leave present-day historians to depend heavily upon ancient town histories and plausible theories.

I believe the foregoing theory, or a variation of it, is how, why and when John Ogden arrived in the New World.

࿒

The actual building of the dam and mill, so important in placing John Ogden in America for historical purposes, probably took place during the fall of 1641. When we look at the construction itself, the history is a little cloudy. At a meeting in September 1641, an agreement was made with Ogden and Matthew Mitchell to build a dam over the swift-moving Rippowam, a job for which the town agreed to bear the charge. Samuel Swayne was hired to build, at a common charge, the frame and body of a mill, "the other parts [to be built] by those of the town who were fit to do such work."[17] Swayne was not one of the forty-two "accepted" freemen at the end of 1641, or one of the fifty-nine such men at the end of 1642; so I don't know where he might have come from.

On the other hand, while historian Majdalany also gives Ogden and Mitchell credit for building the dam, she says the two also built the gristmill ". . . under the direction of Samuel Swayne."[18]

Since the extant Stamford town records of this occurrence are partially damaged and difficult to read, I believe both versions are reporting the same thing: that Ogden and Mitchell built the dam, and worked with Samuel Swayne building the mill.

The work appears to have been completed sometime in the spring of 1642. But the mill was cursed. Soon after it was completed it was the victim of flood. Every homeowner had to pitch

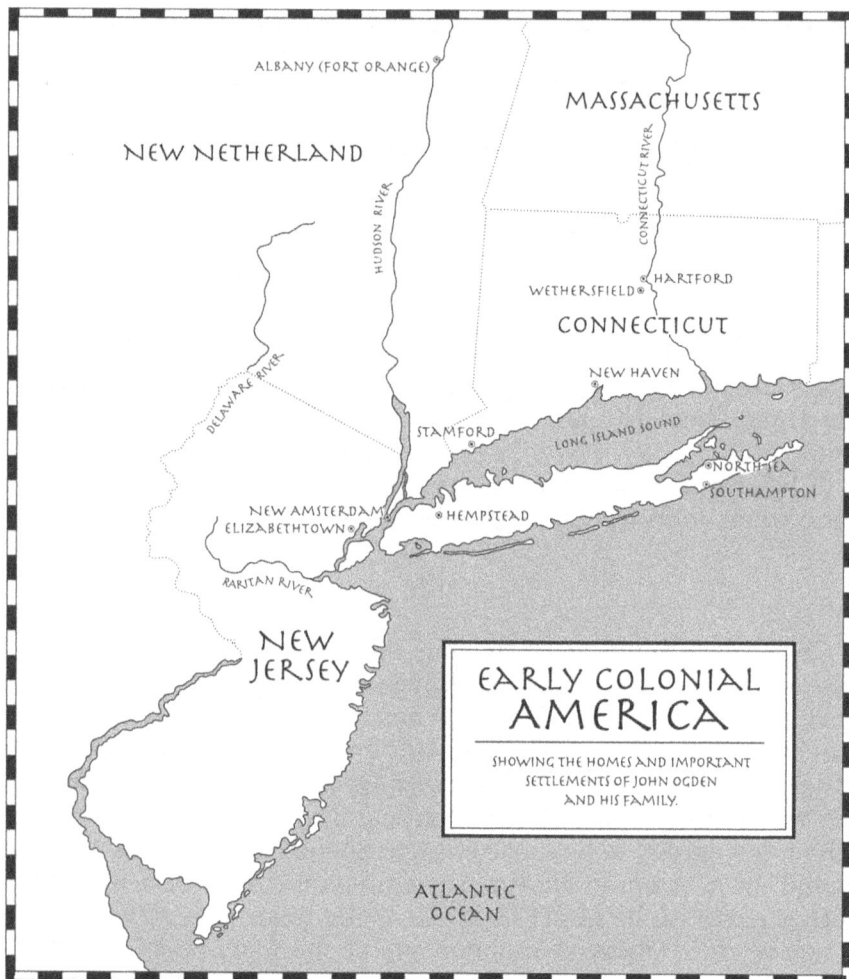

ALBANY (FORT ORANGE)

MASSACHUSETTS

NEW NETHERLAND

HUDSON RIVER

CONNECTICUT RIVER

HARTFORD
WETHERSFIELD

CONNECTICUT

NEW HAVEN

DELAWARE RIVER

STAMFORD

LONG ISLAND SOUND

NORTH SEA
SOUTHAMPTON

NEW AMSTERDAM
ELIZABETHTOWN

HEMPSTEAD

RARITAN RIVER

NEW
JERSEY

**EARLY COLONIAL
AMERICA**

SHOWING THE HOMES AND IMPORTANT
SETTLEMENTS OF JOHN OGDEN
AND HIS FAMILY.

ATLANTIC
OCEAN

MAP OF EARLY COLONIES
This partial look at some of the earliest American colonies indicates the settlements that John Ogden called home during his forty-one years in America. Also identified are a few other settlements that played an important role in his life.

in with hard-gained shillings to cover the expense of rebuilding, this time under the control of Thurston Raynor and Richard Law, who bought the concern from the town for seventy-four pounds and ten shillings.[19]

I believe Ogden did not participate in rebuilding the mill as it was about the same time that he received the substantial commission to build the stone church in New Amsterdam.

Other town business was also being planned and carried out at the same time. At the December 1641 town meeting, it was ordered that every man must fence his personal fields, and his share of the common fields, by April 1, 1642, or pay a fine for every unfenced portion.[20]

It was not long after settling of the town that trouble arose with the indigenous Indians. A constant watch was kept, and each man and boy capable of bearing arms was trained and reviewed. A barricade was built around the meetinghouse, a normal precautionary procedure in most early colonial settlements. The troops were put under the direction of Capt. John Underhill, a man with a checkered past who had gained some fame in the Pequot Wars in and around Wethersfield. Ultimately, this incident would come to nothing, but the settlement, like most of its day, learned to keep a wary eye on the Indians.[21]

Dangerous Indians were not the only problem facing the new plantation. Natural forces were at work too to thwart their progress. The winter and spring of 1641/42 was harsh. It would have been hard for colonial settlers under any circumstances; but Rippowam was a brand new plantation. Newly planted crops, upon which they depended for their sustenance, were just beginning to take hold; and most of the settlers were still living in the crude, temporary houses they had built upon their arrival. They simply would not have been ready for the rigors of an extremely harsh winter and springtime.

We learn of New England's hard winter and spring from John Winthrop Sr. (1588–1649). Winthrop was the leading founder of the Massachusetts Bay Colony, and its first governor. His journals provide much of the firsthand information we have about life in the early colonies:

> January 11, 1642: The frost was so great and continual this winter, that all the bay was frozen over . . . the snow likewise was very deep . . . it was frozen also to the sea so far as one could well discern. To the southward also the frost was as great and the snow as deep . . . [22]

Then three months later:

> April 14, 1642: The spring began early, and the weather was very mild, but the third and fourth month proved very wet and cold, so

that the low meadows were much spoiled, and at Connecticut they had such a flood as brake their bridges, and killed all their corn, and forced them to plant much of their Indian [corn] over.[23]

This flood, or freshet, is undoubtedly what caused the destruction of Rippowam's dam and mill in the spring of 1642, another hard blow for the struggling little settlement.

Finally, once again from John Winthrop, we see the effect of all this bad weather on the Rippowam settlers during the following year:

March 5, 1643: Corn was very scarce all over the country, so as by the end of the 2d month, many families in most towns had none to eat, but were forced to live of clams, muscles, cataos, dry fish, etc. The immediate cause of this scarcity were the cold and wet summer especially in the time of the first harvest; also the pigeons came in such flocks (above 10,000 in one flock) that beat down and eat up a very great quantity of all sorts of English grain . . . and . . . the mice also did much to spoil in orchards, eating off the bark at the bottom of fruit trees in the time of the snow, so as never had been known the like spoil in any former winter.[24]

The Ogdens' life in Rippowam, like that of all their neighbors, was not an easy one. It is impossible for us to understand today how alien this new land and this new life was for these early English settlers. They had new institutions, a new social order, new forms of government and new churches; and it was they themselves that designed this new life, with virtually no experience in doing such things. These townsmen had to change almost every formal institution they had previously taken for granted, as well as the very attitudes and values they held dear. It's as if men today founded a new plantation on the moon, being forced to make significant alterations in every facet of their lives.[25]

Pulitzer Prize-winning historian Sumner Chilton Powell threw new light on just how extensively these Pilgrims had rearranged and reinvented their lives from all they had known in England in writing about the formation of one New World village:

Gone were the court-barons, courts-leets, vestries, out-hundred courts, courts of election, courts of record, courts of the borough, courts of orders and decrees, courts of investigation, courts of ordination and views of frankpledge. In their place came meetings of men to order town affairs. . . .

Abolished too were the quarter sessions, justices of the peace, knights of the shire, king's sheriff, house of correction, Marshalsea payments, king's bench, assizes, Privy Council, and Parliament. The King and Queen were never mentioned. In their places were governors, magistrates, General Court, and town deputy.

Sudbury [in the Massachusetts Bay Colony] was no longer an ancient borough and had no mayor, bailiff, collector of rents of the assizes, chamberlain, chief constable, sergeants at mace, coroner, burgess, aldermen, market overseers, ale tasters, or master of the grammar school. No one met in the Town House or aspired to build paneled rooms for the "select fraternity" who governed the town. There were only selectmen, marshal, clerk and various townsmen doing various specific jobs as assigned by the town meeting.

Life . . . was indeed a "new" England.[26]

Early colonial settlements like Rippowam required that the people of the village support their town through both the payment of taxes and the expenditure of sweat equity. The taxes levied paid for support of the village and the church, while any major building project or defense funds needed were usually raised through a special assessment. When taxes were codified in the early 1640s they combined a "head" tax on every male over sixteen with a property tax. These taxes were recorded each year in a "Grand List," a practice that extended back to early English days.

The first grand list charge in Connecticut was levied in 1637 by the Colony of Connecticut to fund the Pequot War, payable in corn. Stamford's first charge came shortly after the first settlers arrived, to pay for the dam and mill (probably the second one). Tradition has it that the rate for that tax was five shillings an acre of land for the mill, and twelve shillings a home lot, plus five shillings an acre, for the dam.[27]

The "sweat tax" was another important principle of early colonial life. The men spent a great deal of time in community building and maintenance activities. Most New England towns included a significant amount of communal land. The village green, or commons, which was a familiar site in Revolutionary-era towns, was somewhat different in earlier times. It was often very large, fenced in, and used to hold the individual or communal cattle. There was also a large amount of group farming land, where the entire settlement would work together raising food for the common larder. Later on, many towns went to individually managed farms, but many hung stubbornly to the original New England group model. Ownership of the commons and the group farms was divided among all the freemen as town rights.

The men were also expected to arm themselves, at their own expense, and organize into militia bands to defend their town against marauding Indians. Of all the dangers faced by the settlers, the constant threat from the Indians would have been the most frightening. Before arriving in the New World, these people had never seen an Indian; now they were living almost next door to a group of people they considered savages. Two stories exemplify the worst of these fears.

The first is known as the legend of Laddin's Rock. Cornelius Laddin had moved into the Stamford area as a trader with his wife and daughter. He bartered knives, hatchets, and trinkets to the Indians in return for pelts. Often he and others of his kind would cheat the unsophisticated Indians.

One day a band of Indians determined to exterminate the small settlement where Laddin lived. It's possible this was the Stamford massacre of 1643, but we can't be sure. When the attack came, Laddin was working in his fields. He looked up and saw some of the cabins in flame, dropped his hoe and ran toward his cabin to protect his wife and daughter. His horse was tethered at the back of the cabin. He rushed in, barred the doors and windows, and grabbed his old flintlock rifle. One by one, the Indians approached his cabin, bearing flaming torches; but he beat back each charge by shooting them dead. Finally the Indians decided upon a group action, and charged his door, using a log as a battering ram. The situation became precarious. There were so many of them, and he was running low on ammunition. What could be done?

"Fly, husband, fly!" cried his wife. "They will certainly respect our sex," she said of herself and her daughter. After a moment's hesitation, Laddin bolted out the back door and jumped on his horse to bring assistance. At that moment, the front door burst open and the Indians rushed in. Down came their tomahawks with a sickening thud, and the two women lay dead on the floor. Then the Indians rushed out the back door, giving chase. Soon Laddin found himself at the edge of a rocky ledge, with nowhere to turn, the Indians in hot pursuit. After a moment's hesitation, he nudged the horse over the edge, and they were dashed to their deaths below. Thus ends the legend of Laddin's Rock.[28]

The second incident happened in 1643, soon after the Indian fighter Capt. Underhill had been hired to protect the town. A series of events in which the nearby Dutch had inflamed the Indians led to the hostility. More than 1,500 Indians from eleven tribes assembled, ready to attack any white—Dutch or English. Whenever the colonists were found in groups small enough to guarantee an easy victory the Indians sought their revenge.

In the middle of Stamford itself, one of the chiefs, Mayano, found himself in hand-to-hand combat with three Dutch visitors. When the dust settled, Mayano and two of the Dutchmen lay dead. This brought the peril right to the front doors of the settlers. Underhill and an expedition of 130 men set out to find the Indians' encampment and destroy it.

It was winter, and the small expedition was slowed by snow and cold. But finally they met the Indians nearby to today's small town of Bedford, and a fierce battle ensued. Attack and counterattack were employed by each side as the battle raged on; but eventually the bows and arrows were no match for the guns and swords, and the Indian village was burned to the ground. When the smoke cleared, hundreds of Indians were dead, while Underhill and his men suffered only minor casualties.

This was the last serious Indian threat along the western coast of Connecticut.[29]

⚙

For the women and small children of the village, their house and personal grounds were the focal point of their activities. Stamford historian Jeanne Majdalany provides an insightful look into where Jane Ogden and her smaller children would have spent much of their time in Stamford:

> Their first form of shelter was rather makeshift with only a single room, a clay-packed chimney, and probably a thatched roof. This gave way to a more permanent structure, built like those in Plymouth. It was still a single room with space above for a garret under the steeply pitched wood roof, but now a large chimney of stone took up most of one end. When possible, the house faced south for the warmth of the sun. Later still, a second room was added making the chimney a cen-

tral one able to heat both hall (kitchen) and parlor. Windows were primitive arrangements at first and very small; the central door, a strong one.[30]

It was while the Ogdens lived in Rippowam/Stamford that they had their second and probably their third child. Son David was born in the 1642/43 timeframe; and daughter Sarah around 1643/ 44.

Early in 1642, in the midst of their first terrible winter, the Puritans of Rippowam appealed to the New Haven colony for permission to change the name of their plantation. Perhaps they believed a new name would bring new good luck. New Haven Colonial Records of February 6, 1642, tell us "The plantation of Rippowams is named Stamforde."[31] It was named after a town in Lincolnshire, England.

On Sundays men, women, and children alike would put their chores aside. After six long and difficult days of hard labor, both body and soul needed replenishing. That was the job of the Reverend Mr. Richard Denton.

Denton was a small man, and blind in one eye. What he lacked in physical charm, he more than made up for in religious fervor. Cotton Mather, the most famous minister in New England during the seventeenth century, said of Denton, "Though he was a little man yet he had a great soul, his well accomplished mind in his lesser body was an Iliad in a nut shell." In the truest Puritan tradition, Denton not only ruled the church but also held great sway over the political events of the settlement.

The Sunday church outings lasted most of the day, and although it provided a respite from the hard physical labors of the week, spending long hours on the hard wooden benches in the bitter cold of winter must have been challenging. But then, Puritan life was meant to be about challenges.

At some time during John Ogden's tenure in Stamford, his brother Richard had arrived. He is mentioned in neither the 1641 or 1642 year-end landowner reports, so it's doubtful that he bought property.

Near Stamford was another Indian trail that ran from New Haven to New Amsterdam. It was probably on this trail that John and Richard Ogden would trek when they headed for New Amsterdam to build the church.

"SETTLERS OBSERVE THE SABBATH"
"Settlers Observe the Sabbath: Spring of 1642," from a mural painted by Stanley J. Rowland. The illustration depicts the meetinghouse at Rippowam, now Stamford. Note the stockade surrounding the plantation that provided protection from the Indians. Copyright, the Stamford Historical Society.

"SETTING THE BOUNDARIES"
In 1655 the boundaries of Stamford were finitely laid out for the first
time in an agreement between the Indians and the settlers. From a
mural painted by Stanley J. Rowland. Copyright, the Stamford Historical Society.

3

The Stone Church in the Fort

IN MAY 1642, DUTCH WEST INDIA COMPANY DIRECTOR GENERAL WIL-
liam Kieft drafted a contract for the construction of a stone
church in Fort Amsterdam. Rippowam settlers John Ogden and
his brother Richard, probably introduced to Kieft and vouched for
by their old friend Mathew Mitchell, signed to build the church.

Richard Ogden was less than a year younger than his brother,
having been born, it is said, on July 1, 1610. On August 21, 1639,
he married his wife Mary Hall, probably the daughter of David
Hall of Gloucester, England. It is supposed that Richard and
Mary came to America at the same time, and perhaps on the same
ship, as John and his family. Richard was also a stonemason.

Fort Amsterdam was at the extreme southwestern tip of Manhattan Island, well positioned to defend the natural harbor. It
had been part of the original site of the Dutch settlement in 1626.
By the early 1640s, the fort, though only a small part of the entire
New Amsterdam village, was still its nucleus.

From the time the first settlers had arrived, limited religious
services were conducted by "comforters of the sick," or laymen.
The earliest meetings were held in the loft above the Dutch colony's horse mill, which had been built by Sebastiaen Jansz to grind
bark used in tanning hides. The loft was furnished with a few
rough seats. It was located on what is now South William Street,
near Pearl.[1]

On April 7, 1628, the first ordained minister, Reverend Jonas
Michaelius, arrived. This date marks the founding of the oldest
Protestant body in America, part of the Dutch Reformed Church
and now known as the Collegiate Church. It is still an active congregation in New York City, nearly four hundred years later.

For five more years New Amsterdam residents continued to
meet in the loft room. Then a new minister arrived, Dominie Bogardus; and he wished for a more appropriate place for his flock

81

to worship. So, in 1633, during the directorship of Wouter Van Twiller, a plain wooden building was erected on a lane that is now Pearl Street, between Whitehall and Broad. Nearby, the town built a little parsonage for Bogardus, gable-end toward the street, with an elegant brass knocker brought from Holland.[2] But by 1642 the plain wooden edifice that was the church shared the fate common to all the public buildings erected during Van Twiller's administration: it was in such a state of dilapidation that it was considered nothing better than a "mean barn."[3]

It was this house of worship that John and Richard were hired to replace with a larger, more permanent structure.

Why Director General Kieft chose the Englishmen to build the church is open to speculation. Dutch brick makers and bricklayers were considered the best in Europe at the time, there were many of them present in New Netherland, and they already had kilns in operation for firing bricks. The countinghouse, the Company's five houses, the director general's house and the new city tavern were all built of brick. It was true that the Dutch builders were less accustomed to working in stone then the English; but their superior knowledge of the distinctive Dutch architecture, it would seem, would have given them an advantage. If early Dutch builders found the uncut stone a somber medium, they could always add a touch of color by using colorful brick gable-ends, or by using mosaics of brick or tile in the recesses of the window arches.

But whatever the reasons, the Ogdens received the substantial contract.

When John and Richard first arrived at the fort in New Amsterdam to begin their work, they couldn't have been overly impressed with what they saw. Father Isaac Jogues, a Jesuit priest that passed this way at about the same time said, "This fort . . . has four regular bastions, mounted with several pieces of artillery. All these bastions and the curtains were, in 1643, but mounds, most of which had crumbled away, so that one entered the fort on all sides. There were no ditches."[4]

Inside, they found a village that, like New York of today, was a melting pot. Dutch merchants and tradesmen rubbed elbows with English, Germans, French, Walloons (Belgians), Africans, and Scandinavians. There were only twelve to fifteen streets in the entire village, little more than dirt paths.

The small village was outwardly a replica of a European Dutch trading town. Curving streets were lined with quaint, gable-end houses, many of the gables notched like steps; open spaces were a colorful collection of gardens and small orchards, and canals ran through the heart of the town. The low skyline revealed a checkerboard of tile and thatched roofs, many different types of high gabled buildings, a picturesque windmill and a waterfront with busy wharves and slips and protecting batteries. And everywhere there was color. Bricks were blue, red, yellow, and black, and houses and shops were built with a rainbow of designs.[5]

Most of the Dutch houses—only a small percentage of the townspeople were actually of Dutch extraction—featured a large stoop out front. Here families would sit for hours and chat, the men smoking their long pipes, the women busy with knitting or sewing.

Despite all this, however, it would not be accurate to say the Ogdens found the place beautiful. In fact, it was quite the opposite, a real hardscrabble town. ". . . the fort was tumbledown . . . a gentleman's canal—in reality it was a stinking ditch. The lanes of the town were riotous with free-ranging pigs and chickens."[6]

Although the Dutch Reformed Church was the established religion, local officials were quite lenient with followers of other faiths. Dutch was also the official tongue, but the town was a real polyglot. Father Jogues would report that ". . . on the island of Manhate, and in its environs, there may well be four or five hundred men of different sects and nations: the Director General told me that there were men of eighteen different languages. . . ."[7]

The people of the village whom the Ogdens rubbed shoulders with—many were employees of the Dutch West India Company— were a mixed lot as well. To be sure, there were merchants and tradesmen, but there were also, as described by one unknown observer of the scene "footloose bachelors, down-and-out adventurers, fugitive husbands, runaway servants and waterfront riffraff." The women fared little better . . . "shockingly improper, lewd and exceedingly addicted to whoring."

In addition to the visual assault on the senses, the village also had its own sounds and smells. The waterfront was a cacophony of noises: the frantic wing flaps of seabirds, fighting for every morsel of food, the slap of oars on the water, the creaking and crackling of dozens of wooden ships as they bobbed in the harbor. In the town itself, tradesmen shouted noisy insults to one another, the sounds of construction and repairs filled the air, and the crowing, peeping, barking, oinking, and mewing of hundreds of loose animals created a discordant symphony of sound.

The air was redolent with enough foul odors to drive simple country folk back to their forests and streams. A stew of aromas challenged for dominance: boiling cabbage, frying pancakes, tubs of open grease, the excretion of the loose animals, and the miasma of the canals prevailed.

Director General Kieft had made an early effort to tame and improve the town, including his decision to build the church. Before church construction would begin, however, a great deal of old-fashioned politicking, mixed with a good measure of forced conviviality, would add much color to the story of one of America's first permanent churches.

The following information is originally taken from a small book with a very, very long Dutch title, published in 1655 in Holland. It was written by David De Vries, who spent his entire adult life as an adventurer, explorer, and patroon (one who was granted proprietary rights to large tracts of land in exchange for settling them with new colonizers), and translated by Henry C. Murphy in The Collections of the New York Historical Society.

By the early 1640s, when barely five hundred people called it home, De Vries was in New Amsterdam, where he dined often with Director General Kieft. On one such visit, Kieft introduced him to a fine new inn he had had built ". . . in order to accommodate the English who daily passed with their vessels from New England to Virginia, who might now lodge in the tavern."

According to De Vries, "I replied that it happened well for the travellers, but that there was a great want of a church, and that it was a scandal to us when the English passed there, and saw only a mean barn in which we preached; that the first thing which the English in New England built, after their dwellings, was a fine church, and we ought to do so too."

Kieft asked who would do the work, and De Vries answered, "The lovers of the Reformed Religion of whom there were enough," referring no doubt to volunteer labor that could be conscripted from within the community.

Worried about the cost of such a building, Kieft immediately put the arm on De Vries for a contribution of one hundred guilders, to which he added his own donation. Two other men, Jochem Kuyter and Jan Jansen Damen, were appointed, and the four became the churchwardens. Kuyter was chosen because he

DAVID DE VRIES PORTRAIT
David De Vries was an explorer, diarist, and patroon in early New
Netherland. It is from his "Diary of David De Vries" that we have
much of our contemporary description of the land and the important
events that shaped the day, including the building of the stone church
in Fort Amsterdam by John and Richard Ogden.

had ". . . good workmen who could quickly provide a good lot of timber." The largest contributor would be the Company itself; and the churchwardens were confident the remainder would be subscribed by the community.[8]

A propitious event provided Kieft with a golden opportunity. On June 29, 1642, the Rev. Bogardus was giving his stepdaughter in marriage, and Kieft saw the occasion of the wedding as a good opportunity to solicit funds.[9] As De Vries describes the event:

> So after the fourth or fifth round of drinking he set about the busi-ness, and he himself showing a liberal example let the wedding-guests subscribe what they were willing to give towards the church. All then with light heads subscribed largely, competing with one another; and although some well repented it when they recovered their senses, they were nevertheless compelled to pay—nothing could avail to pre-vent it.[10]

Financing secured, Kieft declared that the church would be built within the walls of the fort, which occupied only a small part of the village at the time . . . "to guard against any surprise by the savages."[11] There were many critics of the chosen location, who claimed that the "kerck" (church) would occupy a full one-fourth of the fort area and shut off the southeast wind from the gristmill upon which the settlers depended for the grinding of their corn.[12] It would be located, as described by one opponent of Kieft's chosen spot, "as suitably as a fifth wheel to a wagon." But the autocratic director general would ultimately have his way. The church was built in the southeast corner of the fort, facing south.

With the necessary funds collected or pledged, the work could begin. De Vries reported that the surrounding area "had excel-lent material therefor—namely: fine oak-wood, good mountain stone, and good lime burnt of oyster shells." So the raw materials would have been easy to collect.[13]

The Ogdens would have brought many of the tools of their trade with them from England: trowels and hods, heavy wooden mallets, iron hammers, wedges, levels, and finely honed chisels. The contract (complete translated version appears in the Appen-dix) called for the Ogdens to procure their own stone, and to bring it to shore near the fort at their own expense. To facilitate the transporting of the heavy raw materials to river's edge, the Ogdens were granted use of the Company's boats for up to six weeks. From there, the churchwardens were responsible for having it moved to the work site.

Quarrying the stone and moving it to the building site would have been backbreaking work, and the Ogdens probably enlisted some of the volunteer help for the chore. A team of oxen and a sturdy cart would have been drafted. Moving the stones, particularly the larger ones that would have been used for the below-ground foundation, was difficult. To get these stones to the oxcart, a pair of poles was laid side by side on the ground, and the large stone was rolled along by a number of men until it rested across the poles. Then two or more men would lift the poles and move the stone to the oxcart.

At the work site, the stones were stacked by size in an interlocking pattern so that the piles would not topple. The foundation stones could be misshapen, as long as they were flat top and bottom; but the stones for the walls had to be properly dressed to ensure a good fit and aesthetic beauty. It is not known if the Ogdens had skilled stonecutters available for this purpose, or if they had to do the chore themselves.

It was here at the work site where the Ogdens would have felt completely at home. These were the days before building plans were drawn by architects. Normally, a rough sketch would be provided by the person who had contracted the work. One man, most assuredly John, would be designated as the master builder. He would plan the design; and in addition to his own participation, he would also direct the other craftsmen in their work. It was also his job to calculate the amount of stone that would be required, to ensure that there was always an adequate supply of burned lime and sand for the mortar, and that the carpenters felled enough trees for all the necessary wood.

The Ogdens, like stonemasons for centuries before them, had a love of symmetry. The importance of proportion, the symbolism of various numbers, and the almost magical formulas for working out the correct width of a wall, the angle of a step, or curvature of an arch—these things captivated the brothers.

Root-two to one. This was one of the oldest formulas used by masons, dating to as early as 300 BC when the great mathematician Euclid wrote his groundbreaking book, *The Elements*. Root-two to one was the ratio of the outside width of a wall to the inside, thus giving the thickness of the wall at any point. If ignored, the wall would not be strong enough to support the roof.

Although John and Richard were probably not aware of it at the time, they were about to build one of the most substantial structures in the colonies. In spite of that, the job would probably have created mixed feelings for the brothers.

In truth, it was a house of God they would be building, and that fact in itself was reason for deep personal satisfaction. But as they prepared to begin, they could not have helped but think of what a modest place it would be in comparison to the churches of their boyhood. Even the simplest parish churches in the English countryside would have been places of beauty and simple grandeur. The few cathedrals they may have seen would have been buildings of soaring majesty and awe-inspiring beauty, pulling the eye heavenward with their loftiness.

Though John would have designed and engineered the building, he was given some strict guidelines. The design was to be faithful to Dutch traditions. English Gothic churches normally had one roof over the nave (central part) and chancel (clergy and choir space), with smaller roofs over the transepts, the lateral arms that lead off from the nave. This classic church design shaped the building like a giant Roman cross.

In Holland the churches more often consisted of two or more distinct sections lying side by side, each with its own roof. This fact would explain the double gable-end architecture of the stone church, indicating that there were two adjoining sections.

As the work began, the work site would have been littered with stone, wooden beams, shallow wooden troughs of mortar, and scaffolding hewn from nearby trees and tied together with rope. Supplies would have been carted from place to place in crude wooden wheelbarrows. Since the Ogdens had to ". . . at their own charge pay for the masonry" they would have hired some local men—Englishmen if they were available—to do much of the heavy lifting and carrying. A blacksmith in the town would be placed on call to keep the various tools sharp and in good working order.

Once the work began, the walls of the church went up quickly, laid up with stone. This was the most skilled of the work, and John and Richard would have done this themselves. Each time a stone was brought to one of them, he would first use an instrument shaped like the letter "L" to check that the edges of the stone were square. Then he shoveled a layer of mortar on the wall, furrowed it with the point of a trowel, put the new stone on, and scraped off the excess mortar. A taut string stretched along the length of the wall ensured it was straight. Once the new stone was tapped down, it had to be accurately leveled in each direction. For this, there was an iron triangle with a leather thong attached to its apex and markings on its base. A heavy pointed weight was tied to the end of the thong, making it hang straight down. The level would be placed atop the stone, first lengthwise then cross-wise, and adjustments made as necessary.

For windows and doorways (early drawings show four to six windows in the front, but this could be representational only), arches had to be carefully calculated and laid up on a "falsework" to ensure a perfect fit. The falsework was a wooden arch atop which the stones would be placed. The final piece to be placed was the keystone, a wedge-shaped stone at the top that locks the pieces together and carries all the weight. Then the wooden false-work would be removed, and if the arch had been properly exe-cuted, it would remain standing on its own. Only then would the falsework be mounted on supports on the wall and the stones re-laid and grouted in their permanent position.

Once the work had progressed to a point where scaffolding was employed, a new challenge must be faced: lifting the heavy stones up the wall to where they were needed. This presented a real en-gineering challenge, since the makeshift machinery had to be fixed to the flimsy scaffolding. But it was soon accomplished with a combination of pulleys, lifts, hoists, and old-fashioned brute strength, and the work continued.

Once the walls were completed the church was ". . . to be cov-ered (roofed) by the English carpenters with overlapping shingles cleft from oak, which by exposure to the wind and rain, turn blue, and look as if there were slate."[14]

Partway through the work, however, construction would be halted by ongoing tensions between the village and the nearby Indians.

It had begun about a year earlier, in August of 1641. A garru-lous old Dutchman named Claes Smits, a wheelwright by trade, lived outside the fort's walls in a small house on Deutel (Turtle) Bay, on the Wickquasgeck road. His house was a favored gather-ing place where people would drink, sing, and sit beside a warm fire.

On the fateful autumn day, a passing Indian who wanted to trade some beaver pelts stopped at Smits's door. Smits invited him in and gave him something to eat and drink. While the old man was bending over the chest where he kept his trade goods, the Indian grabbed a nearby axe and cut off the unfortunate wheelwright's head.[15]

Retribution followed quickly. Skirmishes between the two sides would escalate until, on February 25, 1643, Kieft, often referred to as Willem the Testy, ordered a massacre of a local Indian village. More than eighty Lenni Lenape (Delaware) men, women, and children were butchered in their sleep. This incident, and others of a similar nature, lasted off and on for five years and the construction of the church would be delayed, as raw materials couldn't be safely gathered in nearby woods and quarries.

The Ogdens would have made occasional trips home to Stamford to visit their families during this period of inactivity; but the trips would have been few due to the ever-present risk of running into an Indian raiding party. They would probably have waited for times when a larger expedition was heading in the same direction. While in the fort, it's uncertain where they called home; however, they probably stayed in one of two places. There was a sleeping apartment in the old and very small Dutch tavern, which accommodated overnight travelers at night while during the day it served as a public room. Or they could have stayed in Kieft's newer public house, "a great clumsy stone tavern . . . located on the northeast corner of Pearl Street and Coenties Slip, fronting the East River."[16]

The massacre of the sleeping Indians also precipitated a clash between Kieft and Rev. Bogardus that would last to their deaths:

> . . . at the conclusion of hostilities he [Kieft] proclaimed a day of thanksgiving. Domine Bogardus preached, "and a good sermon too," but refused to make any reference to the Director's orders or to the peace. His attitude brought to a climax the quarrel which had long been brewing between him and the Director. Kieft thereafter refrained from church attendance and his example was followed by all those who wished his favor.
>
> This unseemly dispute waxed and waned as one or the other attacked the conduct of his enemy. At last things came to such a pass that Kieft encouraged the baser elements of the community to insult those who were on their way to church, and to play noisy games under the church windows during service. On at least one occasion he com-

CANAL ON BROAD STREET
The canal on Broad Street, New Amsterdam, 1659. According to most contemporary descriptions, the canal, which the Dutch dug to assist in moving and unloading goods by small ships and boats, would have been filled with debris; the streets littered, and pigs, sheep, and dogs running loose everywhere.

manded a company of soldiers to practice shooting near the building while Bogardus was preaching.[17]

There are conflicting stories as to when the church construction was finished. It was probably sometime early in 1644, as the Ogdens moved to Long Island later that year. The Dutch Reformed Church was named St. Nicholas, after a favorite Netherlands saint. The steep twin-gabled roof of the imposing Dutch Gothic building arose over the walls of the fort so that it was the first sight seen as ships sailed into the harbor of New Amsterdam. A square cupola, capped with a low spire, rose up between the two gables, with a weathervane topping the whole. The final structure was seventy-two feet long and fifty-two feet wide,[18] with walls eighteen feet high—an imposing size in early colonial times.

Director General Kieft ordered a stone slab to be erected in front of the church, with this inscription (translated):

1642, WILLEM KIEFT BEING DIRECTOR GENERAL,
THE CONGREGATION CAUSED THIS CHURCH TO BE BUILT[19]

And, on one of the old houses of the village, No. 4 Bowling Green, near the Battery, was once a large bronze tablet, now lost to time, with the following inscription (translated):

THE SITE OF FORT AMSTERDAM,
BUILT IN 1626
WITHIN THE FORTIFICATIONS
WAS ERECTED THE FIRST
SUBSTANTIAL CHURCH EDIFICE
ON THE ISLAND OF MANHATTAN[20]

For their services the Ogdens received 2500 guilders (about one thousand dollars) in beaver pelts, merchandise, and cash. It is unknown if they received the one hundred guilders bonus they were to earn if the work was deemed satisfactory, but we can assume so.

It appears that the people of the village had the last laugh on Kieft, as we see in a 1650 document ". . . the accounts of most of the subscribers were debited accordingly, but they have not yet paid the money."[21]

Eventually Rev. Borgardus and his allies would win the ongoing struggle with the despotic director general, forcing his 1647 recall. He would be replaced by the peg-legged Peter Stuyvesant. It would prove to be a hollow victory for Bogardus, however.

On August 16, 1647, the ship *Princess Amelia*, which had brought Stuyvesant to New Amsterdam, set sail to return to Amsterdam under the command of Captain Jan Claesen Bol. His primary cargo was fourteen thousand beaver pelts. Among the passengers on board were ex-Director General Kieft and his chief protagonist, Rev. Bogardus.

The crossing was uneventful—the two men probably steering clear of each other on the small ship—until Captain Bol made a classic mariner's error, mistaking the Bristol Channel for the English Channel. The ship ran aground off the coast of Wales, and hammering waves dashed it to pieces.[22] Eighty-one souls perished, including both Kieft and Bogardus.

The Ogdens' stone church would gain its greatest historical notoriety thanks to the map-making prowess of the Dutch. The earliest Dutch map of New Netherland seems to be the Adriaen Block map of 1614. After that, it becomes difficult to keep all the Dutch maps straight, as each one was altered, copied, refined, added to, and republished again and again. At some point in time, in order to make the maps more salable, artists and printers began adding beautiful watercolor inset renderings to the maps, most commonly reflecting New Amsterdam and/or the multitude of wild beasts that wandered the New World wilderness.

One New Amsterdam inset, on a map owned by the Austrian National Library and commonly known as the Blaeu view, shows the fort and surrounding town in a sad state of disrepair, almost comically so. Other map insets, like the famous Visscher view or the Montanus view, show the fort and town in a better light. But all the views painted before 1670 had one thing in common: the stone church, with its steep twin-gabled roofs, towered above the walls of the fort and all the other buildings in the town. Some of the maps were used to encourage new colonizers, and they were widely distributed throughout Holland and other western European countries.

Sometime after 1670, the inset of New Amsterdam was repainted on one of the maps that became known as the Restitutio view. In this famous view, the stone church is rendered as having only one high-peaked roof, with a large single-roofed addition to the rear. This means that either the church had been significantly altered by this time, or the artist had been tipping too many strong Dutch beers while wielding his brushes.

One other alteration to the church was also significant. At some point, the original oak shingles had been replaced with tiles, a very typical Dutch touch. But in 1672 the city allowed five hundred guilders for removing the tiles and going back to the wooden shingles, because the tiles were constantly being broken by the concussion of the firing of the cannons in the fort.[23]

Finally, in 1674, the congregation had cast in Holland a bell to hang in the church tower, the first of its kind in the province. The inscription, translated from Dutch, said:

THE AIR IS MADE PLEASANT BECAUSE OF OUR RINGING.
MADE BY P. HEMONY, 1674[24]

VIEW OF THE CITY OF AMSTERDAM (NOW NEW YORK)
After "The Montanus View," date depicted c. 1650. Note the distinctive
twin-gabled church, the largest building in New Amsterdam at the
time. It was built in 1642–44 by John and Richard Ogden, and was the
first sight seen by most voyagers sailing into the Harbor. Museum of
the City of New York.

Less than a century later the church was burned and the com-
memorative slab was buried in the debris. When the fort was de-
molished in 1790 to make room for New York City's Government
House, the slab was recovered and placed in a Dutch Church on
Garden Street, where it remained until both were destroyed in
the famous 1835 conflagration.[25]
    It seems that John Ogden and his stone church came close to
earning some respect in New York City in the early twentieth century. A 1913 article in the *New York Evening Post* carried a
lengthy story that related:

    The proposal to erect, next year, in commemoration of the tercente-
    nary of the city's settlement, a statue in Bowling Green to the build-
    ers of the first church edifice upon Manhattan Island calls attention

to the distinguished career of a man who was perhaps the earliest settler of purely English blood in New York.

The article goes on to describe the church, the circumstances surrounding its construction, and some highlights in the colonial life of John Ogden. In ending, reporter W. Seton Gordon praised Ogden:

A fitting site for the monument to John Ogden would be the Bowling Green. The church he erected there more than two and a half centuries ago has long since become a memory, but the civic virtues of self-sacrificing devotion to public duty and incorruptible honesty in public office, exemplified in his life, can never grow old, and were never more needed in the service of the republic than now.[26]

Apparently the monument was never built, although Bowling Green park, the city's oldest dating back to 1733, still exists.

4

The Great Plains on Long Island

DURING THE CHURCH CONSTRUCTION PERIOD, BACK IN STAMFORD, many of the English settlers, including the Ogdens, were growing restless because of the limited freedoms offered by the governing New Haven colony.

The so-called republic of New Haven was of the most extreme Puritan type. "The word of God," says one old New Haven record, "shall be the only rule attended unto in ordering the affairs of government." In other words, New Haven was a Bible state, ruled with an iron hand by a few men with close ties to the clergy.[1]

While building the New Amsterdam church, Ogden had been told by Director General Kieft about the wonderful lands of western Long Island where families could make a fine home. He reminded Ogden too of the leniency of the Dutch West India Company toward followers of other faiths. Ogden took those words back with him to Stamford.

It is difficult with the passage of so much time to know all of the reasons the group decided to abandon Stamford and begin anew. The weather may have had played a part, and certainly the church did as well. The Puritan church, particularly under the ever-watchful eye of nearby New Haven, was smothering. Rev. Mr. Denton, although very righteous, was also a learned man, having graduated from Cambridge, so he probably questioned many of the tenets the Puritans held sacred. It appears he desired to live not in a theocracy but in a democracy, where every member of the community would have a voice, not only in temporal affairs but also in choosing the minister and providing for the continuance of the religious body.[2]

This belief in democracy resonated with John Ogden, a man who valued personal freedom above all else. The bond between the two men had probably begun in the Pennine hills of Lanca-

96

shire and Yorkshire, long before they came to America. In each of the New World settlements where Denton had ministered, he was forced to preach in a church where some of his values and beliefs were discordant with the core values and beliefs of the Puritan church. As one of his flock, and as his friend, Ogden was forced to accept these halfhearted preachings. Each was eager for the chance to go to a place where they could interpret the Word to their own satisfaction; and this spot on western Long Island, it seemed, offered that opportunity.[3]

In view of all the hardships the Stamford settlers had endured in such a short span of time, it's no wonder they were ready to seek a new home in another place. And so it was that in the late summer of 1643—while the Ogdens were still at work on the church—Robert Fordham and his son-in-law John Carman were assigned to visit the local Indians on western Long Island to negotiate a settlement for occupying the land, and to decide exactly where they wished to plant their settlement. They could not have picked a worse time to travel to the area.

Tension between the Dutch and the Indians had reached a fever point. Conflicts at a number of settlements, including many on Long Island, were escalating. The hostilities were so serious that many Dutch settlers were virtually confined within Fort Amsterdam. It was into this dangerous situation that Fordham and Carman arrived. They must have been aware of the conditions, and had experienced their own Indian troubles earlier in 1643 when a raiding party fell upon their settlement at Stamford.

It's unknown exactly how many others accompanied the two men into hostile territory. Three others had their signatures affixed to the deed, but it's probable that a party of ten or more would have been in attendance. In the end, the group would do a marvelous job. The Hempstead Plain offered a weaving expanse of gray-green grass that almost appeared like a lake. It was fringed by the deeper green of the forest, and nearby was an excellent harbor. It offered both tillable soil and ideal pastureland for the livestock.[4]

The deed from the Indians arrived in late 1643:

December 13,1643. Be it known unto all men by these presents that we the Indyans of Marsapeague, Mericock, and Rockaway whose names are here underwritten, have put over, bargained and sold onto Robert Fordham and John Carman, Englishmen, all that half-part or moiety of the Great Plains [physical description follows] . . .[5]

HEMPSTEAD PURCHASE FROM THE INDIANS
In this mural painted by Robert Gaston Herbert, the Indians of Long
Island sell the land for the plantation of Hempstead to settlers Robert
Fordham and John Carman in 1643. The two men represented a group,
including John Ogden, who wished to leave Stamford. Courtesy of
Hempstead Village, Hempstead, New York.

The area of their intended settlement is known today as Hempstead. The Dutch called it Heemsteed. There were many incon-
sistencies in the deed, and forever after nobody was exactly sure
how much land, and which land specifically, had been deeded to
the Stamford party; nor exactly what price would be paid to the
Indians for it.

However, after receiving their deed from the Indians, the group
applied to New Amsterdam for a patent to plant the settlement.
Ogden's association with Director General Kieft probably helped
their cause, and their application was approved in November
1644. Six patentees, including John Ogden, were mentioned on
the document, which promised:

> . . . a certain tract of land upon and about a place called the Great
> Plains on Long Island from the East River to the South Sea, [ocean]
> and from a certain harbor commonly called Hempstead Bay and west-

ward as far as Matthew Garritson's Bay, to begin at the head of the said two bays and to run in direct line that they may be the same latitude in breadth on the South side as on the North side.

As was customary in such grants, the governing fathers wishing to insure the colonization of the lands under their control, the patent also contained certain obligations:

> . . . the above patentees must settle 100 families upon the land inside five years then they shall have power to build a Town or Towns with necessary fortifications. A Temple or Temples to use and exercise their reformed religions which they possess. . . .

If, after ten years, the quota of one hundred families had not been met, rent was to be levied, payable annually to the Dutch West India Company. Those who farmed would pay one-tenth of their farmed revenue, and those who raised cattle would pay the equivalent of one tenth in butter and cheese.

They were also obliged to elect a ". . . body politic or civil combination among themselves to nominate magistrates not more than eight of the ablest and best approved men among them, and present them to the Governor for him to elect and establish . . ."[6]

A complete copy of the patent from Governor Kieft is in the Appendix.

This document, and the earlier deed from the Indians, makes clear the process required when planting a new settlement. It was twofold. First came the negotiation and purchase of the land from the Indians, or from another party that may have previously purchased it from the Indians (as in the case of Stamford). Then, in a completely separate transaction, a "right to settle" had to be negotiated with the political body that claimed oversight to the land. In this case, it was New Netherland; in Stamford, it was the New Haven Colony.

Technically speaking, of course, the indigenous Indians did not hold legal title to any of the land, but maintained their hold over it by virtue of centuries of habitation. Thus, in some cases, insensitive settlers would bypass the Indians altogether. Of course, the Indians were not without their own brand of deception. The Hempstead land they sold to the Stamford settlers had already been sold in 1639 as part of a large tract to David De Vries and Cornelis van Tienhoven. It does not appear that the two pressed their ownership claims, however, when the new settlers moved in.

Daniel Denton, eldest son of Rev. Richard Denton, wrote in 1670 of the displacement of the Long Island Indians in the first English-language book on the middle colonies: ". . . it hath been generally observed, that where the English come to settle, a Divine Hand makes way for them, by removing or cutting off the Indians, either by Wars one with the other, or by some raging mortal Disease."[7]

Denton's "Divine Hand" theory may ring hollow today, but it made perfect sense to these seventeenth-century Englishmen.

Now that the Stamford settlers had all their permissions in order, the group, which now numbered from twenty to thirty families, was ready to relocate to western Long Island.

It must have been a disappointment to Ogden and Rev. Denton when their good friend Matthew Mitchell decided not to join them in this new adventure. Mitchell's appetite for adventure had dimmed, his misfortunes and failing health finally getting the best of him. He decided to simply stay put for once. He never recovered his health, and died on May 19, 1646, at only fifty-six years old.

When the time came for Ogden and the others to move, according to the Web site of the *New Netherland Project,* ". . . families . . . sailed across Long Island Sound then traveled overland until they reached a broad, flat, fertile plain that seemed to speak to them. This, they decided was home."[8]

Long Island would be the Ogdens' home for the next twenty-one years.

What did this pristine land look like to John Ogden, his family, and friends when they decided to call it home more than 350 years ago? A 1950 book by John Bakeless, taken from very early journals and firsthand reports, describes what America was like when Europeans first set foot on its shores. Regarding Long Island, it says (note: quote marks within the text below indicates statements of firsthand reports):

Eastward stretched Long Island, remarkable for "many fine valleys, where there is good grass," elsewhere forested with elm, oak, nut trees, cedar, evergreens, maple, sassafras, beech, birch, hazelnut, and chestnuts," which yield store of Mast for Swine." One early observer mentions holly. The middle of the island was an open plain, about four by sixteen miles, "upon which plain grows very fine grass." The Hempstead area was never forested. Other wise, "the greatest part of the Island," was, according to a Jamaica resident of the middle seventeenth century, "very full of Timber." It was attractive country, as he described it: "The fruits natural to the Island are Mulberries, Posimons, Grapes great and small, Huckleberries, Cramberries, Plums of several sorts, Roseberries and Strawberries, of which last is such abundance in June, that the Fields and Woods are died red: Which the Countrey People perceiving, instantly arm themselves with bottles of Wine, Cream, and Sugar and instead of a Coat of Male, every one takes a Female upon his Horse Behind him, and so rushing violently into the fields, never leave till they have Disrob'd them of their red colours and turned them into old habit."

Like Manhattan the island was filled with "divers sorts of singing birds, whose chirping notes salute the ears of Travellers with an harmonious discord, and in every pond and brook green silken Frogs, who warbling forth their untun'd tunes, strive to bear a part in this musick." In May the woods and fields "were curiously bedecke with Roses, and an innumerable multitude of Flowers."

Bakeless goes on to describe the wildlife that the Ogdens and their fellow colonizers might have encountered, which included wild turkeys, geese, snipe, ruffled grouse, deer, beaver, black bear, wolves, and many kinds of fish, to name only a few of the species. And finally, "over all of Greater New York was the quiet of the wilderness, broken only by the occasional calls of birds and the rare cries of usually silent wilderness beasts."[9]

The first settlers probably began to arrive in the spring of 1644, the exact date lost to history. It was before the New Amsterdam patent was secured, but because of Ogden's relationship with Kieft, the group was confident of his approval.

This mass departure from Stamford, which included the church leader, Rev. Richard Denton, would have been a hard blow to the town. A third of their number had left homes, fields, town duties, and the church. This would have been especially devastating for the church, as there was now no religious leader in the community. A Puritan community without a ministering father was truly in dire straits.

Late in 1644, probably in conjunction with the patent, Ogden and other settlers were granted freeholder status by Director General Krieft.

Four resettlements since leaving England had sifted these new settlers to those of similar convictions. Their isolation from any other nearby plantations ensured that nobody was near enough to disturb their dearly purchased harmony. When the church was established, it was probably the first Presbyterian Church in America. Rather than being ruled, in effect, by one man, the minister, the new church would be governed by presbyteries, assemblies composed of the minister and the church elders.

The settlers immediately began felling trees. A stream from the east wound an irregular course through the spot chosen for the village, creating a few ponds in its wake; the forest lay to the south, the waving grass of the plains to the north. They began to build: a few dwellings, a church, and meetinghouse with a palisade to encircle it, near a pond that became known as "the meetinghouse pond."

Like all early colonial meetinghouses, it would be built in the center of the new town. These buildings were always very simple, with no ornamentation whatsoever, so as to avoid the ungodly extravagances of the Catholic churches. Inside, pews were roughly hewn log benches, beastly uncomfortable, but meant to be so.

These buildings served a variety of purposes. They were not only the spiritual center of the community but also the political center; and in time of Indian raids, a place of shelter as well.

John Ogden and his family were granted eighty-one acres within the plantation. The other original patentees also enjoyed large holdings. By this time, the Ogden family included John and Jane, and children John Jr. and Sarah. Their third and fourth sons, Jonathan (born 1645–47) and Joseph (born 1646–48) would be born during their residence in Hempstead.

Very soon after building had begun, however, the settlers would have their first skirmish with the Indians. "Breeden Raedt," or Broad Advice, was a Dutch pamphlet of the day, and it is from this source that we find the story of this first trouble. It must be remembered that this was a partisan document, and some of the statements may have been exaggerated; but the basic facts seem to be agreed upon. A translation from the Dutch of part of the story follows:

In April of the year 1644, seven savages were arrested at Heemstede on a charge of killing two or three pigs, though it was afterward discovered that some English had done it themselves. Director Kieft was informed by Mr. Fordham [then leader of the settlement] that he had just arrested seven savages, who were confined in a cellar, but whom he dared not treat inhumanely, as he could not answer for the consequences to himself, because such things were not to be winked at there, or perhaps because the English nation wish to cause a general dislike among the savages to our people. Kieft sent Ensign Opdyke with an Englishman, John Onderhil [Underhill] and fifteen or sixteen soldiers, who killed three of the seven in the cellar. They took the other four with them in the sailing boat, two of whom were towed along by a string around their necks till they were drowned, while the two survivors were detained as prisoners at Fort Amsterdam. When they had been kept a long time the Director became tired of giving them food any longer, and they were delivered to the soldiers to do as they pleased.

The story goes on to give harrowing details of the barbarous treatment of the final two Indians, and their eventual killing.[10]

Other official documents give a somewhat different story, and include a larger force than the sixteen mentioned above; and the fact that some of the force wiped out an entire Indian village at Matsepe. What is agreed upon, however, is that the power of the Long Island Indians was largely broken by this battle.

John Underhill, a key player in the drama, was a man both loved and hated, revered and reviled, in his day. He arrived in the New World in the early 1630s; and when the English made war against the Pequots in Connecticut in 1637, he was among the leaders. He led the savage assault against the Pequots' log fort near present-day Mystic, killing, it is estimated, more than one thousand Indians. But simply conquering the Indian braves wasn't enough for Underhill; he also killed women and children indiscriminately, often torturing them in the process, and torched their villages and wigwams.

Underhill's bloodbath continued when he and his troops attacked a peaceful Indian village near present-day Massapequa, about ten miles east of Hempstead. This time 120 Indians were slain, again in brutal fashion. This battle, called the battle of Fort Neck, was the last Indian battle on Long Island. But in present-day Westchester County, another Underhill massacre shortly thereafter resulted in 180 more Indian deaths.

It is true that Indian problems subsided, especially on Long Island, after Underhill's brutal campaign, a fact often pointed to by his defenders. But his methods of warfare are still condemned to this day. He died in 1672 at his home in Oyster Bay.

Perhaps as a result of the ending of the Indian threat, the settling of Hempstead would not follow the normal New England process for establishing an early colonial village. As late as the time of the Revolution, there were reported to be only nine houses and three inns at the village of Hempstead, and a house within the town might boast seven acres of ground.

Instead of following the custom of building their homes close together for protection, the settlers established themselves in isolated homesteads around the margin of the plain and in clearings deeper in the forest. It was either a very brave or a very foolish plan; but these people were not timid. Their freedoms were hard-won, and they'd live as they pleased.

Like all early settlements, Hempstead set aside significant acreage for the common pasture. In 1658 the town hired a herdsman to attend their growing cattle herd. We read of the richness of their land in an 1828 history by Silas Wood:

> They drove their cattle as far as Cow-Neck to pasture, and it is supposed to have taken its name from that circumstance. The openness of the country was very favorable to the increase of stock; and the plain around the town of Hempstead is peculiarly so, and their cattle became quite numerous within a few years after the settlement of the town. In 1658, the people of Hempstead had 84 cows, which brought them 82 calves that year.[11]

That Hempstead sat in the midst of one of the most beautiful natural surroundings in the New World cannot be denied. And all the early settlers were of one mind, so harmony within the group was perfect. The Indians, after the earlier hostilities, or perhaps because of them, were hospitable neighbors. So if there was ever paradise on earth, this should have been it.

Unfortunately we will never know as much about early Hempstead, and John Ogden's activities in the community, as we'd like to know. All the old town records for the first decade of the settlement have long since disappeared, probably forever, so our knowledge will never be complete.

As fine a place as Hempstead seemed to be, however, the Ogdens eventually discovered that there is no paradise on earth. John Ogden was a righteous man, a fair man to a fault. He and his family must have loved living in such a wonderful community. But he was concerned. The Dutch authorities had proven they had little patience with the Indians, and their credo seemed to be to shoot first and ask questions later. I have not seen it written, but I have no doubts that Ogden would have implored his friend, Director General Kieft, to act in moderation when dealing with the Indians. But that was not Kieft's nature.

Thus, after a few years of watching this brutal treatment, and being convinced that he could not affect a change, Ogden's conscience would not allow him to stay. He and his family would have to move again. After some consideration he decided to relocate to the eastern end of Long Island, to Southampton. Here, the Dutch political oversight of the colony was nominal. It was also the home of his sister, Hannah, and her husband Robert Bond, who was Jane Ogden's brother.

It is difficult to determine the exact date when the Ogdens left Hempstead. Probably the best source we have is an article from the *Nassau County Historical Journal,* which says that Rev. Robert Fordham left Hempstead "about 1649" in the company of some twelve or more families, heading for Southampton. The group also included the Ogdens, Thurston Raynor, Thomas Topping, Jonas Wood, John Lum, Christopher Foster, Thomas Pope, Samuel Clark, and Bartholomew Smith.[12] The 1649 date was important. It marked the end of the original five-year period written in the Hempstead patent. Had these founders left the community before that date, and had the community not met its target of one hundred families, penalties could have been assessed, up to and including the confiscation of the patent. It's doubtful that senior members of the original patent like Ogden and Fordham would have violated their promises to the other settlers and left early.

When the 1654 list of residents was compiled by the village lister, ten years after the Kieft patent had been issued, there were but twenty-three of the fifty original patentees remaining in Hempstead. John Carman, who with Rev. Fordham had negotiated with the Indians for the original deed, had died in the town a year earlier.[13]

Southampton historian Abigail Halsey says that of the first company (those that settled Southampton in 1640) most returned sooner or later to New England. "But," she says, "during the next few years their places were taken by . . . Robert Bond . . . John Ogden . . . and others."[14]

Richard Ogden and his family would remain in Hempstead for another seven years. In the Hempstead town records of February

27, 1656, it is recorded that Richard Ogden sold his house and all his land to a neighbor, Thomas Carle.[15] He and his family removed to the small town of Fairfield, Conn., located on the coast just across Long Island Sound and about halfway between Stamford, his earlier home, and New Haven. He purchased six acres on Old Mill River from a Giles Smith that appears to have had an active gristmill in operation on it. Richard became the miller for the town.

He and Mary would eventually have seven children, and he remained in Fairfield until his death around April 18, 1687. He became the stem ancestor for the Fairfield Ogdens, another line that endures to this day.[16] His son John, born about 1672, moved to South Jersey in about 1705 and became the stem ancestor for that line of Ogdens.

5

Southampton Calls

LONG ISLAND WAS FIRST EXPLORED BY THE DUTCHMAN ADRIAEN Block in 1614. He gave it the name it still enjoys today, Lange Eylandt. The Indians before him had called it Paumanack.

Southampton was the first English settlement in today's New York. It was founded by a group of settlers, called the undertakers, from Lynn, in the Massachusetts Bay Colony. Though Lynn was only an eleven-year-old plantation at the time, many of the settlers felt straitened, or closed in, as new settlers poured in. So the undertakers decided to seek better lands to the south.

A group of the men bought a sloop to transport their families and possessions to their new home, paying eighty pounds for the vessel. Then they turned ownership of the sloop over to one of their number, Daniel Howe, in return for his promise that he would make three trips each year for two years to transport needed goods from Lynn to the new plantation. It was a good arrangement all around.

John Winthrop Sr. wrote of the move:

> In April 1640 . . . divers of the inhabitants of Linne finding themselves straitened looked out for a new plantation, and going to Long Island, they agreed with the Lord Sterling's agent, one Mr. Forrett [James Farrett] for a parcel of the isle near the west end. . . .[1]

Actually, the arrangement with Farrett called for the settlers to receive eight square miles of land wherever on the island they might elect, but their first choice was to go to the closer west end. That turned out to be a big mistake, however.

When the group arrived they found nailed to a tree a plaque that featured a likeness of the Dutch West India Company's director in Holland, indicating that the territory belonged to the Dutch. But the settlers tore down the sign and in its place had carved "an unhandsome face." They proceeded to clear some of the land and began building their settlement. When word of the trespass reached the Dutch authorities, a small troop of about two dozen soldiers was dispatched to apprehend "the strollers and vagabonds."[2]

Eight men, two women, and a child were found at the site, some of the others having already returned to fetch their families. Six of the eight men were arrested and taken back to New Amsterdam where they were questioned and imprisoned for a few days. The main sticking point for the Dutch seemed to be the disrespectful treatment of the director's image, rather then the encroachment itself. One of the six men blamed an unknown Indian for the dastardly deed, while another pointed a finger at Farrett himself as the culprit.

Finally, after a stern warning, the men were released, and in June they returned to their friends and ". . . deserted that place, and took another at the east end of the same island [present-day Southampton] and being now about 40 families, they proceeded on their plantation."[3]

Although the Dutch held sway on the western end of Long Island, and would tell all who would listen that they also had dominion over the east end, the English did have some grounds to lay claim to it. King Charles I, in 1636, requested his Plymouth Colony to issue a patent to William Alexander, Earl of Stirling, for Long Island and the islands adjacent. They did as they were told, and on April 20, 1637, the Earl gave his power of attorney to James Farrett to dispose of the lands. In late 1640 when the Earl, now Lord Stirling, died with no viable male heirs, his grant defaulted back to the king. For a short period of time, Southampton was in and of itself an independent colony until Charles II granted it to his brother, the Duke of York, in 1664, an event we'll watch unfold in the next chapter.[4]

This was wild, uncharted territory for white men in the early 1640s. As wild as it was, however, it was not entirely unpopulated. A priest who had passed through at the time, said "there are many Indians on the greater part of this Island who at first settling of the English there did much to annoy their Cattel with the multitude of Doggs they kept, which ordinarily are young wolves brought up tame, continuing of a very ravening nature."[5]

Daniel Denton wrote eloquently of the eastern end of Long Island in his book:

There is several Navigable Rivers and Bays, which puts into the North-side of Long-Island, but upon the South-side which joyns to the Sea, it is so fortified with bars of sands and sholes, that it is a sufficient defence against any enemy, yet the South-side is not without Brooks and Riverets, which empty themselves in the Sea; yea, you shall travel a mile, but you shall meet with one of them whose Christal streams run so swift, that they purge themselves of such stinking mud and filth, which the standing or low-paced streams of most brooks and rivers westward of this Colony leave lying.[6]

The Indians had earlier been described as bold, hardy, and warlike. However, most local Indians were peaceful to the whites, probably because they depended upon the settlers to protect them from neighboring tribes. Five different tribes lived in the area, but two, the Shinnecocks and the Montauks, were the most numerous. The Shinnecocks had a long history on the island, having come to it more than ten thousand years before as the first hunter-gatherers. Both tribes spoke Mohegan, one of the Algonquian languages.

The Shinnecocks occupied the land that made up Southampton, and in December 1640, parceled out eight square miles to the early settlers from Lynn. In return, the Indians were to receive ". . . consideration of sixteen coates already received, and also three score bushels of Indian corne to be paid upon lawful demand the last of September, which shall be paid in the year 1641, and further in consideration that the above named English shall defend us the said Indians from the unjust violence of whatever Indians shall illegally assail us."[7]

Seventeenth-century Indians had a very different concept of land ownership than Europeans. To them, land was like the air we breathe; it didn't belong to anyone and nobody could "own" it. When they "sold" a piece of land, it was to them a two-pronged agreement. First, that they would share the land in return for some tangible items like hatchets, clothing, or blankets; and second, that a defensive alliance would be created between the two groups where they would help protect one another from other tribes and villages.[8] To the English and the Dutch, however, the meaning of a sale was quite clear: the land in question was now theirs to do with as they pleased.

The settlers also initially agreed to pay the Earl of Stirling an annual quitrent for the right to settle. The task of arriving at a fair price was handed to John Winthrop Sr., Governor of the Massachusetts Bay Colony. He fixed the price at four bushels of Indian corn, a low price that took into consideration that the settlers had already paid once, and that the country was a wilderness.[9]

Having finally found a home, the settlers began to plant their village. Before leaving Lynn they had formed a joint-stock company, owning the land as tenants-in-common. Each man was entitled to a house lot of four acres (later changed to three when it began to get crowded), twelve acres for farming, and about thirty to thirty-five acres of meadow and grazing land. Each also received shares in the undivided common lands according to the amount of money he had invested in the project.[10]

By 1645, Southampton was a thriving community. That year, town fathers decided to unite with the Connecticut Colony, across Long Island Sound, probably as an additional defense against Dutch encroachment. The official document of this union indicates that although they lost some independent powers, they retained most of their right of self-rule.

The first church edifice had been built in 1640 or 1641, within a year after the settlement of the town. Located on Meeting House Lane, it was probably in the middle of the town, a wooden structure with a thatched roof. The first minister was Rev. Abraham Pierson, who had been appointed in Boston to lead the spiritual lives of the Southampton settlers. A pious man, he was tightly attuned to the rigid Puritan standards of the Congregational Church's New Haven Colony. Joining forces with the Connecticut Colony, which was Presbyterian, was too much for Pierson, and he soon fled to Branford, Connecticut with part of his congregation.

The Connecticut Colony had been formed by the union of the three River Towns—Hartford, Windsor, and Wethersfield. The colony had not been anointed by the English crown, as the Massachusetts Bay Colony had; and even though their permission to settle in the rich Connecticut River Valley had been granted by the Boston-based colony, they managed to establish secular and political independence. The founding fathers of the colony claimed legitimacy by virtue of the Warwick Patent, a 1620 patent of Connecticut lands supposedly made by King James I to Robert, Earl of Warwick, and his associates. The fact that the Warwick Patent had probably never advanced beyond the draft stage didn't seem to dampen their resolve to claim land under its auspices.

The Connecticut Colony vested executive power in the Governor and a bench of magistrates. Each town within the colony selected one or more of the magistrates to represent the town at the semiannual General Court in Hartford. Southampton had always elected three magistrates before joining the colony, but only two would be allowed to attend the colony's meetings in Hartford.

In 1647, while still living in Hempstead, John Ogden petitioned the town of Southampton for permission to plant a settlement of six families at Great Peconic Bay, about three miles north of town in an area that served as the harbor for the inland village. He gained his patent, but did not act upon it until 1650, after moving to Southampton.

At that time he planted his settlement, and it became only the second permanent English settlement in New York.[11] The village would be known as North Sea, or Northampton. It appears that Ogden wished to plant a settlement where he could be among men of similar interests. In the *Winthrop Papers*, a letter from one Josiah Stansborough of Southampton to John Winthrop Jr. in 1650 describes the new town this way ". . . mr. Ogden begins a towne on our north side for tradesmen . . ."[12]

On September 3, 1650, Southampton town records indicate that Ogden and his group were granted 324 acres of land upon the following conditions:

> It is granted by the major parte of the towne that Mr. Odgen and his company shall have Cow Neck and Jeffery Neck for their owne proper Right; also, that they shall have for their planting Land in either or both of said necks three hundred 24 Acres of said Land provided they settle upon it and upon the same grant they are to have all the side of the Island . . .[13]

The document was signed or marked by all the town proprietors, including the Indian chiefs who called the land home. It was recorded in "ye office at New York October 3 1665, by Matthias Nicolls, Sec.," fifteen years later, after the English had taken New Netherland from the Dutch.

North Sea was a perfect spot for a settlement. It had a small natural harbor surrounded by accessible meadows and woods; and the nearby encampment of Shinnecocks was friendly. The colony was close enough to Southampton to help ensure safety, and was a jurisdictional part of the older town. In addition to the Ogden family, John's brother-in-law Robert Bond was there, as were John Scott and Robert Smith.

The Ogdens had finally planted roots, and were to remain in Northampton for the next fifteen years. By this time, the New World non-native population had grown to about 50,400.

Later that year, in September 1650, another event was unfolding that would provide the east-enders, as they were called, with relief from their ongoing tension with the Dutch.

The English encroachment into Dutch territory had been a concern to New Netherland for a number of years. In fact, just the year before, in July 1649, one of New Netherland's governing bodies, the Board of Nine Men, had written to the authorities in Amsterdam to present the problem:

> It is highly necessary that this [taking action] should be done, inasmuch as the English have already seized, and are in possession of, almost half of New Netherland, a matter which may have weighty consequences in the future. It is therefore heartily to be desired that Their High Mightinesses will be pleased to take this subject into serious consideration before it shall go further, and the breach become irreparable.[14]

With only a small military force in the New World, the Dutch were hesitant to militarily challenge the English in those settlements. Realizing that this balance of power was in their favor, the English settlers of Massachusetts and Connecticut colonies pushed for an agreement with the Dutch that would put to rest the constant boundary disputes.

Peter Stuyvesant, then Director General of New Netherland, agreed to a meeting in 1650, to convene in Hartford. The result was a treaty known as the Hartford Agreement, where a permanent boundary between the two parties was established. The north-south line ran through Long Island and the mainland, and gave the eastern two-thirds of the island to the English. In truth, the treaty was a victory for Stuyvesant, because the only lands he ceded were those that had already been lost by de facto settlement of the English.[15] Charles II would ignore the treaty in 1664 when he granted all these lands to his brother, the Duke of York.

Shortly after establishing his village, Ogden would embark on another project that would lay the economic cornerstone for the thriving New England whaling industry of the eighteenth and nineteenth centuries. John Ogden was a financially astute man. He did not depend solely upon his trade as a stonemason, or upon his frequent real estate transactions. He was one of America's earliest entrepreneurs, constantly on the lookout for new business opportunities. It is purely speculation, but it's very possible that the poverty that surrounded him in his boyhood and young manhood in rural Lancashire was always buried somewhere in the back of his mind. That could explain why he was always on the lookout for a good business opportunity.

On January 30, 1650, an entry in the *Southampton Town Records* noted that a company he had formed was granted an exclusive license to hunt and kill whales in the waters around Long Island:

> It is ordered at the saide generall court that Mr. John Ogden Senior of Northampton shall have free liberty to kill whales upon the South sea [ocean] at or within any part of the bounds of the saide towne for the space of seaven yeares . . . as alsoe the saide Mr. John Ogden nor his company shall not deny the townes inhabitants claiming privilege formerly belonging to them in the dead whales yt shall be accidentally cast upon the shoares . . .[16]

This was the first commercial whaling enterprise on Long Island, and probably the earliest in all of the colonies.

Whaling historian Alexander Starbuck's (1841–1925) whaling chronology also points in that direction: "This would make the commencement of this industry date back not far from the year 1650."[17] And from *The History of the State of New York:* "Southampton may have been the first American town to organize expeditions which sailed along the coast in search of the quarry, with its rich content of oil and bone."[18]

Finally, Daniel Denton also writes of this new business: "Upon the South-side of Long-Island in the Winter, lies stores of Whales and Crampasses, which the inhabitants begin with small boats to make a trade, Catching to their no small benefit."[19]

Whaling in the New World was certainly not a new endeavor. Long before the white man came, coastal Indians pursued whales on land and in the ocean. The wily Indians, knowing the tides and currents, would pursue the shore whales in their canoes, driving

them into shallow water or onto the beach, where they would kill
the giant beasts by shooting many arrows into them. Whales far-
ther out to sea were killed by harpoons fashioned of bone and
wood, connected to a cedar log float by a strong rope made of
twisted vines and reeds. It could take up to a half day to kill and
beach a whale; and if not done properly, the whale would sink to
the bottom and be lost.[20]

The Indians found many uses for the by-products. Oil boiled
from the blubber was mixed with peas and corn as a staple of
their diet, and they ate cooked or dried blubber when normal food
supplies became scarce. Greasy chunks of blubber were used as a
form of preservative and waterproofing on moccasins, leggins,
and other leather goods. Of course, they also used the oil in crude
lamp-like devices for illumination.[21]

The Indians also had one other use for the giant beast, a very
important use in their culture. The Indians' supreme deity was
called Caulkluntoowut, meaning one who possesses supreme
power. Mutchesumetook, on the other hand, was the great evil
spirit. The highest sacrifice that could be made to the good god
was the tail or fin of a whale. When one was procured, a prolonged
feast and powwow was scheduled. The goal was to keep the evil
god outside the circle of their incantations, where violent gesticu-
lations, loud cries, and laborious movements of limbs and body
continued until a trancelike state was achieved. Once these methods accomplished the defeat of the evil one, the feast could com-
mence.[22]

The Ogden company's method of catching their prey sounds
like a cross between the Indians' earlier efforts and those of later
Nantucket Island whalers:

> Two or three boats put off shore at a time, each one manned by a crew
> of six men at the oars, the boat steerer who stood in the stern and
> steered with an oar, and the boat header who stood in the bow to
> throw the harpoon into the whale. When the whale came up to
> breathe, the boat header threw the harpoon and made it fast to him.
> The whale, when wounded, dived and towed the boat in a long swift
> race before he rose to the surface. Another boat then came and put
> another harpoon into the whale. Then the adventure would begin in
> earnest.[23]

We have no written record of whether John Ogden actually participated in the whale hunts, or simply directed the company as

its owner. However, since he seemed to be deeply involved in all his endeavors, it's probable that he would have participated from time to time in the dangerous work of the hunt and the kill.

Because the practice was so difficult and dangerous, the early colonists and the Indians before them would never pass the opportunity to harvest a drift-whale, which would occasionally wash up on shore. As early as 1644 in Southampton, colonists were assigned responsibility for portions of the beach where a drift-whale might make land. The men were divided into four wards of eleven people each, to attend to any drift-whales that might be cast up on their assigned turf. The beasts would be killed by the appropriate crew, if necessary, then butchered and divided up among the entire community's adult citizens.[24] So although the value of the giant beasts was recognized early, John Ogden was the first person in America to seize upon the commercial possibilities in whaling.

Whales provided many useful by-products for the colonists too, and for export overseas. Whale oil was the principal source of fuel and tallow for lamps. Whalebone was used for corsets, combs, stays, stiffeners, jewelry, buttons, and other everyday objects; ambergris was used for perfume.

Ogden's whaling license was extended in August 1654[25] and as we shall see, he continued to be active in the whaling industry when he later relocated to New Jersey.

By 1687, according to town records, there were fourteen whaling companies in Southampton, of twelve men each. The estimate of the total catch that year, in terms of whale oil, was 2,148 barrels.

Nantucket Island settlers, envying the whaling success of their Long Island brethren, soon entered the whale fishery business themselves; and by the early 1700s, this small island dominated America's whaling industry. Hunting from the shore for the smaller right or Greenland whale remained the norm until 1712 when whaler Christopher Hussey was blown off course and came across a sperm whale. The whaling industry thus discovered the value of the pure liquid oil in the head of the sperm whale and the hunt for this great leviathan of the sea, in the whaling ships that have now become famous, began in earnest.

☙

Over the next few years Ogden also became a successful land speculator. He purchased additional land from the Indians, including one large parcel called the Quogue Purchase in 1659. This was the second largest purchase of Indian lands on Long Island, eclipsed only by the Southampton purchase itself, thus it was often referred to as the "Second Purchase." Signed by Wyandance, sachem (or chief) of the Montauks and his son Wiacombe, this purchase included an unidentified amount of land, and appears to have cost Ogden about four hundred English pounds. This was not the first time this land had been sold, nor would it be the last; and indeed one of the transactions would later become quite a cause celebre on Long Island. There were also a couple of oddities surrounding the purchases that provide an interesting perspective on the times.[26]

Quogue, called Quaquanantuck by the Indians, means "the land which trembles under foot."[27] Including prime parts of the long spit of land that stretches along the entire coast of southern Long Island, this parcel was topographically valuable and extremely rich in salt meadows, which provided excellent fodder for the cattle, sheep, and hogs. It was also the site where many drift-whales would come ashore.[28]

Lion Gardiner, an early Southampton settler, first bought the land from the sachem Wyandance in 1658 "for a considerable sum of money." Shortly thereafter, he transferred the land to John Cooper who agreed to keep up the payments to the Indians and give them all the drift-whales.[29] By some method, the land was available once more in 1659 when John Ogden bought it.

Gardiner was an interesting and colorful figure in early Long Island history. A military engineer by training, he was born in England in 1599, and came to the New World in 1635 to head an expedition to draw plans and build towns and forts at the mouth of the Connecticut River. He designed and built Fort Saybrook, and remained in the area for four years, participating extensively in the Pequot Wars.

In 1639 he bought an island from the Indians called Manchonat, at the eastern end of Long Island. The three thousand-acre island that remains in the Gardiner family to this day was the first English settlement in New York, preceding even Southampton. Because it was privately held, however, it never gained the distinction of being first.

Gardiner was highly regarded by the Indians, and was said to be a very good friend of Wyandance, and often an overnight guest in the wigwam of the powerful chief.

In reality, when Ogden bought the land from Wyandance, Quogue belonged to the Shinnecocks, not the Montauks. How Wyandance came to be selling the Shinnecocks' land to Lion Gardiner, then to John Ogden, adds another interesting twist to the story.

The incident had its beginning ten years earlier in 1649 when a Mrs. Thomas Halsey of Southampton was murdered. Wyandance was summoned to appear before the town's magistrates to answer for the deed; however, he was innocent. His tribal counselors advised him to ignore the summons, fearing that he would immediately be put to death.

By coincidence, his good friend Lion Gardiner happened to be lodging in his wigwam that same night. Wyandance sought his advice. Gardiner encouraged the sachem to immediately go to Southampton and answer the summons, promising to the concerned tribal counselors that he would remain in the camp as a hostage to ensure their beloved chief's safety.

The trip was twenty-five miles, and Wyandance set out on his own to answer the charges. Along the way, in a script that could only have been written in Hollywood, he had the good fortune to come across the real villains, apprehend them, and deliver them to the magistrates. They were not local Indians at all, but Pequots who had been sent over to Long Island to stir up trouble. They would eventually be sent to Hartford (where capital cases were heard) and executed.[30]

At a great assembly arranged to celebrate the outcome—the Indians could never be accused of understatement in such matters—Wyandance was officially absolved of guilt. Mandush, the young sachem of the Shinnecocks, was so impressed with the wisdom and courage of Wyandance that he cut a chunk of turf and presented it to sachem as a token of respect. The other Shinnecock elders manifested their agreement by the custom of stroking Wyandance on the back. The ritual was also a way for the Shinnecocks to pledge their allegiance to the stronger Montauks.[31]

Some years later, in a dispute between the Indians and the settlers over the land, Thomas Halsey of Southampton swore before the town magistrates that he had witnessed the aforementioned event.[32]

By virtue of this incident, Wyandance was in a position to dispose of the Shinnecocks' lands for them, and thus the sales to Lion Gardiner and John Ogden. Wyandance kept the money or trade goods received for himself, it appears; but as part of his deal with the Shinnecocks, he became surety for their debt, the result of fines they were assessed for burning the homes of some earlier settlers.

There were a few restrictions on Ogden's Quogue deed. One, which was not unusual in dealings between the Indians and the white settlers, stated "it is agreed that wee [the Shinnecocks] shall keep our privileges of fishing . . . fowling . . . hunting . . . or gathering of beryes." The second restriction allowed two other men to continue to cut salt hay and retain grazing rights on two small plots within the Purchase.

In 1653 Ogden sold part of the Quogue Purchase to John Scott, who immediately resold it to the town of Southampton for seventy pounds, reserving five acres of salt hay for his horses.[33] Ten years later, the town fathers decided that the valuable salt meadows should never be settled or farmed and that the inhabitants of the town should be taxed for its upkeep.[34] The remainder of the Quogue Purchase Ogden retained, then eventually sold to Southampton in 1667, after he had moved to New Jersey.[35]

Finally, local legend gives us another story that neatly puts an end to this incident as far as John Ogden was concerned. His negotiations for the Purchase, the legend says, took place under a large red cedar tree just west of what is today known as Penniman's Pond. After the deed was given by Sachem Wyandance to John Ogden, the principals retired to a structure then standing nearby on what is now Quogue Street, and all enjoyed a glorious feast. The cedar tree was cut down in the 1920s when the Montauk Highway was constructed.[36] [See a complete copy of the Indian deed for Quogue Purchase in the Appendix.]

Hatfield, in his *History of Elizabeth* . . . ascribed yet another vocation to Ogden: "During his residence at Northampton, Ogden, by frequent visits as a trader to New Amsterdam, had kept up his acquaintance with his old friends and neighbors. . . ."[37]

A number of enterprising men in Southampton and nearby East Hampton, like Ogden, were busily engaged in the sea trade. Their small shallops and pinnaces carried firewood, lumber, salt, hides, and farm produce throughout eastern and western Long Island. Using the small, shallow harbor at North Sea, Ogden also carried products from his whaling business to New Amsterdam, and probably to other ports in New England.

By this time, New Amsterdam had grown considerably in the twenty-plus years since Ogden built the stone church, and it had improved. Writing of the town and its trading practices a few years later (after it would become New York) diarist Daniel Denton said:

> New-York is built most of Brick and Stone, and covered with red and black Tile, and the Land being high, it gives at a great distance a pleasing Aspect to the spectators. The Inhabitants consist most of English and Dutch and have a considerable Trade with the Indians, for Bevers, Otter, Raccoon skins, with other Furs; As also for Bear, Deer and Elke skins; and are supplied with Venison and Fowl in the Winter, and Fish in the Summer by the Indians, which they buy at an easie rate; And having the Countrey round about them, they are continually furnished with all such provisions as is needful for the live of man; not only by the English and Dutch within their own, but likewise by the Adjacent Colonies.[38]

The town had built a proper wharf at the foot of Pearl Street, and was already in the infant stage of becoming one of the great shipping ports of the world. The chief product remained beaver pelts, bound for Europe, but tobacco was quickly gaining ground. The town itself was also undergoing a transformation. Brick houses replaced wooden ones, tile roofs replaced thatched, roads were paved with cobblestones, and pigsties and chicken coops were forced off the streets. The "gentlemen's canal" that had been chopped through the center of town, described as "a stinking ditch" when the Ogdens were building their church, had now been widened into a proper canal, its banks reinforced and crossed by pretty stone bridges.[39]

John Ogden would have found a ready market for the products he carried regularly to this bustling new place, providing him with another prosperous business venture.

❧

The Ogdens raised most of their own food, as did all early colonists. What they did not raise, they traded for. Though John Ogden was very busy with his civic and business responsibilities, it's a safe bet that he also found time to help in the fields and

FIRST FERRY
The first ferry between Long Island and Manhattan Island was started in the mid-to-late 1640s.

gardens. Jane, too, would have spent much time outdoors, help-ing to grow the food that she would prepare daily for her growing brood.

By the early 1660s, John Jr. would have been in his early twen-ties, and would undoubtedly have been shouldering a larger share of the workload. He was the only child who made the voyage to America with his parents. He probably toiled in some of his father's business endeavors as well.

David and Jonathan, a few years younger, were now old enough to tackle most of the "heavylifting" chores. According to the fam-ily's chronology outlined in chapter 9, I believe David was born while the family was in Stamford and Jonathan while they were in Hempstead.

Joseph, in his early teens, would have been old enough to till, plant, weed, and harvest the crops, and tend to the chickens, pigs, sheep, cows or whatever other livestock the family owned. Joseph too, would have been born in Hempstead.

Benjamin, probably born shortly after the Ogdens arrived in

Northampton, would have been too young to provide much help; but there were chores designed even for the youngest members of the family.

Sarah (or perhaps her name was Mary; sources differ) has not been age-dated by any historian or genealogist. However, I believe she too was born when the family was in Stamford, or perhaps soon after they relocated to Hempstead, making her in her late teens. As the only girl, she would have carried a heavy load assisting her mother looking after the six males in the family. However, it was around this time that she married John Woodruff Jr., so she would have had her own family to tend too.

Men and women in early colonial America spent most of their lives working side by side. Family members, down to the smallest children, were interdependent, with each family member contributing to the welfare of the whole. Individual autonomy was secondary to the welfare of the family, which served as a productive economic unit.

Within the larger framework of community life, there was not equality of the sexes. But within the family unit, as least as far as practical considerations were concerned, there certainly was. Husband and wife each shouldered his or her own burdens, and when necessary, they took on the burdens of their spouse as well.

In selecting a wife, a man usually looked for a good temper, a virtuous demeanor, and a pious "helpmeet." A woman primarily wanted a good provider, but a kind nature was also highly desired. A husband received his mandate as provider from God as well as man. A sermon of the day preached that a man ". . . should contrive prudently and work diligently, that his Family, and his Wife particularly, may be well provided for."

There is no written record on the strength of the bond between John and Jane Ogden. That they remained married for forty-five years, and that no town record exists of either ever being punished for sins against the other, would lead us to believe that their marriage bond was a strong one. The wording in Ogden's final will, dated December 1681, does indicate a strong bond: ". . . Jaan Ogden is my Deare and beloved wife. . . ." He provided well, and she handled the home front equally well.

I feel confident in saying that he was a good father too. He and Jane raised five boys and at least one girl, and each child became a pious and contributing member of the community in his or her own right. What more could be asked of parents?

Day-to-day life for the Ogdens, as well as the other colonists on Long Island, would have been an ongoing challenge:

> They raised on the farm Indian corn, wheat (both winter and summer varieties), oats, barley, beans and peas, but no potatoes. The waters abound in fish, clams and oysters, though the shellfish seem to have been used but sparingly. Cows, oxen, goats and sheep were raised in considerable numbers, both for home consumption and for export.
>
> Heavy farm work was done with the help of oxen. The only vehicle in use for a long time was the two-wheeled ox-cart. Men and women traveled on horseback, and when the horse was wanting, on one occasion at least, a bovine was pressed into service.
>
> The transmission of news was only by letter and the last comer. For twenty years after the settlement [at Southampton] not a newspaper was yet in existence in the mother country.[40]

One of the leading crops farmed by Ogden and the other settlers was flax. It had been grown in the New World in New Netherland since 1626. Flax stalks, which grow to two or three feet, are hollow tubes, like bamboo. When pounded with a wooden mallet, they separate into hair-like fibers which, when dried and hetched, or combed, become linen thread. Flax was picked and "cured" in late fall; and during long winter months, the women would turn it into thread, then into heavy linen cloth, which resulted in an extremely serviceable fabric for long-lasting clothing.

In 1660 the Southampton settlers leased pastureland from the Montauk Indians at the extreme southeastern tip of Long Island, near today's town of Montauk. In an annual event that smacks of the Old West, but predates it by nearly two hundred years, each June all cattle from Patchogue, near the center of Long Island, eastward, were rounded up and driven to the leased land to graze for the summer. Each November brought the fall drive back to the villages. This practice was followed for nearly two-and-a-half centuries.[41]

Prior to these cattle drives, the people of Southampton kept their herd at Sagaponack, a meadow about halfway between the town and East Hampton, as we see in this May 10, 1652 town record: "It is concluded by the major pt of the towne that the cattle heard shall be left for this ensuing year at Sagabonack where they were kept the yeare last past."[42]

The area in and around Patchogue also provided one of the few recreational diversions for the Ogdens and their neighbors. Daniel Denton described it:

> Towards the middle of Long-Island lyeth a plain sixteen miles long and four broad, upon which plain grows very fine grass, that makes exceeding good Hay; and is a very good pasture for sheep or other Cattel; where you shall find neither stick nor stone to hinder the Horse heels, or endanger them in their Races, and once a year the best Horses in the Island are brought hither to try their swiftness and the swiftest rewarded with a silver Cup, two being Annually procured for that purpose.[43]

This event could certainly have been one of the earliest organized horse races in the colonies; and must have provided a grand day of feasting and merriment for all the towns on eastern Long Island.

෫

Politically, Southampton was, at its original founding, a pure democracy. The town *was* the people, and for the people, and not the people for the town. Governance was entirely *by* the people. A town meeting, or General Court as it was called, was held semiannually, composed of all adult males of the town, who were obliged to attend under penalty of a fine.

This court exercised the extraordinary powers of both a legislative and judicial branch. They defined the powers and limits of the magistrate's court, received and decided appeals from that court, were the tribunal for trying crimes punishable by death (though that was very rare), set economic regulations and taxes, settled civil cases, allotted lands, elected officers, settled disputed with neighboring towns, conducted relations with the Indians, and enacted the code of laws. All these powers were defined in an act of the first General Court, passed in 1641.

As a leader in his community, Ogden felt duty-bound to serve the towns he had helped found. His history of public service is first recorded in October 1650, when he was named a freeman in the town of Southampton, which retained political authority over Northampton.[44] A freeman was one who had taken the Oath of a Freeman, a kind of pledge of allegiance to the commonwealth. In order to take the oath, one had to be male, churchgoing, and have had a transforming religious experience. The oath stated that the

THE OATH OF A FREEMAN.

I **·A·B·** being (by Gods providence) an Inhabitant, and Freeman, within the iurisdictiō of this Common-wealth, doe freely acknowledge my selfe to bee subject to the governement thereof; and therefore doe heere sweare, by the great & dreadfull name of the Everliving-God, that I will be true & faithfull to the same, & will accordingly yield assistance & support therunto, with my person & estate, as in equity I am bound: and will also truely indeavour to maintaine and preserve all the libertyes & privilidges thereof, submitting my selfe to the wholesome lawes, & ordres made & stablished by the same; and further, that I will not plot, nor practice any evill against it, nor consent to any that shall soe do, butt will timely discover, & reveall the same to lawefull authoritee nowe here stablished, for the speedie preventing thereof. Moreover, I doe solemnly binde my selfe, in the sight of God, that when I shalbe called, to give my voyce touching any such matter of this state, (in which freemen are to deale) I will give my vote & suffrage as I shall judge in myne owne conscience may best conduce & tend to the publick weale of the body, without respect of personnes, or favour of any man. Soe help mee God in the Lord Iesus Christ.

"OATH OF A FREEMAN"

The Oath of a Freeman, printed in the Massachusetts Bay Colony in about 1639, was the first document printed in the New World, followed the next year by the Bay Psalm Book. The Oath was required by all freemen in every settlement operating under a royal or proprietary charter.

colonist would uphold the laws, support the commonwealth, not act against it, and act against those who did. In return for taking the oath, the man was granted the right to be free in the society and was allowed to vote. [A complete copy of the Oath of a Freeman appears in the Appendix.]

Freeman status was a duty, not simply an honor; and the General Court had decreed that any man chosen to be a freeman who refused would be fined forty shillings.[45]

Ogden was first elected as a magistrate in 1650, was re-elected to the post in 1651;[46] and annually from 1655 through 1662. He was also chosen to represent the town at the colony, or provincial, level in Hartford as a magistrate from 1656 through 1662, 1661 excepted.[47] Jane Ogden's brother, Robert Bond, who by this time had resettled in East Hampton as an original patentee, was that town's representative at Hartford for four terms as well.

Ogden and his fellows' duties as town magistrates were laid out on January 2, 1641:

> The Magistrates shall govern according to the laws now established and to be established by General Courts hereafter. They and either of them shall be able to send out warrants to any officer to fetch any delinquent before them, and examine the cause and to take order by sureties or safe custody for his or their appearance in court. And further, to prevent the offenders lying in prison, it shall be lawful for the Magistrates or either of them to see execution done upon any offenders for any crime that is not capital according to the laws that [are] established or to be established in this place.[48]

For the most part, the duties were simply to carry out the directives of the General Court (the citizens), whether from the town or, later on, from the provincial government in Hartford. In effect, they carried out the laws passed by the General Court, or the people themselves.

The first town meeting on record was held on April 6, 1641. By an order of the General Court on December 22, 1644, four quarter courts were to be held annually, in March, June, September, and December, these being the magistrates' courts. At the same time it was ordered that an annual General Court be held on the first Tuesday in October for the purpose of electing town officers.

From the founding of the town in 1640 until John Ogden left for New Jersey in 1664, a litany of the laws passed by the General Court provide a look into the problems that faced the small community. They covered issues ranging from raising and training a militia to sufficiently fencing "little piggs"; from regulating the amount of alcohol that could be served in a year's time to penalties for failing to vote on a community issue; from paying someone to beat the drum calling the men to a meeting to laying a bounty on killing wolves; and from stealing a neighbor's fruit from his tree to paying a fine of a penny for having your goat returned by another. It was upon such issues that the safety and serenity of community life depended.

But the town faced serious matters as well as trivial. A problem that seems to have occurred every few years had to do with the fragile peace they maintained with the Indians who surrounded them. The Town Records of April 14, 1653, ordered that all men between sixteen and sixty be appointed to keep watch.[49] Then a few months later the town purchased twenty-three pounds of gunpowder and 175 pounds of lead.[50]

Historian Howell reported that 1653 was a touch-and-go year for maintaining peace. The Narragansett Indians from the nearby Colony of Rhode Island, perhaps allied with the Dutch, tried to seduce the tribes at the eastern end of Long Island into an alliance for the purpose of exterminating the white settlers. It was unsuccessful, but the apprehensive settlers increased their preparedness nonetheless.[51] East Hampton went so far as to pass a law that no Indian was to even come into town except on special business; and the sentries were ordered to shoot to kill any that tried to pass them after dark.[52]

Again in 1657 the Narragansett tried to stir up trouble. On April 30, half-a-pound of powder was allotted to each of forty freemen in the town, including John Ogden.[53] The following month, on May 4, another town order instructed half of the town's men to stand guard, while the other half went about their normal duties, "provided they goe together and work soe neere together that in the judgement of those appoynted as a centinell, the company that soe goe forth may come together before any danger in respect of assault . . . and are to have their armes with them . . ."[54]

This threat was also reflected in the records of the Connecticut Colony when they took action to assist their Long Island neighbors. In the records of April 1657, it was reported that Major John Mason of Saybrook was appointed to ". . . saile with your men to South Hampton . . . meet with the Magistrates there belonging to this Collony [John Ogden and another] . . . inquire and search out the injury there done & when."

The May 1657 records reflected the outcome of Mason's visit, and set out a course of action: ". . . Whereas the aforesaid Committee have received credible information of severall insolent injuries & insufferable outrages committed against the inhabitants of South Hampton, by some Indians upon Long Iland neare to the said South Hampton . . . send you with 19 men under yo[ur] command where you are to consider of all matters & things whatsoever that may appear necessary. . . ."[55]

The records do not reflect that any further violence came out of this incident; but it again indicates the constant vigilance the settlers had to maintain living among the Indians.

At about this time, town records give us an indication of how the tiny settlement of North Sea must have grown since its inception, in relation to Southampton. Either that or the residents of the town had a very heavy thirst for strong spirits. The records reports that ". . . John Cooper has sole privileges of selling strong drink in Southampton, the total amount to be no more than nine ankers (about ninety gallons) a year. "North Sea, was directed to find a man to be licensed whose total sales were to be "three ankers by the yeare and not to exceed."[56]

Then on November 29, 1659, another town law is passed that is somewhat difficult to fully understand. In it, John Ogden agrees to pay about sixty pounds to have flooring and seating installed in the meetinghouse; then, within five years, to pay an additional forty pounds to some members of the community who had claims against the Indians for some unspecified damages. In return, Ogden was to receive all the proceeds awarded by the court at Hartford against the Indians for those damages, the amount also unspecified. The remaining language appears to indemnify the town in case the Indians refuse to pay the amount in question.[57] This probably relates to the 1657 Indian incident that was discussed earlier in the chapter.

There could be any number of reasons for such an arrangement. My guess would be that the town felt Ogden had the best chance of collecting the debt from the Indians, as they had always trusted him. So the town was probably willing to accept less than full face value on the debt in order to off-load it to Ogden. For his part, Ogden was probably confident of his ability to collect, and felt the risk-reward ratio was in his favor. We can only assume that both parties benefited from the arrangement.

∞

In 1660, the restoration of Charles II to the throne in England awakened fears in the New World that the new government would again attempt to impose its will on the colonies. Connecticut Colony Governor John Winthrop Jr., Ogden, and the other magistrates decided that the Connecticut Colony needed a royal charter to legitimatize it. Obtaining a royal charter—or "letters patent under the great seal," as it was formally known—was a tedious and expensive process. The procedure was defined by a 1535 English law that remained virtually unchanged until the late 1800s.

Once the decision was made to pursue the charter, Winthrop hastily gathered together all the magistrates he could find on short notice. These men, including John Ogden, agreed to recommend to the next General Court, scheduled for March 1661, that they immediately send a delegate to London to petition the king. In May a committee was appointed to perfect the address, which had been drawn up by Winthrop. Their petition also included a statement of what the colony hoped to gain by the charter. Winthrop was appropriately chosen to be the delegate, and five hundred pounds was approved to meet official costs, along with eighty pounds for his personal expenses. He was instructed to also seek confirmation of the original Warwick Patent; and finally, to see that "the liberties and priviledges inserted in the Pattent" were "not to be inferiour or short to what is granted to the Massachusetts." It was also desired that the grant be made to several patentees, including John Ogden, who had authorized and drafted the documents; and that they be assured of the right to conduct their own political affairs. With all his papers in hand, Governor Winthrop set sail for London in July 1661.

He spent the next ten months in London waiting for a decision. But finally, in May 1662, under the name of the "Company of the English colony of Connecticut in New-England, in America," the charter was granted. It gave the colony the right to govern itself and to elect its own leaders. The charter was so well drafted it served as the constitutional basis for Connecticut's government for over 150 years.

The document also spelled out the line of governance among the patentees for the colony: the Governor, John Winthrop Jr; the Deputy-Governor, John Mason; and a committee of twelve assistants. The patentees themselves, including Ogden, were to serve as the assistants, or council, for the first year. As such, Ogden was considered not only one of the leaders of the entire Connecticut Colony but also one of its original patentees. He would retain his position until he left the colony in 1665 to establish the first English colony in New Jersey.

The signers of the document, in addition to Winthrop, Mason, and Ogden were: Samuel Wyllys, Matthew Allyn, Henry Clark, John Topping, Richard Lord, Henry Wolcott, Richard Treat, John Talcott, Daniel Clark, John Clark, Thomas Wells, Obadiah Bruen, Anthony Hawkins, John Deming, and Matthew Canfield.[58]

But the most amazing part about Connecticut Colony's royal charter was still to come. Winthrop was staggered when he learned about it: King Charles II had given the colony a grant that extended from the border of the Massachusetts Bay Colony south, including the Dutch territories and the New Haven Colony, and west to the Pacific Ocean . . . wherever that might be. It was more than he had been told to ask for, and more than he had ever dreamed of achieving.

When word of the charter reached America, the Dutch Colony of New Netherland was incensed. This wasn't the king's land to be giving away; and besides, the Hartford Agreement had established boundaries years earlier between the two powers. But if the Dutch were angry, the New Haven Colony was even angrier.

They had always been independent, completely separate from the Connecticut Colony. New Haven was a colony of Congregationalists, Puritans in the most extreme sense. Winthrop's colony was Presbyterian. The New Haven folks were convinced that to mix with the ungodly Presbyterians would lead to eternal damnation.

It didn't take Charles II long to realize he'd made a terrible mistake. After all, he was new to this king business, and he was much more accustomed to dealing with frivolous court matters. His brother James was the Duke of York and the head of the Royal Navy. He developed a plan: let's take most of it back, by force if necessary. We'll see this drama play itself out in the next chapter.

Most of the foregoing details about the Connecticut royal charter, unless otherwise noted, come from a small booklet prepared for the state's Tercentary celebration in 1933.[59] The tale ends with a delightful bit of minutiae about the document itself. When it was granted, the charter was issued in duplicate, each copy with its own official seal and each one called a duplicate within its text. One of the two copies was mutilated in 1817 when, either in an act of historical ignorance or millinery munificence, it was cut up to form the lining of a lady's bonnet. The only nearly complete extant copy, minus its seal, resides in a vault in Hartford; and the remains of the bonnet copy is in the custody of the Connecticut Historical Society.

One other charter legend is worthy of retelling. When, in 1687, James II ascended to the throne in England, he decided to consolidate all the uneasily maintained American colonies under the formal Dominion of New York and New England, with one royal governor, Sir Edmund Andros. Most colonies gradually abandoned their patents and charters except for Connecticut, who hung tenaciously on. Finally, Andros and seventy-five of his men decided to pay a personal visit to Hartford and wrest the charter from them, by force if necessary.

At Sanford's Tavern, Andros met with Gov. Robert Treat and demanded the surrender of the document. Treat refused. The two sides argued back and forth until night fell, and candles were lit to continue the discussion. During a brief pause, all the candles were suddenly extinguished and the room became pitch black. When the candles were relit, the charter had disappeared!

It is said that one of the colonists, Capt. Joseph Wadsworth, snatched the huge document (it measures about three feet wide by seven feet high), whisked it from the premises, and buried it within the trunk of a huge oak tree—forever after known as the Charter Oak.

This largely symbolic gesture kept Andros from obtaining the document, but he nevertheless incorporated the Connecticut Colony into the Dominion of New York and New England. But the small victory kept the people of the colony in high spirits for the brief two-year period before James II was replaced by William and Mary. Andros was returned to England, and Connecticut voted immediately to return to the original charter, which served it well until a new constitution was written in 1818.

❧

In Southampton, at the town level, another important office was that of townsman. This was an unpopular position, thus often difficult to fill. Their primary responsibilities were to assess taxes and fines, and see to their collection. Sentinels, or wards, were chosen, whose job was to stand guard of the town when deemed necessary by the constable, whose main job was to keep the peace.

Among the minor crimes of the day, most of which were punishable by either monetary fine or time in the stocks, were failing to vote, lying, issuing a false alarm, and drunkenness.

Most early colonial towns also had a number of other important positions that needed to be filled by the freemen. Here are a few of the more notable ones:

- Surveyor
- Lister, one who made up tax lists
- Town clerk
- Fence-viewer, who kept an eye on the general condition of all fences
- Chimney-viewer, who made provisions to watch for fires and check the condition of chimneys
- cattle-herder, cow-keepers, sheep-masters
- Pounder, who impounded loose livestock
- Meat-packers
- Horse-branders
- Leather sealers, who inspected the work of tanners and curriers.[60]

All freemen, including Ogden, served in most of these positions at one time or another. The town clerk and the constable would be paid an annual stipend, but the others served with no pay.

To run the town, taxes were charged, almost always on land, but occasionally on livestock. In the earlier days, taxes would often be paid in commodities: wheat, butter, peas, cheese, pork, beef, or hemp. These products were then bartered to men who would be hired to perform town services: build or repair bridges or common buildings, road construction, military expenses, or maintaining the parsonage and church. It was a good system, and it worked well for the first fifty years or so in colonial America

Ogden is also mentioned a number of times in the town records of the day, often in court proceedings, some of which he appears to have won and others not; and often as being appointed to one or more of the aforementioned town positions. As an example, at a town meeting in 1657, it was voted that "all unlawful cattle or horses (that shall be adjudged so) by Edward Howell and John Ogden shall be turned out of the ox pasture, and also the above said men shall have the power to Judge of the fence of the ox pasture whether it bee sufficient, and whosoever is found defective in their fence shall make the same sufficient by this day senit [seven days]."[61]

6

Nova Caesarea: The Land West of "Hudsons River"

IN 1664, WHEN JOHN OGDEN WAS FIFTY-FOUR YEARS OLD, HAVING spent twenty-four years on Long Island, he and his family decided to relocate again, this time to the west of the Hudson River to what would become New Jersey. It is guessed he saw greater opportunities for material advancement and personal freedom in his new home; and he was never one to pass up an opportunity. It also seems that John Ogden had quite a bit of old-fashioned wanderlust in his soul, an itch that constantly had to be scratched.

As it would turn out, however, Ogden's new home wouldn't come at an easy price. At a time when he probably yearned for a little hard-earned peace and quiet, Ogden would become embroiled in controversies that would haunt him to his grave. Still, at no time since he arrived on American soil would his leadership qualities be so vital, and so tested.

The land west of the Hudson River was virtually unsettled in 1664. Achter Kol, as the area was called by the Dutch, meaning "behind the bay," was part of their New Netherland holdings. In northeastern Achter Kol, where Ogden would relocate, only a few Dutch farms broke the solitude of the surrounding wilderness. The Dutch had established a number of plantations years earlier, but in 1643 they massacred nearly one hundred unsuspecting Indians at Pavonia. In 1655, seeking revenge, the Indians slaughtered a number of settlers in Pavonia, Hoboken, and Staten Island. That put an end to any European settlements in that part of Achter Kol.

In southern Achter Kol, the population was slightly greater; there, Swedes were located at Salem and in several other tiny settlements. Nearby Pennsylvania still remained unsettled; it would be nearly twenty years before Philadelphia would be planted by the Quakers.

Europeans had first set foot on this land in 1609 with Henry Hudson's exploration of the area. The good ship *Half Moon* was manned by twenty men, Dutch and English, who were exploring a passage to China and the Indies, by the northwest route. The day after their arrival they were visited by the local Indians who seemed ". . . very glad of our comming, and brought greene Tabacco and gave us of it for Knives and Beads."

The Indians were friendly at the time, probably more curious than hostile, as most had never seen a white man. As the ship approached, they were led finally to regard it as ". . . a mighty canoe under the guidance of the Great Spirit, and navigated by inferior divinities." The sailors described their hosts, saying "They go in Deere skins loose, well dressed . . . they had red Copper Tobacco pipes, and other things of Copper they did weare about their neckes."[1]

A 1648 publication, "A Description of New Albion," (the English name for New Netherland) says that the Indians in this section of the continent were under the dominion of about twenty kings; that there were "twelve hundred under the two Raritan kings on the north side next to Hudsons River."[2]

By 1664, a full half-century after Hudson's voyage, Achter Kol was virtually unchanged, though now nominally under Dutch rule. But the world scene was changing, and it would have a profound effect on this vast wilderness area.

In 1660 the crown was restored to power in England. The civil wars were over, and the military dictatorship of the Puritan-friendly Cromwells had been ousted. Charles II was on the throne, and the country's leaders were determined to restore things to normal. This included their overseas colonies, which had been virtually ignored for almost two decades.

Just before the Restoration, two separate groups had simultaneously sought to gain permission from the Dutch proprietors to establish a colony in Achter Kol. The first proposal of English-speaking people had been sent in early 1660 in the form of a petition to Governor Petrus Stuyvesant from John Strickland, representing groups from Huntington and Jamaica on Long Island. A second group, New Haven Puritans, followed shortly after with their petition.

Soon, however, both groups began to have suspicions that

Dutch land claims in Achter Kol might not stand up because of England's renewed interest in the colonies. These groups also resented the political jurisdictional control and the assessment of taxes by the Dutch West India Company. So they did not push for approval of their patents.

Other groups went ahead and sought to buy lands in Achter Kol directly from the Indians without even bothering to seek Dutch approval, but without success.

To study the situation in America, and recommend a course of action, Charles II appointed a special committee, composed of Lord John Berkeley, Sir George Carteret, and Sir William Coventry. Despite Dutch claims in the New World, England had never relinquished her claims to these lands as a result of their first sighting in 1497 by John Cabot. In January 1664 the committee recommended to the overseeing Council for Foreign Plantations (of which Lord Berkeley also happened to be president) that New Netherland could probably be taken from the Dutch with only three warships of the fleet, three hundred soldiers and 1,300 New England colonists. The committee's estimate turned out to be prescient.[3]

Armed with this recommendation, King Charles met with his brother James, the Duke of York, in March 1664. James, only twenty-seven at the time, was three years younger than his brother. Charles, who never had much of a head for business, still realized that the American colonies could be an economic boon for the mother country, if handled judiciously. With that in mind, he pledged to James a vast tract of land in the New World that stretched from southern Canada to the Carolinas, and included almost the entire eastern coastline. The grant, which took only a few days to sail through all the proper channels, wiped out any and all previous grants that had been made. This included much of the land Winthrop had earlier been granted.

James was also given the right of government, or sovereignty, over the entire area, but only in the name of the king, a fine distinction that would have long-term ramifications.

James named Colonel Richard Nicolls to be commander of the expedition to take New Netherland. Whitehead, writing in 1848, said ". . . a fleet was dispatched, consisting of two vessels of fifty guns each, and one of forty guns, having on board 600 soldiers, besides a full complement of sailors, to put the duke in possession . . ."[4]

Nicolls blockaded New Amsterdam harbor with his ships. In all of New Netherland there were barely seven hundred Dutch men; and in New Amsterdam itself, only about 150 soldiers. The outcome was crystal clear from the onset, even to Peter Stuyvesant, the Director General of the province.

A Dutch view of the brief affair, undoubtedly given to a little flight of fancy, was offered by Rev. Samuel Drisius in a September 15, 1664, letter to the Classis (church elders) of Amsterdam:

> I cannot refrain from informing you of our present situation . . . On the 26th August there arrived in the Bay or the North River, near Staten Island, four great men-of-war, or frigates, well manned with sailors and soldiers. They were provided with a patent or commission from the King of Great Britain to demand and take possession of this province, in the name of His Majesty. If this could not be done in an amicable way, they were to attack the place, and everything was to be thrown open for the English soldiers to plunder, rob and pillage.
>
> Our Director-General and Council . . . took the matter much to heart and zealously sought, by messages between them and General Richard Nicolls, to delay the decision . . . but every effort was fruitless. They landed at Gravezandt, and marched them over Long Island to the Ferry opposite this place. The frigates came under full sail on the 4th of September with guns trained to one side. They had orders, and intended, if any resistance was shown to them, to give a full broadside on this open place, then take it by assault, and make it a scene of pillage and bloodshed.
>
> Our Hon. Rulers of the Company . . . were inclined to defend the place, but found that it was impossible . . . No relief or assistance could be expected, while daily great numbers on foot and on horseback from New England, joined the English, hotly bent upon plundering the place . . . our authorities found themselves compelled to come to terms . . . The English moved in on the 8th, according to agreement . . .
>
> Your willing colleague, Samuel Drisius[5]

So it was that the peg-legged Stuyvesant surrendered and hobbled out of Fort Amsterdam without a shot being fired. New Amsterdam now became New York, after its new owner, the Duke of York; and Fort Amsterdam became Fort James. Achter Kol became, though only briefly, Albania.

With England now in control of the land west of the Hudson, John Strickland lost no time in re-applying for the establishment of a colony. Richard Nicolls was by now the Deputy Governor, and he had instructions to colonize as swiftly as possible. Thus in late September 1664 he granted the request of Strickland's association to seek a purchase from the Indians, saying "I do consent unto the proposals and shall give the undertakers all due encouragement in so good a work."[6]

The Long Island associates made their way to the wigwam of the Raritan Sachem Mattano on Staten Island and bought the land across the river that was to become known as the Elizabethtown Purchase. Negotiations had to be conducted in sign language and with rough sketches etched in the dirt with sharp sticks. The deed was made out to John Bailey, Daniel Denton, and Luke Watson and their associates, and obliged the association to pay the Indians twenty fathoms (120 feet) of trading cloth, two coats, two guns, two kettles, ten bars of lead, and twenty handsful of powder for the land. One year after settling the land, the Association was to pay four hundred additional fathoms of white wampum.[7]

All totaled, the price of the land was equivalent to 154 English pounds, certainly a bargain price for approximately five hundred thousand acres. The Purchase encompassed all of today's Union County, and substantial portions of Essex, Morris, Somerset, and Middlesex counties. The original deed for the purchase still exists with the New Jersey Historical Society. Appended to it is a receipt, dated one year later, giving proof that the associates were paying on the final installment of the purchase price: "Received of John Ogden in part of the above-specified foure hundred feet of wampum, I say Received one hundred fathom of wampum by mee the 18 of August 1665." The receipt was signed by the mark of the Sachem Mattano, and witnessed by two of the associates. On November 24, 1665, the deed was finally endorsed as fully paid.[8]

In November 1664, Deputy Governor Nicolls confirmed the group's title to the Elizabethtown Purchase. By this time, there had already been ownership changes in the association. John Ogden Sr. of North Sea, along with John Bailey, Luke Watson, and John Baker, were now the four principal stockholders in the purchase named in the confirmation to the deed.[9]

A second group, the irate New Haven settlers, similarly concluded the Monmouth Purchase, in order to get out of reach of Winthrop's Presbyterians.

So all these associates would be encouraged to colonize immediately, and to encourage others groups to re-settle in the Duke of York's new land, Nicolls drew up and published a set of rights and privileges that they could expect to receive. The privileges were broad and sweeping, allowing the settlers to:

—buy land from the Indians, then record it with the Governor without having to pay a tax for the privilege;
—establish a settlement thereon;
—be free of any assessments, taxes or rents for five years; thereafter, only pay yearly quitrents at the prevailing rate of the day;
—retain ownership of the land in perpetuity, to hold or sell as they pleased;
—retain "liberty of conscience", or the right to religious freedom;
—have the right to independent town government, with a free choice of officers;
—every associate could become a freeman and was entitled to a town lot, the right to vote and hold office, except servants and hired laborers.

The settlers could not have hoped for more. If only it had turned out to be true.[10]

What occurred next is one of the strangest twists in the early colonization of America, and an event that would have a profound effect on the people of New Jersey.

Unbeknown to Deputy Governor Nicolls, and while he was following his orders to settle the land as quickly as possible, the Duke of York began dividing the spoils. He kept New York as his own, and to his longtime friends Lord John Berkeley and Sir George Carteret he gave all the lands that included present-day New Jersey. Their tract was described as:

. . . Lying and being to the Westward of Long Island and Manhitas Island and bounded on the East part by the Maine sea and part by Hudsons river and hath upon the West, Delaware Bay or River extendeth Southward to the Maine Ocean as farre as Cape May at the mouth of Delaware Bay or River of Delaware which is fourty-one degrees and fourty minutes of Lattitude and Crosseth over thence in a Straight Line to Hudsons River, in fourty one degrees of Lattitude which said Tract of Land is hereafter to be called by the name or names of New Cesarea or New Jersey.[11]

Berkeley and Carteret were not entirely new to this proprietor largess. They were among eight friends of the royal court who had previously been given proprietorship of the Carolinas. However, just as Deputy Governor Nicolls was unaware of the two new proprietors, they were unaware that he was busily giving away part of their holdings.

As we'll see, this wasn't the end of contradictory land claims in New Jersey, but only the beginning. In any volume of histories of the earliest colonies, you will invariably find less written about New Jersey than any of the others. The reason is simple: New Jersey colonial history is so convoluted that few historians want to tackle its complexities. On a timeline, control of the land (or claims of control) alone would look something like this:

the Indians>the Dutch> the English>the Connecticut colony>the colonizers> The Duke of York>Carteret & Berkeley>the Dutch (again)>Carteret & two English Quakers>Carteret, one English Quaker & William Penn>the Duke of York (again, but this time nullified)>the 12 new proprietors>the 24 new proprietors>the English Crown (who made it a royal province.)

And all this was within the brief span of 37 years.

Is it any wonder that these multiple, overlapping claims on the land in New Jersey were to seriously complicate life, a fact that continued to hound early settlers and their descendents well into the nineteenth century.

But land ownership was only one problem; there was also the issue of political control over the colony. It's important to understand these two issues, as they would become a central focus for John Ogden and thousands of other early New Jersey colonists.

Let's look first at the land issues. There was a profound difference in worldview between these new English proprietors and the New Jersey settlers. Carteret and Berkeley wanted to create a hierarchical society dominated by large estates, with land ownership under their control, much as they enjoyed in England. In fact, their plan called for the lands to be divided into seven parts, one of which they would keep for themselves, and the other six divided among all settlers. The settlers would pay rent to them in the form of quitrents, a kind of feudal taxation system.

The colonizers, on the other hand, wanted to live in communities with distribution of freehold property among the qualifying men of the settlement. These colonizers had left England twenty-five to thirty years earlier to get away from exactly the kind of property ownership system the proprietors now seemed bent on installing. They had braved danger and uncertainty to forge a new home; and for many years, while England was absorbed in its own problems, they had been left to build their own economic and political systems. They would not willingly or easily step back.

At the heart of the land ownership question was the fact that seventeenth-century Anglo-American legal concepts had no fixed meaning, and the boundaries of institutional authority were undefined. McConville, in his landmark book on the struggle for property and power in early New Jersey, summed it up:

> A concept as important as property was governed by a jumble of contradictory laws, institutions, and customs that had been made even more incoherent by the profound turmoil of the English Civil War and the Protectorate (1642–60). The infant English colonies of North America all inherited this confusion, and each of them struggled to escape its grip. New Jersey never truly did, as its endemic property disputes amply demonstrate. The resulting ownership disputes endured until the eighteenth century's end.[12]

The second issue had to do with sovereignty: who would rule, and how. Ostensibly, the proprietors were prepared to create dual governance. The colony would be ruled by the proprietor-appointed governor and his appointed council, aided by the assembly, made up of the settlers' appointed representatives. While it may have had a nice ring to it, in fact the assembly, or house of burgesses, would in truth exercise only as much or as little power as the governor wished to grant it.

This is indeed the political system that was installed in New Jersey by the proprietors. However, when we examine the entire issue of political control through the lens of English law at the time, we find a loophole large enough through which to drive a team of sturdy oxen.

The essential question is this: did the proprietors of New Jersey legally possess rights of government? This question arose from the fact that New Jersey, unlike the other colonies except New Hampshire, did not originate from an immediate grant of the crown. The charter to the Duke of York contained no authority for him to delegate governmental powers to others; in English law, such powers can pass *only* by an express grant from the king himself. So the duke's deed of lease and release to Carteret and

Berkeley was, in point of English law, only a grant of the soil and nothing more. All the subsequent documents that passed from London to America promising political control to the proprietors was therefore improperly drafted, and did not constitute the weight of law.[13]

In his book, *As We Were: The Story of Old Elizabethtown*, author Theodore Thayer praises Ogden and the other colony leaders, perhaps inaccurately, writing:

> Governor Nicolls deserves honor for conferring upon the infant colony the blessings of a free government. But it must be remembered that it was the pioneers themselves, who had insisted all along on having New Jersey founded upon republican principles of government. It is therefore primarily to them that we owe the foundation of liberty upon which the future [of New Jersey] was to rest.[14]

Thayer's terminology, "free government," "republican principles," and "foundation of liberty" ring well; but were perhaps a little overstated as it turned out.

This leads us to the most intriguing conjecture in early New Jersey history: did John Ogden and his contemporaries understand that the proprietors had no standing in law to govern them; or were they simply standing behind their moral convictions that no distant government had such rights? I believe it was the latter. Some of Ogden's acts of civil disobedience over the next twenty-three years were so unabashed they would indicate he knew he was on solid legal footing, but I don't believe that was the case. I believe his moral indignation was so intense that he took his positions without questioning the legal foundation. Had he and the others known their legal rights, the settlers would undoubtedly have pursued them. Even when they asked John Winthrop Jr. to write a letter in their support to present to the king, they asked only for character references, not to argue points of law. So it's probable they were never aware that they were on legally sound footing to ignore the proprietors' grab for political sovereignty.

This entire political issue has significant overtones for American history, I believe. In some circles, and I have seen it expressed in a number of history books, these New Jersey colonists have been called malcontents, dissidents, and even seditionists for their opposition to the proprietors' political rule. But in light of existing English law, they were correct, even if they didn't know it, and the proprietors were wrong. I contend this makes these American pioneers not wrong-minded but right-minded; not anarchists but nationalists; and not seditionists, but patriots.

So as we take one final look at the dual issues of property and power in early New Jersey, it is now apparent that in law, power did not belong to the proprietors. As to property, that issue would not be resolved in court or in fact. It took the War of Independence, more than one hundred years later, to finally determine that America, and the land underneath it, belonged to Americans, not to the British.

❧

None of this, of course, was in the mind of John Ogden in 1664 when, Southampton records indicate, he began to dispose of his real estate holdings. He eventually passed many of his holdings on to his son-in-law John Woodruff Jr., who was married to his daughter Sarah.

Blithely unaware of the problems before them, most of the Elizabethtown Purchase associates decided to wait until the following spring to move their families. In their application to Gov. Nicolls, they had asked him to ". . . answer with as much expedition as may be; because some of them, by reason of not having any accommodations where they then resided, were put upon thoughts of removing into some other of his Majesty's dominions." John Ogden found himself in this situation, having sold his property, so he and three other men, probably accompanied by their families, wasted no time, and on or around November 24, 1664, sailed to their new ground, and built temporary huts at the site of the future town. Ogden's thinking was that much work could be accomplished over the winter: felling trees and working the logs into beams and planks, clearing land for early spring planting, and establishing trade with the Indians who ordinarily took their winter furs to the Dutch.

This became the first English settlement in present-day New Jersey.

Daniel Denton was one of the associates on the original Indian deed for the Elizabethtown Purchase. The oldest son of Ogden's good friend, Rev. Richard Denton, Daniel then decided not to resettle west of the Hudson, and sold his rights to John Ogden. A few years later, during a business trip to England, Denton was constantly asked about the New York-New Jersey area from which he had returned. Inspired by those questions, he wrote and published a small book in London in 1670 describing the place. It was the first printed description in English of what is now one of the most populous and important areas in the world.

Denton described the area "Westward of Achter-Kull River" that is today New Jersey:

> . . . about 18 or 20 miles runs in Raritan-River Northward into the Countrey, some score of miles, both side of which River is adorn'd with Spacious Meadows, enough to maintain thousands of Cattel, the Wood-land is likewise very good for corn, and stor'd with wilde Beast, as Deer, and Elks, and an innumerable multitude of Fowl, as in other parts of the Countrey: This River is thought very capable for the erecting of several Towns and Villages on each side of it . . . upon this River is no town setled, but one [Elizabethtown] at the mouth of it.[15]

Thayer adds some descriptive color of his own about the beautiful land that would become New Jersey:

> As the Elizabethtown pioneers surveyed the wide expanse of meadows and the dense forest rising like a wall to the westward, a great thrill must have seized the heart of everyone. It was truly a great land of boundless promise—for them, for their children and for generations to come. Now that it was autumn, the pioneers saw the waters alive with ducks, geese and other varieties of water birds. Almost everywhere along the shore, bushels of clams, oysters and scallops could be gathered in an amazingly short time. The streams and the salt waters teemed with fish, large and small. Perched in the tallest trees or circling aloft, hawks and eagles were having a final feast before flying off to warmer climes. On penetrating the forest, the men came upon great numbers of wild turkeys, grouse and other game birds. In the spring would come immense flocks of song birds from the south as well as clouds of passenger pigeons, so thick in the sky as fairly to obscure the light of the sun.[16]

The Dutch government had also heaped praise on Achter Kol, describing the land in 1661 when they were attempting to colonize it:

> It is under the best clymate in the whole world . . . seed may bee thrown into the ground, except six weekes, all the yere long, and there are five sorts of grapes which are very good and grow heere nat-

urally, with divers other excellent fruits extraordinarily good . . . the land very fertile, produceth a great increase of wheat and all other grane whatsoever . . ."[17]

❧

Like the earliest town records of many seventeenth-century colonial villages, the first records from Elizabethtown were lost in the eighteenth century, only a few pages somehow remaining. Thus our knowledge of how these pioneers governed their earliest day-to-day activities can only be guessed at.

Early in 1665 the remaining associates and their families began to arrive. They were followed by boatloads of eager colonizers from western and eastern Long Island and from settlements along the shores of Connecticut. Since sloops could navigate the narrow Mill River (now the Elizabeth River) only as far as the site chosen for the town, that's how most arrived.

It was understood that any freeman was entitled to purchase a share and become an associate until a quota of about eighty families was reached. Ogden, as a 25 percent owner of the original association, had sold shares to his eastern Long Island neighbors for the equivalent of four pounds, payable in beaver pelts.

In the spring of 1665 enough men had arrived to warrant calling a meeting for the purpose of laying out rules for the town, and establishing the town lots for their houses. Ogden was selected chairman of the committee to carry out and enforce the new rules. From the beginning, he was the designated leader of the settlement. Hatfield called him "the leading man of the new colony," while Thayer said, "the leadership of the whole community fell to him."

This land was still a wilderness, and it was widely recognized that to travel alone or in a small group was foolish. The Indians here, as in other territories once ruled by the Dutch, did not trust the white man. The Dutch had given them good reason. So in laying out their town, the associates decided to use the old New England plan, which congregated them all together around a common green.

It was normal practice for migrating groups to give their leaders first choice in selection of town lots. John Ogden selected first. His lot was the most centrally located in town, at the head of navigation on the river where a dam could be built for mills. His homestead was recorded in 1691, after his death and probably in the name of his son John Jr., describing it as "Bounded South by a highway, West by Mill River, North by lands of the said Elizabethtown for a place of burial." Today, the main branch of the Elizabeth Public Library stands on the property, while the river's banks are held in place by concrete retainers.

John Bailey and Luke Watson probably chose next, with the remainder of the associates drawing lots for their parcels.

There were three classes of lots distributed to the associates, based upon their standing in the community and the amount of money they had invested in the project: first lot rights earned its owner a house lot of approximately six acres; second lot rights received twice the amount of land as the first; and third lot rights received three times the lot size of the first. Of the eighty associates, thirty-three had first lot rights, twenty-six had second lot rights, and twenty-one had third lot rights. Ogden had two third lot rights, his own and the one he had purchased from Denton.

The choicest town lots were laid out on both sides of the river and measured four chains wide and twelve to fifteen chains deep (264 feet by 790–990 feet). After these areas were taken, other lots were laid out along the old Dutch trail to the Delaware River, which became King's Highway. Three of the Ogden boys, John Jr., David, and Jonathan, now in their mid-to-late 20s, received first lot rights, while John's brother-in-law, Robert Bond, received a second lot right.[18] Most of the associates also had fifty to one hundred additional acres outside the town proper for farming and grazing land.

Home lots, if not occupied, would be forfeit, and owners would have to occupy their lots for three years before being allowed to dispose of them.

Meanwhile, while the settlement was being laid out, the two new proprietors had chosen Philip Carteret, a distant cousin of Sir George Carteret, to act as governor of their new colony. Philip was twenty-six at the time, a handsome, congenial young man. He was also known to have a strong will and solid determination, qualities that he would certainly require, as it turned out. A bachelor, he left behind a young lady whom he hoped would eventually become his bride, but she refused to leave England for the New World.

In mid-1665, Philip Carteret set sail from England with a small coterie of assistants and servants who would become settlers in the new colony he was to rule. Landing in New York in August, he sought out the Duke of York's man, Richard Nicolls, and presented his credentials. If he had expected a warm welcome, he was mistaken. Nicolls was furious. This was the first he'd heard about new proprietors, or a new governor. He'd eventually send two letters to the Duke in London, trying to convince him to reconsider, telling him that he'd given away the best part of his territory, but to no avail.

Philip Carteret stayed in New York only a short time, very uncomfortable with the hot-tempered reception he had received. He figured he'd be more welcome in his new colony, and set sail aboard his ship, the *Philip*, for the short trip across the bay to Achter Kol. But by this time, word of the new proprietors and governor had reached the Elizabethtown settlers who were laying the foundation for their town, and they were not pleased either.

As the *Philip* approached the settlement, it was Carteret's turn to be surprised and dismayed. On the sloping hill before him, he saw only a few crude huts edged by roughly tilled gardens. *That* was New Jersey? This was not what he had expected at all.[19]

The ship made land at the foot of the settlement. Aboard with Philip Carteret were a French surveyor, Robert Vauquellin, who had been appointed surveyor general of the colony, and his wife; a sea captain from New York; eighteen men of the working class; and a group of unnamed servant women—thirty people in all.

The townspeople went to the landing to meet them, and Carteret presented his credentials, signed by Nicolls, among others. Among his documents were the proprietors' grant that announced that the colony would henceforth be known as Nova Caesarea, or New Jersey, and a document called the "Concessions & Agreements," the instrument by which the colony would be governed.

The name part was easy. The settlers preferred the English name to the Latin one, and Nova Caesarea was never in common usage.

John Ogden, as leader of the town, stepped forward and produced the association's credentials: the approved patent from Nicolls, the deed from the Raritan Indians, and Nicolls's approval of the deed. It must have been an awkward moment for both men.

Regaining his composure, Carteret pointed out that his grant from the Duke of York preceded the associates' patent by almost five months, and declared that ". . . the Grants of Colonel Nicolls

JOHN OGDEN MEETS PHILIP CARTERET
In 1665 Gov. Philip Carteret landed at Elizabethtown after journeying from England to take control of the province as its new governor. Joining Carteret were his surveyor general, Robert Vauquellin, and a number of servants. They were met by John Ogden and the other early settlers who had just begun their new plantation late the year before. From the Collections of the New Jersey Historical Society.

is Posterior to our Patent, and therefore both in law and equity the right is solely in us."[20]

Ogden's rejoinder has not come down in history.

Just when it seemed a stalemate had been reached, Carteret backed down and seemingly agreed to the associates' rights. No doubt he simply wanted to avoid a nasty confrontation there at the edge of the river, believing ultimately in the expression that "might makes right." Besides, he had decided to make the town the seat of his government and his personal home, and probably felt that for the time he would simply try to fit into the community.

[In the Essex County Courthouse in Newark, N.J., is a large mural that details that first meeting between the settlers and Carteret's party, at the foot of the river. A photo of that mural appears in this chapter. Among the small group of settlers assembled there stands a large, hawk-nosed man with a high forehead, long hair gathered at the back in a ponytail. To my mind, this *is* John Ogden, the artist's imagination having captured him just as I saw him in my own mind.]

Carteret expressed his desire to become an associate of the town, and eventually purchased the rights of John Bailey who had decided not to re-settle there. In a number of subsequent purchases, he also bought up the land of other associates who had died or decided to sell. So, in this strange twist, Carteret became both the official representative of the proprietors and an associate of the settlement. The other associates agreed among themselves that by virtue of becoming one of them, Carteret had tacitly agreed that the rights granted them in their original patent were valid. That was a very good sign.

According to a legend passed down through many generations—a legend that I've seen extolled in some histories, damned in others, and ignored altogether in still others—Philip Carteret then led his twelve new settlers and eighteen servants up from the banks of the river with a hoe on his shoulder, signifying his wish to become one of those who tilled the soil.[21]

There were now two documents that set down rules for governing the colony, the original list of rights and privileges proclaimed by Nicolls and the Concessions & Agreements proclaimed by the proprietors. This fact would provide the underpinning for most of the disagreements between the two factions in the years to come. In truth, the differences in the two were, in most cases, rather subtle. Both granted the same degree of religious and political freedoms to the associates, and both promised generous inducements in their desire to see the lands settled.

But the differences, though subtle, were important. Both demanded that the settlers proclaim their allegiance to the king, a common condition in any agreement of the day. But the Concessions added a little extra language, requiring that all the settlers swear to be faithful to the interests of the lords proprietors of the province as well. Those not swearing such allegiance could be barred from being freemen, owning land, and voting.

Another difference was that the Concessions gave the surveyor general the responsibility to lay out all lots and issue land titles, a task that had already been accomplished before Carteret and his party arrived. And finally, the Concessions did not bar servants and hired laborers from owning land, as the original rights and privileges had, a fact that would be at the core of another huge disagreement between the two sides. Both documents demanded quitrents of the settlers after a grace period had passed.[22]

The Elizabethtown and Monmouth associates stubbornly stuck

to the rights and privileges granted them in their original patent over the years. To waver from that to the smallest degree, they must have felt, would have been to grant legitimacy to the proprietors' claims, something they simply would not do.

❦

In early colonial towns, the first public building to be put up, right after the individual homes and whatever fortifications were necessary, was the meetinghouse and church. It was only one building, but served both purposes. Puritans did not believe in consecrated places, so they had no problem conducting both religious and secular business under the same roof.

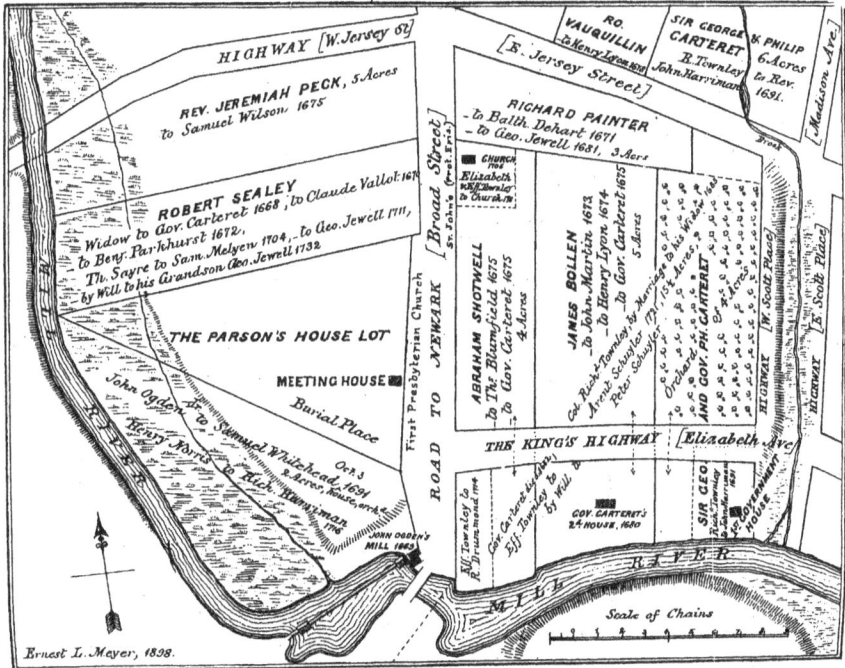

MAP OF ELIZABETHTOWN SETTLEMENT, 1665
A map of the original settlement at Elizabethtown, the first English town in present-day New Jersey, drawn in 1898. Note "John Ogden's Mill" in the bottom center of the map, on the Mill (today Elizabeth) River. Ogden's house lot was situated immediately to the left of his mill, identified on the map as the plot that was sold by John Ogden Jr. to Samuel Whitehead in 1691.

The original meetinghouse was on the Road to Newark, which is today Broad Street. It was only a short distance from the Mill River where John Ogden had built his gristmill, and was sandwiched between the house lots of John Ogden and Robert Sealey. The lot was about eight acres. Matthias Hatfield, one of the original associates, was the first owner of the land on which the meetinghouse sat, and he donated it to the settlement for the church and burial ground.

Ogden was a noted stonemason, as was his son David, and there were a number of carpenters among the original group. Together with other townspeople, they probably built the meetinghouse. Historian Hatfield guessed that the gathering in which sixty-five of the men took the oath of allegiance in February 1666 was held in the new building.

Though its original size, cost, and general appearance cannot be estimated because of the lost records, Hatfield thought that a similar building constructed in Newark at around the same time might provide clues. That building was erected ". . . with a Lenter to it all the Length which will make it Thirty Six foot Square with the doors, and Windows, and Flue Boards at the Gable Ends." Hatfield said the Elizabethtown meetinghouse was ". . . a frame building, and, probably, somewhat larger and more sightly than the one at Newark."[23]

The original Elizabethtown building was replaced by a new structure in 1724, and named the First Presbyterian Church. In 1762, the trustees of the church decided to put the "Church-Edifice" in order. It was voted that:

> . . . the Burial Ground be inclosed with a close cedar Board Fence with red Cedar Posts and that a sufficient Number of Posts be set up before the said Fence for the Convenience of fastening Horses &c.[24]

It was burned by the British in 1780, and rebuilt in 1789. It has since been added to many times. The tall steeple was lost in a fire in 1946, and has never been replaced. Still, today's "Old First," as it is often called, is still grand, and is now on the National Register of Historic Places.

Another of the early structures was the old stone bridge across the Mill River, just below Ogden's mill. The river narrows at that point, making it an ideal place to locate a passageway from one side to the other. I cannot determine with certainty if Ogden built the bridge, but it is a very safe assumption that he either built it himself or in concert with other townsmen. The bridge, like the mill and Ogden's house nearby, stood until sometime in the nineteenth century.

The first official town meeting was held on February 19, 1666. By that time the little town had received its name, Elizabethtown, in honor of Elizabeth Carteret, the wife of proprietor Sir George Carteret.[25]

Another order of business was required. Each male inhabitant of the town was required to take the oath of allegiance, a normal process in any new English town. The list of names totaled sixty-five, "Mr John Ogden Senr" being listed first. It's also telling that on the original document, as on many early New Jersey documents, only Ogden is addressed as "Mister." The honorable designation was reserved only for clergymen and the most distinguished men of the colony. Also signing were John Jr., David, and Jonathan Ogden, Robert Bond and his son Joseph, and all the other men of the settlement except Capt. John Baker, who was in Albany at the time.[26]

The first sixty-six families to arrive were not strangers to each other. Many were sons, or second-generation colonists, of the men who came to Achter Kol. Almost all of them came from Long Island or Connecticut. By and large, they were close personal friends of one another; many had previously been patentees together in founding other colonies. John Ogden, John Strickland, Capt. John Baker, Robert Bond, Luke Watson . . . they knew each other well, and trusted each other implicitly.

These founders brought with them their religious habits, manners, and customs. They were of one mind and one heart. The only disturbing element among them was the group that had arrived from England, Carteret and his entourage. They were not welcomed into the town. Many of them, Hatfield states, were probably Roman Catholic, and the remainder, of the Church of England. These were not men who added character to the town.[27] As a result they were not invited to the town meetings nor welcome in the church nor included in any of the social festivities. The small group became pariahs in Elizabethtown.

Despite these differences, the town continued to grow and develop:

> Also by this time the town had begun to take shape. All the houses were small and made of planks set on end with the butts anchored in

the ground and the tops fastened to risers. All were one story, or one-and-a-half (with a loft) with eaves barely six feet from the ground. Because of low foundations, the doors opened nearly on a level with the street. The massive stone chimney, the first of which were made of clay and timber, covered almost one complete end of the house. At first, some of the pioneers may have made thatched roofs from the course meadow grass, as was customary in New England. Just outside the back door was a rain barrel kept filled with water for washing and fire protection. Inside the house, the large eight or ten foot fireplace dominated the main room, which served as a kitchen, dining room and living quarters. All the houses had plastered walls made with a mixture of clay and ground seashells. To conserve heat the ceilings were very low and the windows small. A trap door in the main room or kitchen led down into a small cellar used for storing vegetables and other commodities requiring cold storage.[28]

Once the houses were built, fencing was the most pressing need. The fencing provided protection against wild and domestic animals for the gardens and fruit trees, and against animals and Indians for the livestock.

Next, the fields were cleared for planting. Oats, wheat, rye, corn, and buckwheat were the standard crops, providing food for both the settlers and their livestock.

While Ogden and the other men and boys were busy with the building and planting chores, the women and girls had their responsibilities too. Jane had brought their spinning wheels, looms, candle molds, kettles, and tubs, and soon all were put to use. Cooking at the massive fireplaces was an endless chore, and washing at the river and putting up food for the winter were also important. Soap making, sewing, knitting, and spinning were chores always waiting when time allowed.

It wasn't long after establishing the town that the need arose for a sawmill. Utilizing his skill as a stonemason, Ogden set to work building a dam on the Mill River, the first step, and by the end of 1666 the dam was built and a sawmill in operation. But Ogden, always the entrepreneur, had in mind more than just a sawmill for his dam across the Mill River.

Using his engineering skills, within two years he had added to his property a gristmill for grinding corn and grains. It stood about two hundred yards below the dam, on the east bank of the river, while the sawmill probably sat on the west bank. It is assumed that John hired a miller to run his gristmill, as he was much too busy for the task himself. Thayer says the men and boys who came to the mill never became tired of watching Ogden's miller, covered with flour dust, as he stood by the chute and tested with his thumb the fineness of the flour as it flowed from the grinding stones.[29]

Early colonial gristmills were once as common as meeting-houses. Every settlement needed one. For that reason, the miller and/or the gristmill's owner were as important to the town as the blacksmith and his forge. At the heart of a gristmill were the two huge grinding wheels: flat, round stones that often weighed thousands of pounds. One laid flat, while the other stood on edge and rolled around the flat one, crushing the grain between the two. The remainder of the working parts were, as one writer described it, ". . . like being inside a giant clock, midst a fascinating collection of wooden gears, pulleys and shafts that translate the power of wind and water to millstones, saws and pumps."[30]

On October 9, 1668, perhaps due to the expenses of starting all his business ventures, Ogden needed capital. Cornelius Steenwyck, a wealthy New York merchant and mayor of the city, was probably an old friend. Ogden sought and gained from him a mortgage on his gristmill for 191 pounds, "one fourth part thereof to be paid in good Wheat . . . one fourth part in good drie Ox hides . . . one fourth part in good merchantable Tobacco . . . and one fourth part in Good Corn fed fat Pork."

As security he pledged "A certain Water Mill now in my Tenure or Occupation, near unto the Mansion or Dwelling House of Gov. Carterett in Elizabeth Towne."[31]

In 1693, eleven years after Ogden's death, Ebenezer Wilson, a second-generation inhabitant of the town, came in possession of the mill, "possibly by foreclosure of Ogden's mortgage to Mr. Steenwyck." Ogden's youngest son, Benjamin, and Rev. Harriman leased the mill from Wilson for twenty-four pounds a year for the next seven years. Nathaniel Whitehead ran it for the men.[32]

As testament to Ogden's building skills, the old mill by the Stone Bridge, as it was later known, was still in operation as late as the 1850s.

Leather was another commodity in great demand in pioneer communities, and again it was John Ogden who met the needs of Elizabethtown.

Ogden built a tanyard on one of his properties. When cows,

horses, deer, even oxen, died naturally or were killed for food in the town, Ogden purchased the hides. He wasted no part of the animal: even hair and bristles were used in making clothes and brushes. The business of turning the hides into leather was a long, messy, and foul-smelling process that could take up to a year to complete.

Tannin, harvested from the bark of the oak or hemlock tree, was the primary material used in tanning, and early New Jersey abounded in such forests. The bark was ground to a fine powder in one of Ogden's mills. The end result was hard, heavy leather that could be made into boots and shoes, and soft pliable buckskin for work clothing. Early settlers learned many new uses for leather from the Indians: leather moccasins, coats, breeches, boots, canoes, and shelters earned for the frontiersmen the title "Leatherstockings." Before long there were other tanneries in Elizabethtown, and by 1690 it was recognized as one of the leading leather centers in the colonies.

The Ogdens remained in the leather business for generations, until well into the 1800s. When Gov. Aaron Ogden moved into the Belcher-Ogden house in 1797, he claimed he could recall hours spent working in the family tanyard in the days before the War for Independence.[33]

Few colonies had a founder more versatile that John Ogden. Before he even finished the corn mill, he began organizing a whaling company like the one he had started at Southampton twenty years earlier. A three-year license issued by Governor Carteret on February 15, 1669, to the Elizabethtown Whaling Company, granted Ogden and twenty others exclusive whaling rights in all the nearby waters ". . . along the coast from Barnegat to the Eastern part of the province, one twentieth part of the oil in casks to be given to the Lords Proprietors." The charter also said:

> In case Statten Island falls within this government, some convenient place or tract of land upon the said Island, near unto the water side for the Settlement of a town or Society to consist of 24 Famelies, and that they shall have a competent proportion of Land allotted to each Family or Lott with Meadow Ground as well planting Land and free commonage upon the Island.

This rather bizarre section in the whaling license agreement appears to propose establishing a fishing and whaling village on

Staten Island, which would be given to the whaling company to settle at some future date. It appears, however, that Carteret overreached, and a short time later he was informed from London that Staten Island belonged to New York, and was not his to give out.

Nonetheless, this whaling license was even better than the one Ogden had been granted at Southampton, in that it did not grant beached whales to the community but rather to the whaling company. In fact, East Jersey colony records reported that a whale cast ashore at Navesink during the contract period was delivered to the company.[34]

Early colonizers had to be jacks-of-all-trades. They could build their own houses and furniture, make and repair shoes, turn out their own tools, and make almost anything required around the house or farm. But as towns developed, most men and women would go to one of their neighbors who specialized in one craft for something a little better. So it was in Elizabethtown. Within a few years, the new town had carpenters, bricklayers, stonemasons, coopers, cordwainers (cobblers), weavers, brewers, tailors, and a broad assortment of other craftsmen. Some would work out of their home, but many began to open small shops where they could combine workshops with space to display their goods, the beginning of retail commerce in the town.

Of course, one of the first public buildings to be erected in each town was a church. Taverns went up as well, and those that also had rooms for weary travelers were called ordinaries. One of the most famous and enduring of these taverns in later years was located next to the old mill in a building Theodore Thayer surmises may have been John Ogden's original house.[35]

In the 1730s it was called the Nag's Head, and thirty years later the Marquis of Granby. It was a popular watering hole for officers and soldiers of the Revolution. After that, under a succession of owners, it was called the Sign of the King's Arms (which would probably have infuriated John Ogden), and the Red Lion Inn, and just after the turn of the nineteenth century, the Indian Queen.[36]

In 1764, to celebrate the centennial of their town, Elizabethtown citizens roasted an ox in front of the Marquis of Granby tavern. Ogden, who was buried not too far away, probably watched the proceedings with pride from a perch high above in the heavens.

℀

Today, in Elizabeth, New Jersey, stands a grand old home called the Belcher-Ogden mansion, now a museum. The home was named after two early New Jersey governors who lived there, Jonathan Belcher, a Royal Governor, and Aaron Ogden, a Constitutional Governor. It sits on land originally awarded to John Ogden Jr. when Elizabethtown was first settled in 1665. It is doubtful that the two-story brick house dates from 1665, but it is entirely possible that an orange brick section in the kitchen, today in the basement of the house, dates back to 1680 when it was one of the first brick buildings in Elizabethtown.

The original Ogdens probably had a hand in building it since many of them were masons and bricklayers. A beehive oven in the old kitchen and other original brick sections have the type of wide orange bricks that were made locally, so it's very possible that they could have made by John Ogden, the Pilgrim, in a brickyard he is said to have owned.

The house was visited by many important people over the years: George Washington, Alexander Hamilton, John Adams, John Hancock, and French soldier and statesman Lafayette, to name only a few. In fact, Aaron Ogden had been Lafayette's aide-de-camp in the Virginia campaign during the Revolutionary War.

During Gov. Jonathan Belcher's residence, he awarded the College of New Jersey its original charter in 1746. The next year the college opened, its initial goal to train ministers in the Presbyterian faith. Gov. Belcher presented the college with his library of four hundred books that set it on its course to be an institution of general learning. In 1756 the college moved to Princeton, N.J., and took on the name of its new home. Because of this history, the Belcher-Ogden mansion has been referred to as the cradle of Princeton University.

The house is well worth visiting, and if you listen carefully, you may even be able to hear the ghosts of Ogdens past whisper to you.[37]

7

Seeds of Revolution

As new colonizers joined the Elizabethtown settlement, Governor Carteret attempted to ingratiate himself with the townspeople. On October 26, 1665, he commissioned the settlement's acknowledged leader, John Ogden, as justice of the peace, the commission reading:

> Whereas, I have conceived a good Opinion of the ability prudence and integrity of you John Ogden Gentleman, In the management of Publique affairs, I have therefore thought fitt, & doe by these presents Constitute and appoint you the said John Ogden to beare the Office of a Justice of the Peace in the Province of New-Jarsey, Giving you full power and authority to execute all such Laws, as are or shall be made for the good government of the said Province . . .

Less than a week later, on November 1, he appointed Ogden a member of the Governor's Council, the highest of the two legislative councils: ". . . to be one of my Councellours for the affaires of the saide Province, And to be assistant to mee your said Governor or my Deputy for the time being . . ."[1]

Over the next seven years, Carteret probably often mused on how he could have appointed as deputy governor and chief law enforcement officer a man who would become such a thorn in his side.

It's difficult from this great distance in time to guess why the men of Elizabethtown so blithely allowed themselves to be subservient to the crown's man, just as it is difficult to guess why he, in his turn, accepted their deeds and patents as being legitimate. Perhaps each side was trying to "play" the other to its ultimate benefit, or perhaps they all considered it of no great importance either way. Maybe they just wanted to get along with each other. We just don't know.

Soon, people from other New England communities began to

covet all the open lands in New Jersey. The Elizabethtown Purchase was vast, much more land than Ogden and his neighbors could ever hope to occupy. A group from Newton, in the Massachusetts Bay Colony, came first, followed by a group from New Hampshire. Each was sold a tract of land, the first sale bringing in eighty pounds sterling itself, which more than compensated the original associates for half of their purchase price. The new settlements were named Woodbridge and Piscataway.

A group from Milford, in the Connecticut Colony, came next, and purchased land for their settlement, which they called Newark. All of these deeds of sale were approved by John Ogden and Governor Philip Carteret, and all were based upon the promises made in the original patent.

For a time, all seems to have been peaceful in the new colony. Hatfield reports that the settlement's second winter was excessively cold, with heavy snows, making travel to or from the place almost impossible.

In the spring, a new problem developed. The surveying of the house lots and the planting fields had been a haphazard affair, probably done by New Amsterdam's city surveyor before the surveyor Vauquellin came to the town. The descriptions of the lots were so imperfect as to render them almost useless. Seventeen men of the town signed a petition, probably in December 1667, requesting that some remedy be sought for the problem. Many among the group of seventeen were second-generation sons: Jonathan and Joseph Ogden, Joseph Bond, and others. Vauquellin had been sent back to England on an errand, so he was not available to assist. The petition to the Governor said, in part:

> We . . . do humbly petition . . . that we may have our lands laid out unto us, according to the Agreements made by the inhabitants and consent of the Governor with them, as may more fully appear in the Town Records . . . if it cannot be granted, we do not see how we can possibly subsist in the Town, but shall be forced to look out somewhere else for a livelihood.[2]

The surveying problems did not end there. There was also a dispute arising among the people of Newark who challenged the boundary line between their town and Elizabethtown. Ogden, Bond, Luke Watson, and Jeffry Jones were appointed to look into that matter.

They met with the delegates from Newark on May 20, 1668. According to court testimony given more than a quarter century later, it was reported that the issue was resolved to everyone's satisfaction; and that ". . . Mr. John Ogden prayed among the people, and returned thanks for their loving agreement."[3]

As to the earlier dispute within the town itself, re-surveying the property would eventually become one of the thorniest issues between the settlers and the proprietors.

Even though these early years were relatively peaceful ones, tensions were building between the townsmen and the proprietors. In 1665, a great plague had swept through London, claiming an estimated one in five Londoners. The following year, the great fire of London raged for six days and destroyed most of the town. To the Puritans in the New World, these twin catastrophes, coming one on the heel of the other, proved that God was not on the side of these foreign interlopers, and assured them that their cause was just.

The rights that had been originally extended to the settlers in their patent, and the Concessions as well, called for a General Assembly to meet annually. Carteret, however, did not hold the first one until the third year. He issued a proclamation on April 7, 1668, requiring the freeholders of each of the towns now established in the colony to choose two able men to be their burgesses and attend the assembly, set for May 25th in Elizabethtown. The purpose was to set laws for the entire colony.[4]

In practice, the government of most English colonies was composed of a governor and a bicameral legislature. Members of the upper chamber, called the council, were usually appointed by the governor, while in the lower chamber, called the assembly or house of burgesses, members were elected by the freemen of each community. Robert Bond and Vauquellin the surveyor were two of the six council members.

In 1665, John Ogden had been appointed one of the first members of the council from Elizabethtown. By now, however, he wanted no part of the governor or his council; so he was elected by his townsmen to serve as a burgess. The colony's burgesses were:

"For Bergen, Gasper Steenmetts and Balthazar Bayard; for Newark upon Pishawack River, Captain Robert Treat and Samuel Swarne [(Swayne]; for Elizabethtown, John Ogden , sen'r., and John Brackett; for Woodbridge, John Bishop and Robert Dennis; for Middletown, James Griver and John Bound, and the last named also represented Shrewsbury."[5]

The legislature remained in session for five days, and passed a variety of laws or acts. The laws passed were simple ones, many taken nearly verbatim from the Hempstead Code that had previously been written by many of the same men. The laws reinforced the rights that had been given to them in their patent; but also added some crime-and-punishment acts. These laws may seem draconian today, but they must certainly have served as a clear deterrent against crime:

—That men from 16 to 60 years of age, should provide themselves with arms, on penalty of one shilling for the first week's neglect, and two for every week after.
—That for burglary or high-way robbery, the first offense, burning in the hand, the second, in the forehead, in both, to make restitution; and for the third offense, death.
—For stealing, the first offense, treble retribution, and the like for the second and third offense, with such increase of punishment as the court saw cause, even to death, if the party appearth incorrigible; but if not, and unable to make retribution, they were to be sold for satisfaction, or to receive corporal punishment.
—That conspiracies, or attacks upon towns or forts, should be death.
—That undutiful children, smiting or cursing their father or mother, except provok'd thereunto for self-preservation, upon complaint of, and proof from their parents, or either of them, should be punished with death.
—That in case of adultery, the party to be divorc'd, corporally punished or banished, or either, or all of them, as the court should judge proper.
—That for nightwalking and revelling after the hour of nine, the parties to be secured by the constable or other officer till morning, and then not giving a satisfactory account to the magistrate, to be bound over to the next court, and there receive such punishment as should be inflicted.
—That the meeting of the assembly should be always on the first Tuesday in November, yearly, and oftener, if the governor and council thought necessary; the deputies of each town to be chosen on the first of January, according to the concessions, that any deputy absenting himself at such times, was to be fined forty shillings for every day's absence: that thirty pounds should be levied for provincial charges . . .

—That no son, daughter, maid or servant, should marry without the consent of his or their parents, masters or overseers, without being three times published in some public meeting or kirk [church], near the party's abode . . .

—That fornication should be punished at the discretion of the court, by marriage, fine or corporal punishment.

—That no life should be taken but by virtue of some law, and the proof of two or three witnesses.[6]

The burgesses also agreed that some form of central government was necessary for the growing colony, and that funds would be required. So they voted New Jersey's first tax of five pounds from each town, payable annually. It's understandable that Carteret, not sensitive to the staunch resolve of these people, might misread their willingness to pay taxes; but the burgesses also misread their neighbors. New Jersey yeomen would not entertain any kind of tax. Period.

Almost immediately Carteret began to understand what he was up against. Middletown residents refused to post the laws set by the assembly; those in the Monmouth Patent refused to take the oath of allegiance, sensing it would weaken their land claims under the Nicolls's patent; and Woodbridge residents began re-selling some of their land without consulting the surveyor general.

A decision was also reached to move subsequent General Assemblies to November each year, and so it was held that following November. The meeting began amiably enough, and a few new laws were passed. It was decided

. . . that every town within the Province shall have a brand mark for their Horses, to distinguish the Horses of one Town from another, besides which everyone is to have and mark his Horse or Horses with his own particular brand mark, also that every Town shall have a Horn brand mark, for all the Cattle from three Years old and upward . . .

A fine was laid down for every town not abiding by the new branding law, and a second law, also with a fine attached, was also passed: "Every town shall provide an Ordinary for the Relief and Entertainment of Strangers." And finally, John Ogden was appointed and empowered ". . . to take command of the Country's Charges and Rates, and to order the disposal of the same for the best Ease and Benefit of the Country." It was an appointment that delegated him to collect and distribute fines, assessments, etc, a position similar to that of a treasurer.[7]

The easy part now over, simmering tensions between the settlers and the governor finally erupted.

The council members had been appointed by Carteret, so were for the most part of the same persuasion. He had little trouble enforcing his will with this group. But assembly members, or burgesses, paid little heed to the wishes of the governor. The differences grew over a number of issues, until finally the burgesses sent a message to Governor Carteret stating they would no longer meet with him as a group to discuss these issues:

> Honored Gentlemen:
>   We, finding so many and great inconveniences by our not setting together, and, your apprehensions so different to ours, and your expectations that things must go according to your opinions, though we see no reason for, much less warrant from the Concessions, wherefore we think it vain to spend much time of returning answers by writings that are so exceedingly dilatory, if not fruitless and endless and therefore, we think our way rather to break up our meeting, seeing the order of the Concessions cannot be attended to.

Carteret responded:

> In answer to your last proposition, we desire you to appoint two of your deputies to consider with us, in what point we act contrary to the Concessions, it being too late to-night to entertain so long a debate, we will be ready to-morrow morning to give them a hearing and if reason will satisfy you, we shall be very well pleased that you proceed accordingly to the Lords Proprietors Concessions, and the trust imposed upon you, if not you may do what you please, only we advise you to consider well of your resolutions before you break up.[8]

But Ogden and his fellow burgesses did break up, as threatened, without even honoring the governor him with an answer.

Carteret was incensed. So much so that he ignored The Concessions and did not call for another General Assembly for a number of years, ruling instead by himself with the tacit approval of his council.

Bigger problems, however, were brewing across the ocean that would again profoundly affect the struggling little colony.

The two proprietors were both in trouble at home. Berkeley had been "detected in the basest corruption," and had been kicked from office. Carteret was accused of looting the treasury of the navy, of which he was the treasurer. Both men would soon agree to give up New Jersey. A letter from the Royal Commissioner, Samuel Maverick, to Connecticut Colony Governor Winthrop on June 29, 1669, spells it out: "New Jersey is returned to his Royal Highness . . ."[9]

While the problem rested, awaiting word as to what would transpire next, we see evidence of another problem raging throughout all the colonies in another letter from Maverick ". . . The autumn of this year was made memorable, as well as that of the previous year, from the prevalence of fatal disorders. The flux, argues and fevers, have rained both in cittie and country, & many dead, but not yett soe many as last yeare. The like is all N. Engld over, espetially about Boston."[10]

The dire letter referred to a yellow fever epidemic that scourged many of the New England and middle colonies in 1668 and 1669. Rarely seen outside of the tropics, the disease is spread by mosquitoes. No word can be found about the extent of the disease in New Jersey, so we can assume the colony was not among the hardest hit.

Back in England, the fortunes of the two proprietors took a turn for the better, aided perhaps by the intervention of their old friend the Duke of York with his brother, King Charles II. When news of his rekindled powers reached Governor Carteret, he decided to press ahead with another unpopular issue. The original patent had granted the settlers a tax-free five-year period, following which they were expected to pay annual quitrents. The grace period was over.

Even though this condition had been part of the original patent, the settlers now decided that it was unwarranted. They had purchased the land free-and-clear from the Indians, not received it as a gift or a lease from the proprietors, so they should owe rent to nobody. Also, they felt that to pay the fees would weaken their claims to the land under the prior patents and Indian purchase. The bad feelings between the governor and the settlers grew when they ignored his order to pay the quitrents.

New Jersey founders were not alone in their indignation at the Royal Commissioners for trying to bring them under subjection. Long Island, now under the Duke of York, and other colonies as well, smarted under these attempts. They had been left virtually alone since arriving in America, and were not kindly disposed to have new masters.

A number of other events of distinction occurred over the next three years, each testing the patience and resolve of the settlers. The freemen had allowed Carteret to attend the Elizabethtown town meetings, as he was an associate, but refused to let him control the proceedings. Finally, he went too far, giving away one of his lots to a servant, a direct violation of town laws (from the Nicolls's patent, but not from the proprietors' Concessions) that held that new owners must be approved by all freemen.

While the town's citizens were trying to decide how to proceed against this breach, Carteret repeated the process, unilaterally giving a house lot to another servant, Richard Mitchell. This was too much.

A meeting of the associates was hastily gathered at the home of Goodman Carter to discuss Carteret's breach. The record of this meeting, on June 19, 1671, states: ". . . it was agreed by the Major Vote that Richard Mitchel should not enjoy his Lott given him by the Governor . . . it was agreed that there some should goe the next morning and pull up the saide Mitchel's fence."[11]

A group of men, including John Ogden Jr. (who had the same passionate independent streak that his father had), William Meeker, and Luke Watson went to Mitchell's house and tore down his fence. Others soon joined in, tearing down Mitchell's palisade and even the clapboards off his house. The fence to his garden gone, the town's wandering hogs now invaded his garden and rooted up most of his crop.[12]

William Pardon, an ally of Carteret and the Council's secretary, witnessed the event. Historian Hatfield called him "the Governor's obsequious parasite." A number of the associates also turned out to watch, many claiming it was one of the most memorable incidents in their pioneer life. Indeed, the event did mark a turning point, the Elizabethtown settlers moving from simmering but passive anger to open and determined resistance to the usurpation of their rights.

With public opinion against him, Carteret seethed inwardly but took no direct action against the men.

At about this time, Sir George Carteret's second son, Captain James Carteret, arrived on the scene from England, on his way to a political assignment in the Carolinas. He decided to stay on for a while in Elizabethtown. In New York, unrest among the Indians again became a hot topic, and a meeting was held to discuss how well armed and equipped the various settlements were to deal with any uprising. Gov. Carteret attended, and invited his distant cousin Capt. Carteret to accompany him. It was decided that New Jersey should call a General Assembly to assess the readiness of their settlements. It was set for October 3, 1671 in Elizabethtown.

When the meeting convened, the Indian threat was glossed over lightly. It became apparent that Gov. Carteret had another agenda. He appointed a court of seven men to meet, any three of them, the following February in Elizabethtown to decide punishment for the so-called rioters against Mitchell's property. When they met, a jury was seated of seven men from Woodbridge and five from Bergen, not a single man from Elizabethtown or Newark being included.

The accused men refused to enter a plea and walked out of the proceedings. They felt Carteret's kangaroo court would find them guilty regardless of what they said. The trial proceeded without them, with no defense being offered. They were found guilty, and each man was fined from three to five pounds. The marshal was instructed to collect the fines, or seize the property of the guilty— but he was powerless in the face of overwhelming opposition from the entire community. The fines went unpaid.[13]

The other English towns in New Jersey, now numbering six, had thus far kept their distance from Elizabethtown's problems, but they now realized that if Carteret could abuse the rights of one town, he could do the same in their towns. They now became united against Governor Carteret and his small clique. At a January 1672 town meeting in Newark, a committee was appointed: ". . . Mr. Treat and Lieut Swain are deputed, to Take the first opportunity to Advise with Mr. Ogden, or any other they see Cause, what may be the Safest and Best Course to be taken for the Town, about our Lands and Settlements here."[14]

The burgesses decided to hold their own General Assembly, with or without the governor or his council. It convened on March 26th, and re-convened on May 14th. Gov. Carteret refused to attend either meeting. So it was that Capt. Carteret, who had by now switched loyalties, was elected president of New Jersey, the burgesses saying that Gov. Carteret had forfeited his office by virtue of his wanton disregard of their rights.

The Governor was not pleased with the proceedings of the two meetings, and instructed the secretary, William Pardon, to destroy the minutes, which he apparently did.

On May 25, 1672, testing his new powers, Capt. James Carteret issued a warrant for the arrest of Pardon, directing the constable to keep him in custody until he delivered the acts (or minutes) of the General Assembly. Pardon refused, and magistrate John Ogden ordered an attachment on his movables (personal property). Capt. Carteret followed up by issuing another attachment against his houses and land, stating that Pardon—who had escaped from the constable—had gone to England.

Gov. Carteret, fearing for his safety, moved his headquarters to Bergen. From this safe vantage point he labeled Ogden and the other leaders of the rebellion as "Mutineers and as enemies to the Government," adding, "and if by this means there should be any blood shed We do hereby Cleer our Selves before God and Man from the Guilt thereof."[15]

So, just as land ownership in New Jersey was convoluted, now too was the government. Gov. Carteret had no more cards to play. His council advised him to go to England, and sent along their own letter encouraging the authorities ". . . to endeavor the curing of the wound by speedy medicine, which delay might cause to gangrene."[16] As fate would have it, aboard the same ship was a letter the settlers dispatched to Sir George Carteret telling their side of the story, and asking that their rights under the original patent be honored under their new proprietor, Capt. James Carteret.

In London, the Duke of York and the two proprietors immediately drew up documents reinforcing Gov. Carteret's right to rule. They appointed John Berry deputy governor, and sent him back with a list of imperatives. He also carried a letter from the king himself, confirming the governor's authority and requiring him to exact from the settlers all due obedience.

Sir Carteret's son James was the first to be dealt with. He was told unceremoniously to mind his own business, and be on his way to Carolina. His tail between his legs, he promptly did as he was told. Second, all wrongdoers in the mini-revolution were to present themselves in Bergen to seek the pardon of the governing authorities. And third, in order to put the land claims mess to an end, every colonizer in all the towns of the Elizabethtown Purchase and the Monmouth Patent were to have their land surveyed and patented by proprietary officials, or forfeit their lands.

Things seemed worse than before. The New Jersey towns, in concert, decided to once again send a letter to England. This time, however, they would enlist the support of John Winthrop Jr., the most distinguished gentleman of New England and a personal acquaintance of both Carteret and Berkeley. Winthrop knew many of these men well—John Ogden had been one of the original patentees and signers of his Connecticut Colony charter that had fared so well—so he quickly agreed to intercede. On July 2, 1673, he wrote for them a character reference, saying in part:

> Right Honourable: There having divers persons of good repute and approved integrity who were formally improved in publicke offises in this Colony, viz: Mr. Jasper Crane, Mr, John Ogden, Mr. Robert Bond, Mr. Abraham Peirson, Mr. Brewen with many of their lovinge neighbors and friends wel disposed men, of sober and peaceable conversation did Transplant themselves and famalys into your Honours Province, whoe being persons well known to us, But strangers to your Honour desires us to give you our Carracter of them that soe they might not bee misrrepresnted, whose presence in this colony that good worke of subduing the Earth and replenishinge of it, which in this remote, desert part of the world never formerly inhabited nor Cultivated is A very difficulte work, and requires much hard labour, to subdue so Ruff and woody A wildernesse . . . [17]

Whether or not the letter was ever dispatched to England is not known, as another event began to unfold that would once again change everything.

⊗

The third Anglo-Dutch war had begun in 1672, and five Dutch warships were patrolling the coast of North America. By chance, they intercepted Capt. Carteret's sloop on its way to Carolina. Some members of the Carteret party told the Dutch admiral that New York was currently defenseless. He set Carteret and a few of his party ashore, and immediately set sail north, and in an almost bloodless confrontation, recaptured all the Duke of York's lands.

Only three days later, Ogden, joined by deputies from Newark and Piscataway, petitioned the Dutch supreme military tribunal for an audience. They wished to press for their rights, and secure their independence under the new Dutch rule. They were asked to send their delegation to New Orange, as the town had now been re-named. When Ogden and his group reached New Orange >New York>New Amsterdam, they were warmly received.

The tribunal assured them they would be granted all the privileges enjoyed by any Dutch town, confirmed their rightful possession to all the lands they had lawfully acquired, and instructed them how to set up their town governments under the Dutch system. They were also told that they would not be required to take up arms against England. These same rights and privileges were also granted to the people of Woodbridge, Shrewsbury, and Middletown, who had not participated in the meeting.[18]

From among men who would be nominated by each town, Dutch officials would select three magistrates from each, as well as one "schout" or sheriff and one secretary for the entire colony. All candidates were to be the wealthiest and most intelligent men available in each town.

The schout's job was an office tantamount to that of governor of New Jersey. John Ogden had been a favorite of the Dutch ever since the days, a quarter-century earlier, when he had built their church, and the sixty-five year old was named to be schout in 1673.[19]

As schout, Ogden had the responsibility of laying out highways, building bridges, and erecting public buildings throughout the colony. He also had to lay out land to qualified applicants. The schout was also charged with preservation of the peace and administration of justice. According to early Dutch colonial records, he was charged to:

> . . . take care that the Reformed Christian Religion be maintained in conformity to the Synod of Dordrecht without permitting any other sects attempting anything contrary thereto. [Also to . . .] take good care that the places under his charge shall be cleansed of all mobs, gamblers, whore-houses and such like impurities.[20]

With the power now in their hands, and Ogden at their head, the New Jersey colonizers turned to righting matters the proprietors had upset. Ogden arrested the surveyor general Vauquellin for crimes against the town, and sent him to New Orange for trial, where he was found guilty of sedition and banished from the colony.[21]

Ogden also had to administer the Dutch oath of allegiance to all the inhabitants of the towns. In Elizabethtown, fifty of the seventy-one freemen took the oath, the remaining twenty-one being absent at the time. Among those taking the oath were Jonathan Ogden, John Ogden Jr., David Ogden, Benjamin Ogden, and Joseph Ogden, John's five grown sons. Joseph Bond also appeared, but his father Robert Bond had moved to Newark by this time and took the oath there.[22]

The captain of one of the ships that had re-taken New Netherland, Anthony Colve, was seated as the governor. To Schout Ogden he assigned the following task: to take ". . . all the arms and other goods belonging to the late Governor Carteret" to be delivered to him at Ft. William Hendrick. It proved to be a difficult task, however. Carteret's old friend and ally, the surveyor Vauquellin, who had not yet left after being banished, identified himself as Robert Laprairie, beat them to the stash, and refused to return it. Colve ordered his arrest and detention.[23]

There was a flurry of other official orders from Governor Colve to Schout Ogden, most too mundane to bear repeating. One of interest, however, signed January 2, 1674, indicated that the Dutch feared the English would not give up the province without a fight. It said ". . . the governor is Informed that at your Towne are Lying 2 or three pieces of ordinance for which he hath at present occasion to make use of, you are therefore hereby Required to Cause the said peeces to be sent hether with the first opportunity whereof you are not to faile."[24]

Hidden among all the negative duties Schout Ogden was assigned was one of a very positive nature. The governor proclaimed a "Day of Humiliation and Thanksgiving," for the entire colony, saying:

> Concidering the Manifold Blessings & favours which the Bountifull & Merciful god hath bene pleazed graciously to Bestow uppon this Province and the Inhabitants thereof . . . Know Yee therefore that wee have thought it Necessary & do by these Presents order & Proclaime an universall day of fast humiliation & thancksgiveing which shall be held within this Province on the first Wednesday of every mounth . . .

The proclamation went on to outline all the things that should not occur on these special days, like ". . . all manner of Labour & exercizing of hunting ffishing gaming Excesse in drinking and the Lyke . . ." and ordering the schout and magistrates post the notice and prosecute any who would abridge it.[25]

Like all good things that had happened to the New Jersey settlers, this brief period of relative freedom did not last. Less than a year later, the Dutch sued for peace, and the February 1674 Treaty of Westminster returned New York and New Jersey to the English.

By now the two original proprietors, Carteret and Berkeley, had decided to divide up their lands. By royal mandate on June 13, 1674, Sir George Carteret became the sole owner of the northern part of the colony, henceforth to be known as the colony of East New Jersey. Berkeley, meanwhile sold his moiety (half) of the province for one thousand pounds to John Fenwick, in trust for Edward Byllinge of the Society of Friends, or Quakers. This colony would become known as West New Jersey.

The royal mandate also required obedience from the people of the territory "to the laws and government" of Sir George Carteret, and giving him sole power under the king to settle and dispose of the country as he saw fit. James Stuart, the Duke of York, brother of the king, issued a new lease and release for the entire territory, rescinding many of the freedoms granted in the original Concessions.

In East New Jersey, Philip Carteret was reinstated as governor, and re-established himself in the governor's house in Elizabethtown. He brought with him sweeping new powers that included two requirements that were universally unpopular with the settlers. First, all landholders must re-apply for new surveys and titles for all their lands, and any citizen failing to do so within one year would have his land confiscated. Second, the governor was given complete control over the legislature, depriving the people of the original jurisdiction they had been granted.

Carteret immediately went to the friendlier confines of Bergen and recalled his old council of cronies to his side. A summons was issued to the deputies of each town to meet with him to hear the contents of His Majesty's instructions and orders. Following the meeting a proclamation was issued by Carteret and his council, dated December 11, at Elizabethtown, in which he spoke of "the late past distractions of times," as:

> Occasioned first by the meeting of several male-content inhabitants, and then by the arrival of the Dutch forces in our neighbor Colony,

giving opportunity to those seditious spirits, to cover their former guilt with the mantle of treason.

We find ourselves not obligated to countenance the commissionating any person or persons, to any office military or civil, who have not patented their lands, nor to yield the privileges of a Corporation to any otherwise qualified, than the said Orders of our said Proprietor doth allow.

The proclamation went on to say that the surveyor general would remain in Elizabethtown from April 1 through May 15, 1675, to re-survey and patent all the lands.[26]

In a few mighty strokes of the royal pen, John Ogden and a few other leaders of East New Jersey had been declared to be malcontents, guilty of sedition and treason. It was clear that the sixty-seven year old Ogden's political career was over as long as the governor had any voice in it.

The proclamation also ordered that those persons "who were the chief actors in attempting the making of an alteration in our government" must appear before the governor and his council to seek remission of their offenses. So, in John Ogden's case, he was mandated to two actions: submit to a new survey and title of his land; and appear before Governor Carteret and his council, apologize for his actions, and seek forgiveness.

In March 1675, just prior to the scheduled beginning of the surveying, some of the townsmen decided to seek a compromise, and sent a proposal to Governor Carteret. In it, they agreed to pay twenty pounds per year quitrent for all the lots in the town, if he would recognize the existing patents. Carteret swiftly rejected it by the insulting gesture of simply scrawling on the back of their petition that there would be no compromises.

April 1st arrived, with only one of the townsmen having signed up for the new survey and patent. Prior to May 15th, the last day that the surveyor would be in Elizabethtown, a second man signed up, Robert Vauquellin, the surveyor himself, now returned to the colony. By the end of the year, ten more men had signed up, all fearing that without a recognized title, their land would be seized. It must have been a disappointment to Ogden to see the name of his brother-in-law Robert Bond and Robert's son Joseph on that list (Robert Bond had removed to Newark, but still owned his land in Elizabethtown).

As the one-year deadline of April 1, 1676, approached, other landowners also became fretful. By the assigned deadline, forty-nine of the eighty-four landowners had signed for the surveys and titles. Among the men who met the deadline were Carteret himself and original patentees Luke Watson and Capt. John Baker. Not one of the five Ogdens who owned land had signed up.

The next few months would have been filled with tension and fear for those thirty-five landowners who refused to obey. Each man knew that at any moment the governor's men could show up and evict him from the land he had fairly and honestly acquired more than ten years earlier. The threat became too great for some. By the end of 1676, thirty-one more men would sign, including the Ogden brothers David, John Jr, Jonathan, and Joseph. Now, eight months after the deadline had passed, only four people remained who refused to cave to the pressure: Margaret Baker, the widow of Peter Wolverson; James Haynes; Mrs. Hannah Hopkins; and John Ogden Sr.

Time passed. Carteret was obviously hesitant to take action against the four dissenters who continued to defy him. Two were women, and one, John Ogden Sr. was the figurative leader of the entire colony. To act against such people would have done irreparable harm to the governor's already fragile hold over the citizens of East New Jersey. So while he did nothing, we can fairly assume he privately chaffed against the refusal of the four to fall in line.

Finally, on February 1 of the following year, 1677, Margaret Baker signed for the survey, followed on July 11 by James Haynes. Now only two remained. More than fifteen more months passed, and then on October 26, 1678, Mrs. Hannah Hopkins put her name to the order.

John Ogden Sr. now stood alone. Governor Carteret had the full weight of the English crown behind him, and but one dissenter in front of him. As Ogden figuratively thumbed his nose at the governor, and indeed at the entire English royal establishment, all of East New Jersey held its collective breath. Would Carteret dare evict the old man and take his land?

Three days later, on October 29, 1678, John Ogden felt he had made his point. Still under strong protest, he signed his name to the order with a proud flourish. It was three-and-a-half years after the proclamation had been issued, and two-and-a-half years after its deadline for action.

Once the survey was completed and the title recognized by a grim-faced Carteret, Ogden was recorded as having three hundred acres of land, a sum topped by only the holdings of seven other men.[27]

History has not recorded that Ogden ever appeared before the governor and his council to seek a pardon for his actions during the brief Dutch period. Given his penchant for civil disobedience under the heavy hand of the proprietors, it is very doubtful that he ever did so.

Ironically, the royal mandate that had created the colonies of East and West New Jersey, and set down such draconian measures for their governing, was issued exactly one hundred years before armed Massachusetts militiamen stood face to face with the British advance guard on Lexington Green. On that day in 1774, "the shot heard round the world" would change forever the concept of liberty in America by signaling the start of the War for Independence.

I believe a case can be made that the first seeds of the American Revolution were not planted on the Green that day, or in the Boston Harbor where patriots threw English tea into the ocean, or with the taxing of all printed material in the colonies, or in any of the other laws passed by the crown in England that slowly stripped away the most basic human freedoms in the colonies.

I believe some of the earliest seeds of the American Revolution were planted in New Jersey when the heavy yoke of foreign domination was first put on the necks of a group of law-abiding citizens who wanted only to keep what they had lawfully achieved. I also believe that John Ogden, through his resolute moral courage, planted those seeds; and that he was perhaps the American colonies' first civil dissenter against the tyranny of foreign intervention.

The linchpin document of the United States of America is the Declaration of Independence. No other document so brilliantly outlines an individual's and a community's right to freedom. Yet buried about halfway through this document is a portion that is seldom remembered and rarely quoted. In it, the founders outlined the abuses that caused them to seek freedom from the oppressive English crown. They include the crown's refusal to pass and abide by equitable laws, its dissolution of representative government, and its arbitrary imposition of taxes.

These charges were leveled specifically at the sitting monarch of the day, King George III. Yet more than one hundred years earlier, under King Charles II, the struggling American colonies of the mid-seventeenth century suffered the same deprivations. Was their suffering less than that of their ancestors who would come one hundred years later? I think not.

One eminent historian and author of nearly a dozen American history books, Thomas Jefferson Wertenbaker, shares my sentiment in his 1938 *The Founding of American Civilization: The Middle Colonies:*

> After all, the founders of the nation were the pioneers of the seventeenth century rather than the patriots who declared our independence and made it good upon the field of battle, or the framers of our Constitution or the men who put it into successful operation. However important was the work of Washington, Madison, Jefferson, Hamilton, in giving unity, strength and direction to America, they built on the foundations laid by their grandfathers and great grandfathers.
>
> It was these forces that endowed the Americans with their love of freedom, their self-reliance, their optimism, their desire for democracy, which in turn made political independence possible.[28]

I believe the suffering and the resultant civil disobedience of John Ogden, and perhaps a few others as well, should have earned them the right to stand alongside men like George Washington, Thomas Jefferson, Samuel Adams, John Hancock, and Patrick Henry as the founders of our democracy.

8

A Vigorous Plantation in East New Jersey

THE NEXT FEW YEARS IN EAST NEW JERSEY PASSED IN RELATIVE CALM. The colony's General Assembly was held annually, and many past sins were legally or at least practically forgiven or forgotten. At the town level, Elizabethtown continued to grow and prosper. As in most towns of early colonial America, the citizens strove to attain economic independence, producing as many of their own goods as possible. The town now had a blacksmith, a joiner, a carpenter, a weaver, a brewer, a clothier, a wheelwright, and a shoemaker. While each family continued to produce their own grain, fruits and vegetables, milk, butter, and meat, they turned to their neighbors to purchase shoes, furniture, carts, and hardware. Often the purchase was made in trade. The type of economy that flourished in these towns is reflected in an order for ammunition made by the nearby town of Woodbridge, to be paid for "by the Constable in wheat and pork out of the Treasury," and voting for the minister's salary in the prevailing currency of the country, which meant grain, meat, or other provisions.[1]

Town business continued to be conducted in the town meetings. If the weather was good, the meetings would be held in the meetinghouse. If the weather was too severe and the meetinghouse too cold, the proceedings would move into someone's house where the townsmen would sit by a roaring fire and conduct their business. It's easy to visualize an aging John Ogden sitting in a rocker next to the fire directing a meeting of his friends and neighbors. They might discuss the construction of a good horse bridge to replace a failing one, or how much bounty to offer for killing a wolf within the boundaries of the town, or who to appoint to replace a sheep watcher who had passed away. Thus these pioneers regulated the everyday affairs of their lives.

One of the foremost problems of the time throughout the colonies was an Indian uprising that began in 1675.

175

Algonquian-speaking tribes inhabited the entire coastal region of North America, from Labrador to the Carolinas. These tribes were at the end of their patience with the white man's encroachment on their lands. The young chief of the Wampanoags, twenty-four year old Matacom, called King Philip by the English, decided it was time to put an end to their land-grabbing ways. He and his envoys visited all the tribes from the Hudson to the Kennebec, an area that encompassed virtually all of today's New England. A confederation of four tribes—the Wampanoag, Abenaki, Nipmuck, and Narragansett—joined together for the purpose. In the summer of 1675 Philip held a two-week war dance for the chiefs and warriors of the four tribes. One by one, the names of the English towns were called; at each name a brave would pick up a brand from the fire, go into a wild dance, and end by quenching the fire into the earth to signify victory. King Philip's War was ready to begin!

The Indians attacked town after town, putting them to flame and killing as many men as possible. There were ninety settlements in New England, and more than half of them felt the wrath of the Indians. Over 1,200 colonists would die.

Reprisals came swiftly, and thousands of Indians were slain. The war lasted only a year, and inevitably the Indians were subdued. Matacom (his wife and son captured and many other family members killed) was beheaded. In East New Jersey, the militia had been re-activated, and every man between sixteen and sixty was charged with arming himself and going through four days of military training. Fortunately, the hostilities never reached East New Jersey.

The memory of the horrors of King Philip's War lingered in the minds of settlers all along the East coast for years, even those that had escaped direct involvement. At some point in the late 1670s something happened with the Indians that alarmed the settlers of East New Jersey. We can't be sure what it was, exactly when it happened, or even with certainty which tribe of Indians was involved, but it was serious enough to be an action item at the General Assembly meeting on May 8, 1679, in Middletown:

A Committee Chosen by this Assembly to treat with the Indians at Piscataqua . . . to order, agree and determine of such Things as may conduce to the Peace and Wellfare of the Province with the said Indians . . .[2]

Arguably, the tribe involved was the Raritans. Although they had previously shown no aggressive tendencies toward the settlers, they were the nearest tribe, thus the one the settlers kept the closest eye on. However, another possibility also exists, the clue being the use of the word "Piscataqua" in the aforementioned resolution passed by the General Assembly. The town of Piscataway was originally called Piscataqua, after a group of the settlers who had come there from the area of the Piscataqua River that runs between southeastern New Hampshire and Maine. But by this time, the town's name had long since been changed, so it may be that the reference was to a tribe by the older name and from the same area that may have wandered west after being displaced. Still, I go with the first option as being the most likely.

Good Old John Ogden, as he was now called throughout New Jersey, was approaching seventy, and probably had no need for further adventure. But it wasn't to be. He was appointed one of the six men to "treat with the Indians;" and due to his excellent relationship with all the tribes, he was probably chosen as the leader of the delegation. An accounting of this incident as it may have happened provides a striking example of the diplomatic skills—and the raw courage—this man brought to every task.

The Raritans were a branch of the Lenni Lenapes, and although they had never proven aggressive to the East New Jersey settlers, they did have a long-standing reputation as being hostile. They had suffered greatly at the hands of the Dutch, and undoubtedly trusted no white man. So Ogden and his small delegation were probably skittish as they set off to confront the tribe.

They could have traveled overland, perhaps fifteen to twenty miles southwest, to reach the tribe. However, if the warming signals were strong enough, they probably chose to go by boat where the chance of ambush was lessened. They would have sailed south on Long Island Sound to the tip of Staten Island, then westward up the Raritan River, where they would have found the Indian village.

David DeVries, the Dutch diarist, had visited a number of Raritan villages in his travels. In his journal he described the tribe:

The natives are generally well set in their limbs, slender round the waist, broad across the shoulders, and have black hair and dark eyes.

They are very nimble and fleet, well adapted to travel on foot and to carry heavy burdens. They are foul and slovenly in their actions . . . the men generally have no beard, or very little which some even pull out. They use very few words, which they consider well . . . in their actions [they are] high-minded enough, vigorous and quick to comprehend or learn . . . They are not straightforward as soldiers but perfidious, accomplishing all their enterprises by treachery . . . the desire of revenge appears to be born in them.

Their clothing, both for men and women, is a piece of duffel or leather in front, with a deer skin or elk's hide over the body. Some have bears' hides of which they make doublets; others have coats made of the skins of racoons, wild-cats, wolves, dogs, otters, squirrels, beavers and the like, and also of turkey feathers. They made their stockings and shoes of deer skins or elk's hide . . .

Ornamenting themselves consists of cutting their bodies, or painting them with various colors . . . they frequently smear their skin and hair with different kinds of grease.[3]

As Ogden and his small party approached the village, they saw weather-beaten women and statuesque girls busying themselves at water's edge. Naked children and playful puppies romped nearby. Ogden found the men who came down to greet them as good-looking men with active, muscular bodies. Most, however, were past middle age. Their hair was shaved into scalp locks, with eagle or turkey feathers dangling from them. All had pendants in their ear lobes, and their cheeks and temples were streaked with white and red paint. They made no hostile movements, and the small group of visitors was ushered into the sachem's wigwam.

A long ceremonial pipe was lit and passed around, the custom before any conversations could begin. Though Ogden spoke a good deal of Algonquian, the Raritans' dialect and unusual language habits made an interpreter necessary, and one of Ogden's men had probably come along for that purpose. When the time came, and as diplomatically as he could, Ogden carefully asked if the Raritans had any warlike predilections. Such questions were never answered with a simple "yes" or "no," as Denton describes in his 1670 book:

When their King or Sachem sits in Council, he hath a Company of armed men to guard his Person, great respect being shewn him by the People, which is principally manifested by their silence: After he hath declared the cause of their convention, he demands their opinion, ordering who shall begin: The person ordered to speak, after he hath declared his minde, tells them he hath done: no man ever interrupting any person in his speech, nor offering to speak, though he make never so many or long stops till he says he hath no more to say: The Council having all declared their opinions, the King after some pause gives the definitive sentence, which is commonly seconded with a shout from the people, Every one seeming to applaud, and manifest their Assent to what is determined.[4]

There is no extant written record of Ogden's meeting with the Raritan chief, or of how long the meeting lasted. We can judge it only by its result: Ogden and his small party left the village freely, following the meeting and an obligatory dinner celebration, and East New Jersey had no problems with the Raritans.

If I've guessed incorrectly, and another tribe was involved rather than the Raritans, we still know for a fact that the outcome was the same: peace with the Indians for the East New Jersey settlers.

Ꮚ᎒

Elizabethtown, and indeed the entire colony of East New Jersey, was a desirable place to settle in the early 1680s. There was still plenty of available land, the soil was fertile and the Indians now friendly. A contemporary account of the area is provided in an interesting document, George Scot's *The Model of the Government of the Province of East New Jersey in America,* published in 1685. He gives us an idea of how the colony was populated at the time:

Shrewsbury . . . consisting of about 30,000 acres, including the out plantations . . . the families in town are 80, the inhabitants were computed to be about 400. Colonel Lewis Morris, a Barbados, had iron works and other considerable improvements here.

Middletown, 10 or 12 miles over land northward from the Iron Mills . . . the town may consist of 100 families . . . [out-plantations] of 500 more; and the acres taken up by the town and out-plantations 30,000.

Piscattaway Lyes next 25 or 26 miles from Middletown . . . there are several Plantations all along on the North side of the River [Raritan] . . . and some on the South side . . . the Town consists of about 80 families and of about 400 inhabitants; and of the Acres about the Town about 10,000, and for the Out-Plantations, 30,000.

Woodbridge is over Land from Piscattaway about 7 or 8 miles; it lies up a River . . . on the South side of the entrance into the River or Creek, Mr. Delapairs [the French surveyor and Carteret crony, Vauquellin] hath a neat plantation . . . this Town hath a court house and prison built on their charge. It consists of about 120 Families and 600 Inhabitants. The Acres taken up by the Town may be about 10,000, and the Out-Plantations about 20,000.

Elizabeth Town is the first new place that was settled in 1664 . . . before the Lord Berkeley and Sir George Carteret title was known. This Town lies up 3 miles within a Creek [Elizabeth River] the entrance whereof is opposite to the Northwest end of Staten Island . . . it's but a narrow passage there over to the meadows of Staten Island . . . there is in this town a house, orchards and farm, within the Town in partnership between the Proprietor and Governour Philip Carteret, it being one of the first houses built there, and hath all along been the resident of the Governour, untill of late he hath finished his New house . . . the Town is built on both sides of the Creek, and consists of 150 Families and 700 Inhabitants. The Acres taken up by the Town are computed to be 10,000 and for the Out-Plantations 30,000.

Newark . . . is a Town distant to the Northward over Land from Elizabeth Town, about 6 or 7 miles . . . It lyes on . . . Newark River. In this Town hath been a Court of Session . . . it is the most compact Town in the province and consists of about 100 Families and of about 500 Inhabitants. The Acres of the Town . . . may be about 10,000 and for the Out-Plantations 40,000 Acres.

Berghen . . . is a compact town and hath been fortified against the Indians. There are about 70 families . . . The Acres . . . for the Town about 10,000 and the Out-Plantations 50,000 . . . the greatest part of the inhabitants are Dutch.

Scot also details a number of smaller settlements and individual plantations, mostly located along the rivers, and sums up the colony's population: Upon the whole there were at this time supposed to be about seven hundred families settled in the towns ". . . and reckoning 5 to all Families the Inhabitants in the several Towns estimate to be 3500 Persons." The out-plantations, which were thought to contain half as many more, brings us to about 5,200 Europeans living in East New Jersey at the time.[5]

❧

The late 1670s and early 1680s found Gov. Carteret facing another threat, this one from seemingly friendly forces. The Duke of York had appointed Edmund Andros as Governor of his New

York colony, and the two had seen advantage in trying to extend their power over the New Jersey proprietorships. However, the Duke was cautious not to step on the toes of the two court-favored proprietors, Sir George Carteret and Lord John Berkeley. When Berkeley sold West New Jersey, Andros used the situation to gain political control over that colony. In 1679, Sir George Carteret passed away in England, and Andros set wheels in motion to exert his control over East New Jersey as well. Gov. Carteret was justifiably nervous.

For the first time in years, Carteret and the citizens of Elizabethtown stood together. This incident indicates the character of the colony's leader, John Ogden. Despite many years of acrimony between the two men, Ogden now stood shoulder to shoulder with Carteret during his time of trouble. There was a great deal of threats and saber-rattling on both sides, but Carteret, Ogden, and his fellow citizens rebuffed Andros' efforts at wresting control from Carteret. Exacerbating the situation, Carteret had declared Elizabethtown—which stood at the mouth of New York harbor—to be a free port, throwing a chink in Andros's plan to collect custom fees for any boats entering the harbor area. In retaliation, Andros threatened to build a fort at Sandy Hook, just above Elizabethtown.

In April 1680, Carteret was informed that Andros was on his way to Elizabethtown with 150 armed men, planning to take over the colony by force if necessary. When the ship arrived, however, it held only Andros and a few of his advisors. The two men went to Carteret's house for a discussion. In what must have seemed to Carteret as a flashback to his first day in the colony, each man presented his assorted documents and claimed his right to govern. Andros's letter of patent was read by his secretary: (note: brackets represent unreadable letters in the original documents).

> A while after being gone in, Sir Edmund Andros acquainted Carteret and the rest with the occasion of his coming to underceive the people and to shew his pretensions on hi[ ] Royall Highnesse behalfe to the Govt. Thereupon commanded mee to read the Kings patent to himselfe etc. to receive The place and Country from the Dutch, which was don[ ] Together with GO: Colves orders under his [ ] and seale to all officers to surrender unto the Go[ ] and one particularly to Mr. Ogden then scho[ ] for the surrender of N. Jersey.[6]

As we can see in the language of the king's patent, it had been written over six years earlier, when the Dutch were still in control and Ogden was sheriff of all New Jersey. It makes obvious that Andros and his boss, the Duke of York, had been biding their time for this power move.

The meeting then ended, as it had begun, with each man standing firm. Then, Carteret explained in his account of the meeting, "we went to dinner, and that done, we accompanied him to his sloop, and so parted."[7]

To finish this sad tale of Edmund Andros's grab for power, we turn to Jasper Danckaerts, a German visitor to the scene at the time, to tell the rest of the story:

> He [Andros] sent boats several times to Achter Kol to demand the submission of the place to his authority, which the people of Achter Kol jeered at and disregarded, being ready to uphold the king and their own government, whom they bound themselves to maintain. At night, and unseasonable hours, and by surprise, he took from New Jersey all the staves of the constables out of their houses, which was as much as to deprive them of the power to act. Seeing he could accomplish nothing by force, he declared the inhabitants released from their oaths to the Heer Carteret; they answered they could not acknowledge any release from their oaths, unless by the same authority which had required it of them or the exhibition of a higher one, that of the king.[8]

Andros next struck directly at Carteret, having him violently kidnapped from his bed and conveyed, naked it is reported, to New York. On May 27, 1680, he was taken to trial for usurping the government's powers, but he was found not guilty, to Andros's chagrin. However, appended to the finding was a condition that Carteret could return to Elizabethtown, but could assume no authority or jurisdiction over the colony. He was beaten.

Gov. Andros took over the reins of government, until the Duke of York could name a permanent replacement, one who would answer directly to Andros.

The final act in this little drama, at least as far as John Ogden was concerned, happened a few months later. Andros called for a General Assembly, to meet in Elizabethtown on June 2. The records do not reflect whether Ogden attended. He was seventy-two at the time, but it is difficult to imagine that he would have missed a meeting of such import unless he lay on his deathbed.

Andros again presented his credentials for governing. Then he recommended the enacting of all the laws currently in force in

New York, and reminded them of the protections provided them by the King's letters patent under the Great Seal of England.

The East New Jersey freemen treated him with all due respect, but in their reply they summed up all the principles of free government and democracy they had fought so bitterly for over the past fifteen years. If Good Old John Ogden's hand was not in the writing of their response, there can be no doubt but that his inspiration was behind it:

> As we are the representatives of the freeholders of this province, we dare not grant his majesty's letters-patent, though under the great seal of England, to be our rule of joint safety; for the great charter of England, alias Magna Charta, is the only rule, privilege and joint safety of every free-born Englishman. What we have formerly done, we did in obedience to the authority that was then established in this province. These things which have been done according to the law require no confirmation.[9]

The freemen then presented for Andros's approval the laws already in force, and reasserted their belief in the legitimacy of their original patent from Gov. Nicolls.

Eventually, about four months later, the Duke of York would renounce Andros's efforts at taking control of New Jersey, distancing himself from any culpability in the scheme.[10]

For a very brief period, Philip Carteret was re-installed as governor, but he died shortly thereafter—only forty-four at the time—it is said from the internal injuries he had incurred at the hands of Andros's soldiers when he was plucked naked from his bed. Carteret left only his wife, whom he had married in 1681, though he had stepchildren by her. She was the daughter of Richard Smith of Smithtown, Long Island, and returned to that place after selling off the New Jersey properties she had inherited. Philip Carteret was buried in Elizabethtown.

But it was in May 1682 that the fledgling colony of East New Jersey suffered its greatest loss. John Ogden, about seventy-three years old, passed quietly away. We do not know of what he finally died, but the fact that his will had been drawn the previous December indicates that he knew his time was approaching.

Old age was certainly a curse in early colonial times. "Work was the essence of adult manhood in early New England," says Lisa Wilson in *Ye Heart of a Man*, a look at the domestic lives of men at the time.[11] John Ogden would certainly have felt the infirmities of old age, having spent the majority of his life in hard work.

Forced by failing health to retire at sixty, Josiah Cotton, registrar of wills in Plymouth, spoke for most elderly colonists when he said, "I find old age coming upon me like an armed man." Retirement for these hardy men came only when the body gave out.[12]

Although his family was financially well off due to many shrewd business interests, Ogden must certainly have felt let down by his inability to contribute in his final months. Family responsibility demanded reciprocity in colonial times. Retirement meant loss, not leisure for these people, and it was not welcome in their homes.

Rev. Edwin Hatfield, the eminent New Jersey historian who himself was directly related to a pioneer Elizabethtown family, provided the best panegyric to John Ogden, the Pilgrim, the Father of New Jersey:

> And now "Good Old John Ogden," whose wanderings for forty years had justly entitled him to rank with the "Pilgrim Fathers,"—the acknowledged pioneer of the town, in whose house the first white child of the settlement was born, the accepted leader of the people, a pillar in the church and in the State, honored and trusted by all . . . lies down and dies; leaving the impress of his political and religious principles, not only upon his children, but upon the community that he has so largely aided in founding. A man he was of more than ordinary mark—a man of sterling worth; of whom the town, as well as his numerous posterity, should be gratefully mindful. He was called a "malcontent," and regarded as "the leading malcontent of Elizabeth Town;" but surely the man that was held in such high esteem by the accomplished, sagacious and pious Winthrop—the man who, both at Southampton and here, had been an honored magistrate, loved and trusted by the people, and, during the Dutch rule, the virtual Governor of the English portion of the province, is not to be ranked with restless agitators because of his persistent opposition to arbitrary government. A true patriot, and a genuine Christian, he devoted himself while living to the best interests of the town, and, dying, bequeathed to his sons the work of completing what he has so fairly and effectually inaugurated—the establishment of a vigorous plantation founded on the principles of civil and religious liberty.[13]

The date of the death of John's wife, Jane, is not recorded. However, we do know that the house lot and mill on the Mill

River that he left her in his will, was by 1691 in the hands of John Jr. Thus we can deduce that she died sometime before that date. Where John and Jane were interred is also not known with one hundred percent certainty. Since it was the custom of the early settlers to bury their dead in the burying ground, immediately to the rear of the meetinghouse, it can be fairly guessed that was where they were laid. Hatfield, writing in the 1860s, verifies this opinion, saying ". . . nearly the whole area [the rear of the church-yard] . . . is occupied with the remains of the first two or three generations of the people of the town."[14]

Today, on the site of the original meetinghouse, is the First Presbyterian Church of Elizabeth, and the Ogdens' remains would lie beneath that present-day structure. Rev. Jeremiah Peck had become the town's first minister in 1668. From ten years later, a handwritten record exists, kept by Rev. John Harriman, which contains a list of the money subscribed for the upkeep of the church and its minister. The list shows John Jr. and Jonathan, called Deacon, to be two of the town's leading contributors.

The burial ground behind the present-day church, which has not accepted any new burials since the late 1800s, has nearly a hundred gravestones from the Ogden family. The earliest Ogdens interred there are two of John Ogden's sons, Benjamin, who died in 1722, and Jonathan, who died in 1732.

John Ogden's will left all his earthly possessions to ". . . Jaan Ogden . . . my Deare and beloved wife and soe hath been for above fowerty yeares." [A complete copy of the will appears in the Appendix.]

East New Jersey would go on without John Ogden, of course. It was shortly after his death that the widow of Sir George Carteret sold East New Jersey at auction for 3,400 pounds to a group of twelve new proprietors, which soon became twenty-four, primarily Quakers, under the leadership of Robert Barclay. Barclay seated a London Quaker lawyer, Thomas Rudyard, as deputy governor to run the colony. Rudyard sought to avoid the mistakes and pitfalls encountered by his predecessors by seeking an understanding with the citizens of the towns. This attempt, however, would end in failure.

The twelve Quakers, mostly Scotch, wasted no time trying to entice other Scots to settle in their new land. *A Brief Account of New Jersey*, a pamphlet published by the group, was widely distributed in their homeland. It promised a paradise on earth for

The First Presbyterian Church in Elizabethtown, circa 1840. The original church and meetinghouse, built in 1666, sat on the same ground. John and Jane Ogden were interred in the burying ground immediately behind it. A new church was built on the site in 1724, burned by the British in 1780, and rebuilt in 1789. It is believed that the Ogdens would today lay beneath the present structure. From the Collections of the New Jersey Historical Society.

those willing to make the commitment: temperate air, fertile soil, sober and industrious people, fine provisions, ample jobs, free (almost) land, and friendly Indians. In what was probably America's first planned community, the proprietors would build a new town, Ambo Point ". . . a sweet, wholesome and delightful place," and people it with like-minded Scots. The project met with only lukewarm success, there ultimately not being as many like-minded Scots as they had anticipated.[15]

William Penn became an associate of Elizabethtown, buying out the holdings of Luke Watson. Other leaders came and went, and in 1686 James, the Duke of York, became King James II, following his brother on the throne of England.

Once again, New Jersey was ordered to capitulate to the governor of New York. But James's reign as king lasted only three years, and under the new sovereigns, William and Mary, power was returned to the proprietors once again. The turn of the century saw anti-proprietor sentiment reach such a state that riots, bordering on complete rebellion, broke out across the two colonies. Between 1698 and 1701, mobs of angry townspeople attacked courts, jails, and officials on at least fifteen occasions in East and West New Jersey, causing the proprietary governments of both colonies to collapse.

Finally, in 1702, in frustration over their inability to rule the dissenting colonies, both sets of proprietors turned the government of East and West New Jersey over to the crown, making it a royal colony. The proprietors did retain their land ownership rights, convoluted and challenged as they were.

∞

It is necessary to elaborate on a statement that I made earlier about the disappearance of the early Elizabethtown Town Records.

It was customary in early colonial days for accurate records to be kept of all civil transactions, and recorded in the Town Book by a town clerk or recorder. This included all distributions of land and deeds of transfer of land. These records were invaluable in later settling disputes about land ownership, boundaries, etc. The first Town Book of Elizabethtown, so-called Book A, began in 1665 and was faithfully maintained until 1718 when it disappeared.

In truth, it didn't just disappear; it was stolen. In the second Town Book of Records, Book B, begun on November 18, 1720, and signed by all 111 of the current Elizabethtown associates, it says Book A was ". . . Craftily and Maliciously Stole and . . . Burnt or otherwise destroy'd . . ."[16] Strong words, but not without cause.

Book A included a full statement of the purchase of town lands from the Indians, Governor Nicolls's approval, and the original land distribution to the eighty associates. It was this record the associates used to back up their claims of legal ownership whenever the proprietors tried to disenfranchise them. The original settlers and their descendants obstinately maintained the legality of their holdings, and with the Town Book in hand, rebuffed one assault after another from the proprietors and the crown.

Book B continues:

WHEREAS, the Books of Record, Belonging To The said Elizabeth Town, wherein the Important affairs of The Same Towne were Recorded from the Beginning thereof; have Been privately Taken Away from him unto whose Care And Custody They were Committed; And Are not Likely To be Again Obtained: It is now Therefore, By A free And unanimous Agreement of the freeholdrs Concluded and Resolved; That This present Book Now Is and Shall be Improved To be, A book of Records, for the use and behoof of the freeholders of Elizabeth Town Afores[aid], and for no Other use whatsoever.[17]

The strange and nefarious disappearance of Book A was a serious blow to the associates. In later court cases, the proprietors claimed it was the associates themselves who had destroyed the book because of their fear of bringing it into court. But everyone knew that was just a subterfuge. On August 2, 1720, a committee of seven men was seated to reconstruct the land records.[18] The task took nine years but a new record of surveys and conveyances was finally finished, and all of the associates finally signed off on the new record.

In a strange modern-day twist, the third Book of Records, Book C, covering the mid-1700s, also disappeared at some point. A few years ago, it turned up on eBay at auction. The city attorney of Elizabeth contacted the seller, and he graciously returned the book to the city, and it now resides in the State Archives in Trenton.[19]

Though the Elizabethtown associates certainly suffered a loss with the theft of the irreplaceable Book A, we latter-day historians are also seriously affected. We have few ways to learn what happened in the town during those early years, and that is a loss to all Americans.

∽

Life during the latter half of the seventeenth century in Elizabethtown was more than political and land bickering. It was still a very good place to live, to worship, and to raise a family. Thomas Rudyard, the first governor under the Quakers who took control of East New Jersey in the 1680s, spoke glowingly of living there in a 1683 letter:

My habitation . . . is at Elizabeth-Town; and here we came first; it lies on a fresh, small river; with a tide, ships of thirty or forty tons come before our doors.

We cannot call out habitation solitary; for what with public employ, I have little less company at my house daily than I had in George Yard [England], although not so many passes by my door. The people are generally a sober professing people, wise in their generation, courteous in their behavior, and respectful to us in office among them. As for the temperature of the air, it is wonderfully suited to the humors of mankind . . . I never had better health.

The following year, the second Quaker governor, Gawen Lawrie, wrote similarly of his new hometown:

Here wants nothing but people. There is not a poor body in the province, nor that wants. Here is abundance of provisions; pork and beef at two pence per pound; fish and fowl plenty; oysters I think would serve all England; Indian wheat two shillings and six pence per bushel; . . . cyder good and plenty for one penny per quart; good drink that is made of water and molasses stands in about two shillings per barrel, wholesome like our eight shilling beer in England.[20]

Looking up Broad Street from the stone bridge, circa 1795. The bridge was built over the narrowest point on the Mill (now Elizabeth) River in the earliest years of the settlement. The building immediately behind the bridge sits on the house lot originally granted to John Ogden in 1665. It is too small to be his house, but could be his mill, which by this time would have been a tavern. From the Collections of the New Jersey Historical Society.

Even toward the end of the eighteenth century we still find the charm of Elizabeth being extolled, this time in the journals of a Polish Count who married into a local family: "Elizabeth is a charming little town; there is, one might say, only a single street in the middle. Elsewhere one sees houses scattered about here and there, surrounded by weeping willows, gardens, etc. The Presbyterian church has a very tall and slender spire . . . Who now will have a higher one! The place itself is inhabited by well-to-do people."[21]

Good Old John Ogden and his contemporaries, through their vision, determination, and hard work, had created a wonderful town and colony in many respects. If the story had not had such sad, long-lasting consequences, her ongoing power and land squabbles would have made a marvelous Gilbert and Sullivan comic operetta. It's easy to envision a chorus of seventeenth-century American Pilgrims, dressed in their leather boots and tall hats with a big silver buckle in front, angrily brandishing their staves from stage-left. On stage-right, the proprietors' men in their feather-bedecked hats, their lace collars and velvet jackets would be singing lustily while waving their official documents at their adversaries. What a costume pageant it would have made.

John Ogden was an extraordinary man, in an extraordinary time. The earliest colonial period of America is a fascinating era, packed with brave, resourceful men and women who deserve to be remembered.

Ogden's beloved East New Jersey was unlike any other early colonial American colony. Here, freedom and democracy were not handed out as God-given rights; they were fought for. The character of her people was forged in their hunger for freedom and justice, and their refusal to settle for anything less.

Their determination, their intransigence, was most notably seen in one man, Good Old John Ogden, a man of more than ordinary mark.

ॐ

9
Ogden Family Notes

ONCE MORE, I WANT TO MAKE CLEAR THAT THIS BOOK *IS NOT* A GENE-alogical study. However, I have included these Ogden family notes in the book because I believe they will be of interest to many readers. Also, to properly recount the life of John Ogden, the vital statistics and important events of those people closest to him are a must. Many of them are facts that have been previously published, but are herewith juxtaposed for the first time to reveal new information about the Ogden family. Others are my own theories on the family based upon the extensive research I've done here and abroad. For the most part, they are colorful little shards of Ogden family information which, when positioned properly, help us clarify the mosaic that was John Ogden's life.

The information is taken from a number of sources, including some family genealogies. Most of those works are not sourced, and can often be unreliable, so be forewarned.

As you read in the preface, information from the William Ogden Wheeler book prior to John Ogden's emigration to America is suspect because of the contribution made by the fraudulent genealogist Gustave Anjou. However, I see no reason to doubt the veracity of the genealogical information provided after Ogden's emigration, as there is no indication that Anjou had anything to do with those facts. However, the Wheeler genealogical information is subject to the same warning as issued above. I have also used three other sources whenever possible, as I believe the three, taken with Wheeler's post-immigration information, are the most reliable Ogden sources available.

The first is Charles Carroll Gardner, a noted genealogist in the first half of the twentieth century who is generally recognized as the foremost expert on early New Jersey families. The *Gardner Collection* is a series of handwritten family folders he amassed during his career, which he eventually turned into a sixty-volume series of pre-Revolutionary New Jersey families and individuals.

The second source is a family tree constructed by Francis (Frank) Barber Ogden, Jr. in the mid-to-late 1800s. It is probably the first Ogden genealogy ever done, and was published in 1890, just a year before his death. Wheeler wrote of Frank Barber Ogden, "He was the author of the first Ogden chart, which in a few instances has been found incorrect, yet upon which all subsequent investigators have built . . .[1]"

Frank Ogden's father was very prominent. He served as aide-de-camp to General Andrew Jackson at the Battle of New Orleans. Thereafter, he devoted himself to mechanical science, and is credited with having first applied the important principles of the expansive power of steam in marine engines. In 1813 he received a patent on his engine, and in 1817 built the first steam engine in Yorkshire, England. He went on to become the U.S. Consul at Liverpool.

The third source I've often turned to is *Family Histories and Genealogies* . . . by Edward Elbridge Salisbury and Evelyn McCurdy Salisbury, originally published in 1892. A four-volume work, it is composed of a series of genealogical and biographical monographs on a number of early families, including Ogden.

JOHN OGDEN AND JANE (BOND) OGDEN

I am not able to vouch for the birth date of John Ogden. Wheeler states it as September 19, 1609,[2] but we do not know if this is Wheeler's date or Anjou's date. Frank Ogden dates his birth to 1610.[3] Given Ogden's date of death as May 1682, which we know is reliable, and the reference to him as "Good Old John Ogden" in his latter days, either of these birth date seems plausible. Accepting these dates, he would have died at 72 or 73, certainly not unheard of in colonial times.

(NOTE: The 1752 change from the Julian calendar to the Gregorian calendar in England and all her colonies can hazard a pitfall to those looking for exact dates of early births, deaths, and marriages. Some historians and genealogists have taken this calendar change into consideration when stating pre-1752 dates; others have not. Others still have taken the approach of listing both years, thus 1642/43. So the difference of a year or so that may be shown in two different versions of the same event should be disregarded.)

Jane (Bond) Ogden's vital statistics are not available. It was not an unusual occurrence in the seventeenth century to find little information on the women of the village. We do know that she died prior to 1691, because we find the homestead John willed to her in John Jr.'s name by then. We also know that Robert Bond, described below, was her brother.

We do have a clue we can use in verifying the Ogden's date of marriage. Wheeler states they married on May 8, 1637.[4] In his will, dated December 1, 1681, John Ogden states ". . . Jaan Ogden is my Deare and beloved wife and soe hath been for above fowerty years . . ."[5] That statement, in John's own words, indicates they were married during the late 1630s, so the Wheeler information on their marriage seems to be accurate, or at least close. This would also debunk the claim made by some historians and genealogists that John Ogden did not marry Jane Bond until *after* they came (and met?) in America.

JOHN AND JANE OGDEN'S CHILDREN

"The truth," Oscar Wilde once said, "is rarely pure and never simple."

When he made that observation, Wilde might as well have been talking about the vital statistics of the Ogden's second generation in America. As we begin to examine them, the accuracy of Wilde's quip becomes all too clear.

It has been generally accepted that John and Jane Ogden had six children. Three of them, John Jr., David, and Jonathan, were born before the Ogden's emigration to America, according to Wheeler's information; but I believe that is incorrect.

Wheeler gives the birth date of John Jr. as May 3, 1638;[6] while Salisbury says it was 1640.[7] Either could be correct; and if we've accepted the 1637 marriage date of his parents, and their 1641 emigration to America, either date would mean that John Jr. was born in England.

But when we move on to Jonathan and David, our present knowledge begins to unravel. Wheeler tells us that the two were twins, born on January 11, 1639.[8] We know Jonathan died on

January 3, 1732, and Wheeler says he lived to be 93 years old. The inscription on his headstone, however, says he died ". . . in ye 86th year of his Age,"[9] which would make his year of birth 1646, not 1639. This discrepancy is particularly odd in that Wheeler also wrote the book on the tombstone inscriptions, so how he could postulate different birth dates in the two books is peculiar. It is possibly explained by that fact that Wheeler died in early 1900, seven years before the publication of his massive genealogical study. The book was completed by two others, so one of those editors could have made the mathematical blunder.

From his handwritten notes, Gardner gave the birth date of Jonathan as 1647;[10] Salisbury agrees;[11] but Frank Ogden says 1645.[12]

Jonathan's birth date is doubly important if he and David were twins, as Wheeler believed. If Jonathan's birth date is incorrect, is David's incorrect as well? Or is it possible that they are not twins after all? Let's examine it. It's difficult to accept that Jonathan's tombstone would be incorrect as to his age at death. Accepting that, two possibilities arise. First, Jonathan and David were not twins. Jonathan was born in 1646/47 as the headstone indicates, but David was born at another time. The second possibility holds that the boys were twins, but that both were born in 1646/47. Let's look somewhere else for verification.

Frank Ogden's family tree indicates that David was born in 1643, indicating that they were not twins.[13] I lean toward this option. First, I accept the tombstone inscription, which means Jonathan was born in 1646 (or, it could have been 1645, as Francis Barber Ogden says, or 1647 as Gardner says, the difference being only a matter of the month of birth or the aforementioned calendar change.) That still makes Jonathan an old man when he died in 1732; but it's more believable than that he lived to ninety-three, an incredibly old age in colonial times.

Moving on to David, I also lean toward Frank Ogden's date of 1643, rather than Wheeler's earlier 1639 date. (Gardner and Salisbury offer no birth date for David.) I did not find any further verification of either Wheeler or Frank Ogden's birth date choice, nor does a tombstone inscription exist for David to offer any help. However, as you'll see in a moment, this isn't as simple as it first appears.

As to the other children, Wheeler tells us that the fourth child, Joseph, was probably born on November 9, 1642, and died before

January 15, 1690.[14] If this is accurate, it would make Joseph older than either Jonathan or David, and that was not the case. So we have another big question mark. Francis Barber Ogden offers no birth date for Joseph, nor does Gardner or Salisbury. Also, no Stamford church records for the early years of the settlement exist to verify any births in that place. I did study the earliest town records, beginning in 1641, but found nothing that relates to the Ogden children. We do have one other clue, an old family bible that you'll read about a little later.

This bible, which it is supposed to have belonged to John Ogden, the Pilgrim, has a handwritten notation in a margin that says that one of the children was born on November 9, 1642. Unfortunately, the name of the child was unreadable. Wheeler guessed it to be Joseph, because it fits into his timeline of the order of births of the Ogden boys: John Jr., David and Jonathan, Joseph and Benjamin. I believe that order is accurate. But now that I've moved David and Jonathan forward by quite a few years, it would be impossible for Joseph to have been born in 1642/43 if he is indeed younger than the other two.

Thus, in my opinion, the unreadable name in the bible is not Joseph but David. I believe David was born on November 9, 1642/43, which fits perfectly with the earlier scenario I have outlined.

So having informed you that I believe David was born in 1642/43 and Jonathan in 1645–47, I have to go further out on the ancestral limb and guess that Joseph was born sometime during the 1646–48 period.

From the time of the earliest settlements in America, town records recorded the political happenings of the day, and many early courts recorded the buying and selling of real estate. But vital statistics—who was born, who got married, and who died—were not recorded in the town records. These records were the province of the churches. In many early settlements, it could be one or two years—perhaps more—before the church was built, a minister enticed to join the settlement, and a system of record-keeping put in place. Even then, the records were subject to damage, fire, theft, or any of a dozen other catastrophes. (I've read of numerous cases where mice have eaten the records.) Early cemeteries were also subject to the ravages of time; and whatever headstones may have been used were not really stones at all, but plain wooden markers that have long since turned to dust. So it is normal that no vital statistical records exist in earliest colonial America.

The fifth son, Benjamin, was born circa 1654 (Wheeler and Salisbury[15,16]) or 1652 (Frank Ogden)[17] or 1653 (Gardner)[18] His tombstone tells us he died in 1722 "in his 69th year,"[19] so his date of birth would have been 1653/54, at North Sea, Long Island.

The final child, a girl, has no birth date recorded by any of three gentlemen; as a matter of fact, they don't even agree on her name. Wheeler calls her Mary; Frank Ogden calls her Sarah; and Gardner and Salisbury don't even mention her. The first two agree that she married John Woodruff; and the Woodruff family genealogy calls her Sarah. Despite all the conflicting information, we know for a fact that she existed, and that she was married to John Woodruff, Jr. (sometimes referred to as "The Elder" because he was the eldest of two brothers who were adopted by another family).

In the *Southampton Town Records*, we find the following notation with the date September 7, 1665. This was after John Ogden had left Southampton for Elizabethtown, and was disposing of his Southampton property:

> Sept. 7, 1665. Mr. John Ogden doth acknowledge that what land or housing or privilidges thereto belonging which he bought of his cousin John Ogden [of Rye], hee ye said Mr. Ogden did make over all the same unto his sone in law John Woodruff that it became his.[20]

The Woodruff family and the Ogden family had strong ties. John Woodruff Sr. was an original settler of Southampton, from Lynn Mass. in 1640. His son John Jr. had been born in Kent, England in 1637, and traveled with his family to America. In about 1659, according to some Woodruff family genealogies, he married Sarah Ogden. The same genealogy provides her birth date as around 1643, which would have made her of marrying age— though on the cusp—by 1659. This would have placed her birth at either Stamford or Hempstead.

I do not know when Sarah (Ogden) Woodruff died, however, her husband John died in 1691 in Elizabeth, and had taken a second wife by then. So Sarah died in the 1670s or '80s.

I have no doubt that there will be some hard-core Ogden genealogy buffs reading these words sometime in the future. For you folks—and you know who you are—I have one additional mystery to get your genealogical juices flowing.

Genealogies of New Jersey Families is a two-volume set excerpted and reprinted from the "Genealogical Magazine of New Jersey." In it is an article entitled "The Wife of Stephen Crane of Elizabethtown, New Jersey," by James Thompson. Crane was one of the original associates in Elizabethtown, but apparently little else is known of him. Thompson set about to prove who Crane's wife was, and he cites only the most respected primary source material in reaching his conclusion.

"I'm My Own Grandpa" is a catchy novelty tune written many years ago. The lyrics describe how, through a convoluted series of intermarriages and other ancestral shenanigans, the singer of the tune eventually becomes his own grandfather. Through the same kind of process—but on a much more serious note—Thompson follows a number of colonial familial lines in reaching this rather startling conclusion: "Therefore, the final conclusion of our research based on Daniel Crane's will is that his mother, the wife of Stephen Crane, was a heretofore unknown daughter of John and Jane (Bond) Ogden, and a sister to Sarah, the wife of John Woodruff, and Jonathan Ogden."[21]

Now this was a surprise! The rationale and the records Thompson followed leave little doubt that he's on to something. Not being an expert in these matters, I can neither confirm nor deny that his information is accurate, but I have no reason to doubt it. The lady is question was named Hannah, the same as John Ogden's also heretofore unknown sister (see below).

I find one other clue that may verify Thompson's claim. Elizabethtown historian Hatfield, in his eulogy on John Ogden, includes this brief sentence: ". . . in whose home the first white child of the settlement was born . . ."[22] Since we know with certainty that Sarah and the five boys were all born earlier, Hatfield's reference could only be to an additional child we knew nothing about. If Hatfield is correct, this must have been the unknown Hannah, who would have been born in about 1665.

Here's one additional bit of genealogical trivia that I find fascinating. In writing about a fifth-generation Ogden, also named John, Wheeler refers to a marriage date, then states:

The above marriage is recorded at East Hampton, L. I. It agrees with record in an old Bible owned by Mrs. Cortland Drake of Mendham,

N. J., and which was doubtless the family Bible of "Good Old John.[1]"
[The number 1 refers to the first generation John Ogden, the Pilgrim.] It descended to John[77] through his gr. Grandfather Jonathan[4], son of John[1]. On a blank page at the beginning of the Book of Psalms is written "Jonathan Ogden, his book 1697." In another place "John Ogden son of Jonathan Ogden Dec'd His Bible given him by his grandfather Ogden in the year 1724." At the end of Revelations is "Nov. 9, 1642, my son [name unreadable] was born by gods providence." This birth date is probably that of John the Pilgrim's son David, as I stated earlier—at all events proving that this rare old Bible printed in 1599 was once the property of John Ogden[1].[23]

When I first read this, I became very excited that such a bible might still exist today. Remember, Wheeler's words would have been written over one hundred years ago. I began to search on the Internet for a descendant of Cortland Drake, and found what I'm confident was the correct family, the great-grandson. Unfortunately, he knew nothing of the old family bible, which means it must have passed to another branch of the family in the intervening years. It was a big disappointment.

Another disappointment has been my inability to find a single note, letter, or journal from the hand of John Ogden. Of course, I'm not even sure the man could write. Perhaps someday, someone will come forward with such a document, or with the family bible itself, allowing us to answer a few of these questions.

So, let me summarize the best-estimate vital statistics of John and Jane Ogden's children:

John Jr.: b. 1638–40, d. 1702
David: b. 1642/43, d. 1692
Sarah: b. 1643, d. before 1690
Jonathan: b. 1645–47, d. 1732
Joseph, b. 1646–48, d. 1690
Benjamin: b. 1652–54, d. 1722
Hannah: b. 1665, d. unk.

ROBERT BOND AND HANNAH (OGDEN) BOND

The eminent New Jersey historian Rev. Edwin Hatfield, in writing a brief biography of Ogden's brother-in-law, Robert Bond, said, "His intimacy with Ogden (tradition says that each married the other's sister), . . . his influence was second only to John Ogdens." And then, "His first wife was Hannah, a sister of John Ogden."[24] Bond was by trade a blacksmith.

Wheeler does not mention John Ogden having a sister named Hannah, but again, is this Wheeler or Anjou speaking? He does mentions seven siblings—five brothers and two sisters—three of them dying in infancy. Of the others, we know nothing, except for his brother Richard, who was in the New World with him.

I believe Hatfield is correct in saying that Hannah was John's sister. I have seen three other sources that say the same thing. One is Frank Ogden's family tree. Another is a genealogy on the family of Robert Bond, published in 1872. It lists Hannah as his first wife, and mother of his two sons, Stephen and Joseph. That book provides the following biography of John Bond:

> The ancestors of the Bond family were Puritans. A company of them came from Kent County, England, to New England in 1639. Robert Bond, the first of this name in America, as far as can be ascertained, was at Southampton, Long Island, in 1643, at Lynn, Mass., a short time, and at East Hampton in 1649.
>
> John Ogden, with a few of his friends, came to Elizabethtown in 1664. He was a man of sterling integrity and piety, and Robert Bond was one of his most intimate and influential associates.
>
> After the death of his first wife, Robert Bond married at Newark in 1672, Mary, the widow of Hugh Roberts. She was the daughter of Hugh Calkins, an emigrant from Wales in 1640, first to Gloucester, Mass., and then to New London, Conn.
>
> Robert Bond thus became interested in the Newark Colony, and was elected in the same year their Representative. He continued to reside in Newark, where he died in 1677. His sons were: Stephen Bond who settled at Newark, and Joseph Bond, who settled at Elizabethtown, and died in 1709.[25]

The above passage would indicate that John Ogden's sister, Hannah, died sometime before 1672, the year Robert Bond remarried. We cannot establish if she married Bond before coming to America or afterward. If it was afterward, she probably traveled to the New World with John and Richard.

JOHN OGDEN OF RYE

One group of historians, probably taking their cue from Wheeler, believes that John Ogden of Rye was about nine years older that John Ogden, the Pilgrim, and had arrived in America a few years earlier. They also say the two were first cousins. Another group, including Charles W. Baird, believe John of Rye was the son of John, the Pilgrim's brother Richard, who eventually settled in Fairfield, Conn.[26]

The first group is correct. In the Southampton Town Record cited above, this John Ogden is clearly noted as the cousin of Mr. John Ogden [the Pilgrim].

It is agreed upon that he married twice, to Judith Budd and to Ann Richardson; and that he died in 1682 or 1683, at approximately the same time as John the Pilgrim, a fact that adds to the two often being confused in early records.

WILLIAM BUTLER OGDEN

His brief bio follows in a few pages—he was another very prominent and wealthy man in the direct line of descent from John and Jane Ogden—but I wish to touch here on the contribution he *almost* made to our knowledge of Ogden genealogy.

Quoting from Wheeler's book:

> For several years before his death, William B. Ogden had interested himself in genealogy, intending to trace his family back to the original immigrant [John Ogden, the Pilgrim.] Being a very busy man it was more in the nature of recreation with him than otherwise; yet his wide acquaintance gave him an advantage that enabled him to gather a mass of genealogical information, only to be lost forever at the burning of his Chicago home at the time of the great fire there. A few notes, mostly made from memory, were all that remained at the time of his death in 1877.[27]

Truly, what a pity for the rest of us. It would appear, however, that at least he provided the inspiration that led to Wheeler's monumental genealogical study of the Ogdens, as we see in our next genealogical note.

WILLIAM OGDEN WHEELER

William was born in Delhi, Delaware County, New York, in 1837, and died in 1900. When he was about twenty, he moved to

Chicago to enter the employ of his uncle, William Butler Ogden. At about this time, Ogden had acquired a second residence near High Bridge, N.Y., known as Villa Boscobel, on which he contemplated making alterations and improvements. He entrusted this work to his nephew, William.

William loved the work, and his natural flair for landscape gardening transformed Villa Boscobel into a showplace. After the completion of that job, he traveled for a number of years, both at home and abroad, finally settling in Sharon, Conn. With only the few genealogical notes his uncle had given him, he now set about completing the task his uncle had begun. No expense was spared—he had inherited from his uncle—and he had a staff to assist him in Morristown, N.J., and contract historians in Europe.[28]

At a time before genealogy was popular, he rescued the family history for preservation, which puts all of us in the Ogden line of descent deeply in his debt. Upon his death, responsibility for finishing the book fell to Rev. Charles Burr Ogden and Lawrence Van Alstyne, who finally saw it published in 1907.

ॐ

NOTE: All the following brief bios are taken from Wheeler's book. Any corrections I may have offered above have not been inserted in these bios; though I may have restated some of the copy, all the dates are as written in Wheeler.

First Generation

JOHN OGDEN, THE PILGRIM, b. Sept. 19, 1609; d. Elizabethtown, N.J., May, 1682; m. May 8, 1637, JANE BOND, b. ____; d ____, Elizabethtown N.J.

Second Generation

JOHN OGDEN, JR, b. Mar. 3, 1638; d. Nov. 24, 1702; m. ____ Elizabeth Plum, b. Jan. 18, 1650; d. ____ 1702; daughter of Samuel Plum.

With his parents in Stamford, Hempstead and Southampton. Took the oath of allegiance to King Charles II, Feb. 19, 1665, in Elizabethtown, and was one of the original associates. Appears in the town records as being one of a group that on June 20, 1671, pulled down the fence of Thomas Mitchell who, in the Associates' opinion, had wrongfully been given the privileges of Freeholder by Gov. Philip Carteret.

Took the oath of allegiance to the Netherlands on Sept. 11, 1673, when the Dutch regained New Amsterdam from the English.

John Jr. had one daughter, Jemima.

DAVID OGDEN, b. Jan. 11,1639 (twin to Jonathan); d. circa Feb.1692; m. circa 1676, ELIZABETH (SWAINE) WARD, b. Apr. 24, 1654; d. after 1706, daughter of Capt. Samuel Swaine.

With his parents in Stamford, Hempstead, and Southampton. Took the oath of allegiance to King Charles II, Feb. 19, 1665, in Elizabethtown, and was one of the original associates. Like his father, a stonemason.

Took the oath of allegiance to the Netherlands on Sept. 11, 1673, when the Dutch regained New Amsterdam from the English.

In 1676 David moved his family to nearby Newark. The early records of Newark indicate that David was active in the community, accepting many political appointments. His wife, during her first marriage, was among the group of original settlers in Newark, N.J., it being recorded that she was honored by being the first English settler to set foot on the land at Newark. Her father had arrived in 1635 from England.

David had five sons, David Jr., Josiah, John, Thomas, and Swaine.

JONATHAN OGDEN, b. Jan. 11, 1639 (twin to David); d. Jan. 3, 1732; m. _____, REBEKAH (WOOD?), b. Nov. 1648; d. Sep. 11, 1724.

With his parents in Stamford, Hempstead, and Southampton. Took the oath of allegiance to King Charles II, Feb. 19, 1665, in Elizabethtown, and was one of the original associates.

Took the oath of allegiance to the Netherlands on Sept. 11, 1673, when the Dutch regained New Amsterdam from the British.

In 1692 he was the receiver of taxes for Essex County, N.J. In 1691 he is called Deacon Jonathan Ogden. He is often mentioned in the town records as being a fighter against the proprietors' usurpation of town and individual rights.

Jonathan had five children, Jonathan Jr., Samuel, Robert, Hannah, and Rebecca.

JOSPEH OGDEN, b. Stamford CT, Nov. 9, 1642; d. before Jan. 15, 1690; m. SARAH WHITEHEAD, b. ____; d.____; daughter of Isaac Whitehead.

With his parents in Hempstead, Southampton, and Elizabethtown.

Joseph had two children, Joseph Jr. and Isaac.

CAPTAIN BENJAMIN OGDEN, b. Southampton, 1654; d. Nov. 20, 1722; m. 1685(?) HANNAH WOODRUFF, b.____; d.____; daughter of John Woodruff.

With his parents in Elizabethtown.

Took the oath of allegiance to the Netherlands on Sept. 11, 1673, when the Dutch regained New Amsterdam from the British.

In 1693 he and a partner, Rev. John Harriman, leased the gristmill built by his father for a period of seven years. The two probably dealt in slaves for use in the mill. Like his brother Jonathan, he is often listed in town records as being a fighter against the proprietors' usurpation of town and individual rights.

Was appointed sheriff of Elizabethtown in 1694, and was admitted as an associate in 1699.

Benjamin had three children, Benjamin Jr., John and William.

MARY OGDEN, b. ____; d.____; m. JOHN WOODRUFF, 2d, b.____; d. 1691; son of John Woodruff 1st.

Mary had eight children, John 3rd, Jonathan, Sarah, Hannah, David, Joseph, Benjamin, and Elizabeth.

A Few Notable Ogden Descendents to 1907

GOV. AARON OGDEN (Sixth Generation) b. Dec. 3, 1756; d. Apr. 19, 1839; m. Oct. 27, 1787, ELIZABETH CHETWOOD.

Aaron Ogden was born in Elizabethtown and graduated from Princeton before he was seventeen. Entering the Continental army at the outbreak of the Revolution, he rose to the rank of Brigade Major, distinguishing himself in battle at Brandywine, Springfield, and Yorktown.

Returning to Elizabethtown after the war, he was licensed as an attorney in 1784.

In 1797, during a brief war with France, he again entered the service, rising to the rank of Colonel, the title by which he was known for the remainder of his life. During the War of 1812, he served for one year as governor of New Jersey.

Shortly thereafter he gave up the practice of law and became engaged in the business of running steamboat ferries between New Jersey and New York, a New York state-approved monopoly venture licensed to him by Robert Fulton and Robert Livingston, inventors of the steamboat. Soon another man, Thomas Gibson, began a competing ferry line using a license granted by a federal governmental agency. The issue eventually ended up in the U.S. Supreme Court in the case of *Gibbons v. Ogden*, 1824.

This was a landmark case, as it was to decide whether states—which had always regulated these things before—or the federal government had the right to regulate interstate commerce. In the end, the court sided with Gibbons, arguing that under Article I, Section 8 of the U.S. Constitution, Congress had the right to regulate interstate commerce.

Ogden lost his sizable fortune as a result of the case, and he moved to Jersey City, where he died in 1839.

HENRIETTA FRANCES EDWARDS (Sixth Generation) b. Jun. 28, 1786; d. Apr. 16, 1870; m. Jan. 6, 1817, ELI WHITNEY.

Eli Whitney is best known as the inventor of the cotton gin, one of the most important inventions in the development of the South. He invented the machine while studying law in Georgia.

PETER SKENE OGDEN (Seventh Generation) b. 1794, d. Sep. 24, 1854, m. Julia Reava.

Explorer, fur trader, trapper, mountain man: Peter Skene Ogden was all this and more.

His father was a supporter of the Loyalist side in the early part of the Revolution, thus the family was forced to abandon their property in Newark, N.J. and flee to Quebec, Canada, where Peter was born.

In 1811 he entered the service of the Northwest Fur Company, which in 1821 merged with the famous Hudson's Bay Company, one of the earliest and most important merchant companies in North America. He was transferred to the Western front and established trading posts with the Indians. On one of his expeditions he discovered the Humboldt River in northern Nevada.

Around 1824 Ogden was named one of three chief factors (today's equivalent to a chief operating officer) of the Pacific branch of the Company, located at Fort Vancouver. He continued to be a major explorer of the American West, particularly in the Great Basin, Oregon, and Northern California and the Snake River country. He was the first white man to traverse the intermountain West from north to south.

A number of Ogden's expeditions went into the Utah Territory, and the city of Ogden, UT, as well as the Ogden River and the Ogden Valley, are named after him. He remained in the employ of the Hudson's Bay Company until shortly before his death in 1854.

CAROLINE CARMICHAEL (seventh generation) b.____; d. Aug. 11, 1881, 1st m. Ezekiel McIntosh, 2nd m. 1858, Millard Fillmore.

Millard Fillmore was the 13th President of the United States.

Born in Cayuga, N.Y. on January 7, 1800, he was self-educated, and admitted to the bar as an attorney in 1827. His political life began in 1828 when he was elected to the state legislature, serving three terms. In 1832 he was elected to Congress where he served for ten years.

He was elected Vice President in 1848 running with Zachary Taylor, and succeeded Taylor when he died in July of 1850. Fillmore has been considered one of the lesser U.S. Presidents. Yet he was a statesman whose support for the Compromise of 1850 helped prevent civil war and preserve the union for the next ten years, while also admitting California to the Union. He was also a diplomat whose dispatch of a U.S. expedition to Japan helped open that nation to world trade.

After fulfilling Taylor's term, the Whig party failed to nominate him to run again due to his stand on the Compromise of 1850. He retired to Buffalo, N.Y. where he married Ogden descendant Caroline Carmichael, and lived until his death in1874.

WILLIAM BUTLER OGDEN, (eighth generation) b. Jun. 15, 1805; d. Aug. 3, 1877; m. Feb. 9, 1875, Marianna Arnot.

William's parents left New Jersey in 1789 for a new home in Delaware County in northwestern New York state, eventually settling in Walton, N.Y., where William was born. He had just begun to study for a career in law when his father's untimely death required him to assume management of the family lumbering and woolens business.

William's brother-in-law, Charles Butler, seeing much potential for western commerce, set out on a western trip in 1825, soon after the Erie Canal was finished. He stopped at the small village of Chicago, then numbering about two hundred people, and predicted that the village at the foot of Lake Michigan was destined to become the largest inland city in America. Accordingly, he made a number of land investments in the area.

In 1835 he induced William to take up residence there to manage the holdings. At that time there was little more of Chicago than Fort Dearborn and a few huts, and it is estimated that there were fewer than five thousand white men between Lake Michigan and the Pacific. Convinced of the future importance of the town, William also made extensive real estate purchases.

Over the next few years he laid out and constructed over one hundred miles of streets at his own expense, and built two bridges over the Chicago River to enhance their investments. Nearly all the public improvements of the city were originated by him, and he also built thousands of miles of railways passing through or centered in Chicago.

In 1837, when Chicago was incorporated as a city, William became the first mayor. But it was his foresight in building railroads to the West that made him most famous. He was president of the Galena & Chicago Union R. R. Company, the Chicago & Northwestern R. R. Company, Illinois & Wisconsin R. R. Company, Buffalo & Mississippi R. R. Company, Chicago, St. Paul & Fond-du-Lac R. R. Company and the Wisconsin & Superior Land Grant R. R. Company. Most notably, he was the first president of the Union Pacific R. R. Company, and later president of the Northwestern R. R. Company.

In 1856 William reentered the lumber business, purchasing nearly two hundred thousand acres of pine forest in Northern Wisconsin. And in 1860, he joined with others in organizing the Brady's Bend Iron Company on the Alleghany River in Pennsylvania, a company that employed six hundred people.

After his death, the Historical Society of Chicago heralded William Butler Ogden as "one who, more than any other man, living or dead, had lain the foundations of Chicago's splendor." And the *Chicago Tribune* wrote of him, "No one else in the history of the city better understood its prime commercial position, and no one did more to influence the world to appreciate it."

THOMAS ALVA EDISON (ninth generation) b. Feb. 11, 1847, d. Oct. 18, 1931, 1st m. Dec. 25, 1871, Mary Stilwell, 2nd m. Feb. 24, 1886, Mina Miller.

Probably the most famous and distinguished Ogden descendant, Thomas Edison was born in Milan, Ohio. His great-grandmother, Sarah Ogden Edison, and her husband John, originally from Holland, were loyalists during the Revolution, so had emigrated to Nova Scotia in 1783. The family remained in Canada until 1838, when Thomas's father, Samuel Edison Jr., took the family to Michigan, then on to Ohio.

Returning to Michigan when he was seven, Thomas entered school. He was considered a dull student by his teachers, however, an undiagnosed hearing problem caused his difficulties. Nevertheless, he became a voracious reader, and at age ten he set up a laboratory in his basement.

At the age of twelve he took a job as trainboy on the Grand Trunk Railway, and established a new lab in an empty freight car. He also began printing a weekly newspaper that he called the *Grand Trunk Herald*. During this period, he saved the life of the station agent's child who had fallen on the tracks, and was rewarded by being taught how to use the telegraph. He worked as a telegrapher for six years, during which he began developing a telegraphic repeating instrument that made it possible to transmit messages automatically. By 1869 this invention and others were progressing so well that he left the railway to begin a career as a full-time inventor and entrepreneur.

He moved to New York, opening a workshop in Newark, N.J., where he continued to develop new printing and telegraphy technology. In 1875 he built a new laboratory and machine shop in Menlo Park, N.J. where he would achieve his greatest success.

By the time of his death in 1931, Edison had patented 1,093 of his discoveries. These include the incandescent light bulb, the phonograph, the kinetoscope (forerunner of the movie camera), the storage battery, the electric pen, and the mimeograph, to name just a few. He, more than any man, was responsible for bringing electric power to the masses, and he is still considered the greatest American inventor in history.

MALVINA BELLE OGDEN (ninth generation) b. Cincinnati Ohio, May 7, 1842; d. ____; m. Oct. 16, 1862, PHILIP DANWORTH ARMOUR.

Philip Armour was born in Stockbridge N.Y. in 1832. At the age of nineteen he walked to California and made a fortune there in mining. Returning to Milwaukee, he entered the meat packing business with business partner John Plankington. In 1867 he established Armour and Company at the Union Stock Yards in Chicago, which became the largest pork and beef packing concern in the world.

In later years, Philip became a philanthropist, making huge donations in Chicago. He died in 1901.

Chronology of the Life of John Ogden

Sept 1609	John Ogden born in County Lancashire, England
May 1637	Marries Jane Bond in England
Late 1641	Migrates with his family to Rippowam; builds dam and mill for the town
Dec 1641	Is voted into the Rippowam community
May 1642	Obtains contract to build the first permanent stone church in New Amsterdam
Spring 1644	Is one of original founders of Hempstead, on Long Island
1649	Is original founder of Northampton, Long Island
Jan 1650	Granted America's first commercial whaling license
Jan 1651	Is appointed Magistrate of Southampton, first of nine such appointments
1662	Is original patentee in gaining a Royal Charter for Connecticut Colony
Nov 1664	Is original patentee with three other men for Elizabethtown Purchase, the first English settlement in present-day New Jersey
Mid 1673	Appointed "schout" of all English towns in present-day New Jersey, making him the virtual governor of the territory
May 1682	Dies in Elizabethtown at 72 years of age

Appendix

From Chapter 3. The Stone Church in the Fort

Contract for the Construction of the Church In Fort Amsterdam

"Appeared before me, Cornelius Van Tienhoven, Secretary, in behalf of the general privileged West India Company in New Netherland, the Honorable William Kieft, church-warden, at the request of his brethren, the church-wardens of the church in New Netherlands, to transact and in their name to conclude the following business. So did he, as church-warden, agree with John Ogden about a church in the following manner, viz-

John Ogden of Stamford, and Ritsert [Richard] Ogden, engage to build in behalf of said church-wardens, a church of rock-stone, seventy-two feet long, fifty-two feet broad, and sixteen feet high, above the soil, all in good order, and in a workmanlike manner. They shall be obliged to procure the stone, and bring it on shore near the fort at their own expense, from whence the church-wardens shall further convey the stone to the place where it is intended to build the church, at their own expense. The church-wardens aforesaid will procure as much lime as shall be required for the building of the aforesaid church. John and Ritsert Ogden shall at their own charge pay for the masonry, and provided that when the work shall be finished the church-wardens shall pay to them the sum of 2500 gl. [guilders], which payment shall be made in beaver, cash, or merchandise, to wit: if the church-wardens are satisfied with the work, so that in their judgement the 2500 gl. shall have been earned, then the said church-wardens shall reward them with 100 gl. more; and further promise to John Ogden and Ritsert to assist them whenever it is in their power. They further agree to facilitate the carrying of stone thither, and that John and Ritsert Ogden may use during a month or six weeks the company's boats, engaging themselves and the aforesaid John and Ritsert Ogden to finish the undertaken work in the manner

209

as they contracted. Done in Fort Amsterdam, in New Netherland."
[signed but undated]

Willem Kieft   Richard Ogden   Thomas Willett
John Ogden   Gysbert op Dyck

(source: I. N. Phelps Stokes, *Iconography of Manhattan Island*,
95–96.)

FROM CHAPTER 4. THE GREAT PLAINS ON LONG ISLAND

Governor Kieft's Patent for Hempstead

Know all men whom these presents in any wise concern, that
I, William Kieft, Esq., Governor of the province called New Netherlands, with the council of state there established, by virtue of a
commission under the hand and seal of the high and mighty
lords, the States-General of the United Belgick Provinces, and
from his Highness, Frederick Hedrick of the West India Company, have given and granted, and by virtue of these we do give
and grant, unto Robert Fordham, John Stricklan, John Ogden,
John Karman, John Lawrence and Jonas Wood, with their heirs,
executors. administrators, successors or associates, or any they
shall join in association with them, a certain quantity of land,
with all the havens, harbors, rivers, creeks, woodlands, marshes,
and all other appurtenances thereunto belonging, lying and being
upon and about a certain place called the Great Plains, on Long
Island, from the East River to the South Sea, and from a certain
harbor now called and commonly known by the name of Hempstead Bay, and westward as far as Matthew Garritson's Bay to
begin in direct lines that they may be the same lattitude in
breadth as on the south side as on the north, for them, the said
patentees, actually, really, and perpetually to enjoy in as large
and ample manner as their own free land of inheritance, and as
far eastward, in case the said patentees and their associates shall
procure one hundred families to settle down within the said limit
of five years after the date hereof; giving and granting, and by
virtue of these presents we do give and grant unto the said patentees and their associates, which with their heirs and successors,
full power and authority upon the said land, to build a town or
towns, with such fortifications as to them shall seem expedient,
with a temple or temples to use and exercise the reformed reli-

gion, which they profess, with the ecclesiastical discipline thereunto belonging; likewise giving and granting, and by virtue of these presents we do give and grant to the patentees, their associates, heirs and successors, full power and authority to elect a body politic or civil combination among themselves, and to nominate certain magistrates, one of more under the number of eight, of the ablest, discreetest, approved honest men, and him or them annually to present to the Governor of this Province, for the time being, for the said Governor-general for the time being, to elect and establish them for the execution or government among them, as well civil as judicial; with full power to said magistrates to call a court or courts as the they shall see expedient, and to hold pleas in all cases civil and criminal, make an officer to keep their records of their proceedings, with power for said magistrates and the free inhabitants to make civil ordinances among themselves; also to make an officer to execute warrants, process of injunction, and likewise to take testimony of matters pending before them, and give the first sentence for the deprivation of life, limb, stigmatizing, or burn-marking any malefactor, of they in their conscience shall judge them worthy; and to cause the execution of said sentence, if the party so condemned maketh not their appeal to the chiefe court, holden weekly in the fort Amsterdam, in which case he shall be conveyed thither by order of the magistrates or the town of Hempstead, who shall have power to sit in our said Court, and vote in such causes. And if the said Patentees cannot within five years, procure 100 families to settle on said lands, that they shall enjoy "ratum pro rata", land according to the number they shall procure; reserving from the expiration of ten years—to begin from the day the first general peace with the Indians shall be concluded—the tenth part of all the revenue that shall arise from the ground manured with the plow and hoe, in case it be demanded before it be housed (gardens and orchards, not exceeding one Holland acre, excepted). Given under my hand and seal of this province, this 16th day of Nov. 1644, stilo nove.

William Kieft   (L. S.)

Source: Benjamin Thompson, *History of Long Island,* Appendix.

FROM CHAPTER 5. SOUTHAMPTON CALLS

Wyandanch's Quogue Deed to John Ogden

May 12, 1659 Be it knowne unto all men that by this present writing that I Wiandance Sachem of Paumanacke on Long Island have upon deliberate consideration, and with my sonne Weeay-comboune, both of us together, given and granted unto Mr. John Ogden and his heirs for ever, I say freely given a certain tract of land beginning at the westward end of Southampton bounds, which land is bounded eastward with Southampton bounds, and with a small piece of meadow which I gave to Mr. John Gosmer which he is to enjoy, Northward to the water of the bay and to the creek of Accoboucke [Beaverdam stream] Westward to the place called Pehecannache, and Southerly to Potuncke, three miles landward in from the high water marke, and creeke of acco-boucke, and soe to the west, But from this three miles bredth of land Southward all the land and meadow towards the south sea, the beach only excepted which is sold to John Cooper, I say all the land and meadows I have sold for a considerable price unto Mr. John Ogden for himself his heirs executors and assigns for ever upon condition as followth, first that Thomas Halsey and his associates shall have the privilege of the place of meadow called ququanantuck the term of years formerly granted to him or them. But the land lying betweene Quaquanantuck and three miles northward he shall or may possess and improve at present, but when the years of the aforesaid Thomas Halsey shall be expired, than shall the aforesaid Mr. John Ogden or his assigns fully possess and improve all quaquanantuck meadow with the rest aforesaid, and then shall pay or cause to be paid unto me Wyandance my heirs or assignes the summe of twenty five shillings a yeare as a yearly acknowledgement or rent for ever. And it is also agreed that we shall keep our privileges of fishing, fowling, hunting or gathering of berries or any other thing for our use and for the full and firme configuration hereof we have both parties set too our hands markes and seals interchangeably The date and yeare above written.

    In presence of us
        DAVID GARDINER   JOHN OGDEN
        LION GARDNIER
(Source: Henry Parsons, William Smith Pelletreau, and Edward Foster, *Southampton Town Records*, May 12, 1659.)
(NOTE: Ogden was supposed to have paid four hundred pounds for the land, but that figure is not mentioned in the deed. The additional land that made up the meadows at Quaquanantuck, which had been previously leased to Thomas Halsey, would have its lease reassigned to Ogden when Halsey's lease expired. For

that additional land, Ogden would pay a yearly rental, as indicated in the contract.)

Oath of a Freeman

I [colonist's name] being (by Gods providence) an Inhabitant, and Freeman, within the jurisdiction of this Common-wealth, doe freely acknowledge my selfe to bee subject to the government thereof; and therefore doe heere sweare, by the great & dreadful name of the Everliving-God, that I will be true & faithfull to the same, & will accordingly yield assistance & support therunto, with my person & estate, as in equity I am bound: and will also truely indeavour to maintaine and preserve all the libertyes & privilidges therf, submitting my selfe to the wholesome lawes, & ordres made & established by the same; and further, that I will not plot, nor practice any evill against it, nor consent to any that shall soe do, butt will timely discover, & reveall them to the publick weale of the body, without respect of personnes, or favour of any man, Soe help mee God in the Lord Jesus Christ.
(source: University of California, Berkeley, Sims School of Information Management and Systems.

FROM CHAPTER 8. A VIGOROUS
PLANTATION IN EAST NEW JERSEY

John Ogden's Last Will and Testament

Know all men by these presents that I John Ogden Senior Inhabitant of Elizabethtown in ye province of new East Jersey for Divers good causes and waity Considerations moveing me hereunto but more Espetially for that Jaan Ogden is my Deare and beloved wife and soe hath been for above fowerty yeares Have Given Graunted Alienated and made over unto my above Deare wife Jaan Ogden all my Estate both moveables and immoveables that is to say houses lands cattles goods and what ever else may be my Proper right & Due & what soever Lands not yet Layed out which is my Right & Due I say I Doe by these rights fully and firmly Give Graunt Alienate and make over all Just Debts being payd satisfied & answered: by ye advice & Councell & assistance of such overseers as I have thought fitt to Constitute namely Ben-

jamin Parkis Jonathan Ogden & Joseph Ogden for a full & firm
Ratification & Confirmation of ye promises I have hereunto set
my hand and Seall this one and twenty day of December one
thousand six hundred Eighty and one and in the three and thirty
yeare of his Majesties Raign

Signed Sealed & Delivered in presence of us   JOHN
OGDEN [Seal]

> Isaac Whitehead
> The marke W of
> Jaan Whitehead

Reverse Side of Will

John Curtise of a new-ark & Jonathan Ogden & Benjamin
Ogden both of Elizabethtown Came before me underwritten
Commissionated for taeking ye probate of all last wills & Testa-
ments within ye province of East new Jersey & did solemnly de-
pose upon ye holy Evangelists of almighy God that they were
perfectly well acquainted with the handwriting of John Ogden
decsd Commonly then Called old John ogden & Isaac Whitehead
decsd & then did & still do know their writing very well and yt
they do truly and verily believe in the Consciences yet ye within
written Instruments is ye hand writing of sd Isaac Whitehead &
his name subscribed thereto as a witness is his true hand writing
and yet ye name of ye testator John ogden subscribed thereunto
is ye real and true hand writing of ye sd John ogden & ye sd Jonathan ogden further saith yet this Instrument was delivered to
him very shortly after ye sd John Ogdens death & yt he hath
safely keept it ever since yt time till now Jurat: Decimo nono die
martij anno Dom: 1702do: Coram me

Thomas Gordon

An Inventorie of the Estate of John Ogden of Elizabeth Towne of
Late Deceased Approved by Humphrey Spinniag and John De-
rent by order from the Gouvernor.

To One Corne Mill 140L to one house Accomodation 100L	L 240	00	00
To two Cowes 9L two yearelings 3L Six Hogs 4L 10s	L 16	10	00

To Five sheetes and one table Cloth 2:10:00: two fether bedd 10L	L 12	10	00
To twoo Ruggs five pounds two boulsters two pounds	L 07	00	00
To one fether Bedd and one Rugg	L 05	00	00
To one Blanket and five pillowes	L 01	03	00
To one large Coaste and Trowsses	L 02	01	00
To one Cloth Coate and one Cloth hood	L 01	00	00
To one Wascott made of oyle Leather	L 00	15	00
To one Dynncaster hatt	L 00	18	00
To one Great Bible 1L 10s two peare of stocking 00:07	L 01	17	00
To Thre Neckcloths and two ould Cappes	L 00	05	00
To one Bedd Stid 1:10 to one other Bedstid board and mat 10s:00	L 02	00	00
To one Cubard 2L one table and two formes 2L – 3s	L 04	03	00
To one joyned Stoole 2s two Chests 2L2s	L 02	04	00
To one Box 5s one Carved Chest 0:10s	L 00	15	00
To one Case and Eight Bottles	L 00	10	00
To one ould Coate and one hatt	L 01	00	00
To three Cheares and two ould sheets and two peare of Drawers	L 01	04	00
To foure Chushens and one table	L 00	08	00
To one kneading trough and one ould Cheare	L 00	07	00
Tto Two Barrells and one hogshead	L 00	05	00
To three Ankers and one Chorne	L 00	11	00
To Eight milk Boules and one Funnell	L 00	06	00
To heire Sives and obe Splinter Sive	L 00	05	00
To three peales and two piging and one Little table	L 00	10	06
To one Dussin of trenchers and Dishes	L 00	02	06
To two Earthen potts and two Garres	L 00	07	00
To three Earthen panns and one Nutmeg pott	L 00	02	04
To foure Glass bottles and two Baskitts	L 00	06	00
To foure parrengers and one Dram CupL 00	07	06	
To one Candle stick and one Chamber pott	L 00	11	06
To Eight plates and two pint potts	L 00	03	00
To one pintpott and one puter BasonL 00	09	00	
To one platter two puter Salt Sellers and one Candlstick	L 00	06	03

To one tyn funnell and ould hangings for one Bedd	L 00	05	06
To one warming pan and one Greate Kettle	L 05	03	04
To one small Iron pott one other Iron pott	L 00	09	00
To one Greate Iron pott and one Iron Kettle	L 01	10	00
To one peare of scales and weights and a bras skimer	L 00	05	00
To one frying pann and Atramell	L 00	13	00
To one Iron peale and A Gridd Iron and one pere of tongus	L 00	10	00
To one peare of pott hooks and A broad Ax	L 00	07	00
To one narrow Ax two wedges and Anaddes	L 00	13	00
To one peare of Beetle Tings and one Sledg	L 00	14	06
To Six mill pickes and one mill Chissell	L 01	07	06
To one Smoing Iron and one peare of Stillyerds	L 00	13	00
To two Andirons one Doore Lock and one Cubard Lock	L 000	09	06
To one Iron Crow and one Smale Bible and a pitch fork	L 000	17	06
To one spade and an ould Spade and A hedg hooke	L 000	08	06
To one Smalle hamer and one Ston dish	L 000	02	00
To two Meate Marrells one Tymber Chain and a Lanthorn	L 000	02	00
To A Booke of Mr Backsters one Bedcase and two Blankets	L 001	10	00
To three smale Boxes a Bottle case and one pere moulds	L 000	09	06
To two trowell one stone hammer and two Gudions	L 001	06	00

Sume totle	L 326	09	05
To be Deducted the widdos Bedd Consisting of one feather Bedd			
one Boulster one Rugg	L 009	15	00
9: 15: 0 Subtracted there remaynes	L 316	14	05

This is a true Inventory According to the best of our under Standing and Knowledg

May 30: 1682 In wittness where of we Sett our hands

                                        HUMFREY
                                        SPINNIGE
                                        JOHN DERENT

The Apprisers was Sworne before
me this 30 Day of May 1682:   PHILLIP
                                     CARTERET"

(Source: William Ogden Wheeler, *Ogden Family in America*, 33–35)

Endnotes

Preface

1. William O. Wheeler, *Ogden Family*, 6.
2. Charles Gardner, *New Jersey Families: Ogden File.*
3. Gordon Remington, "Gustave Anjou." *Swedish American Genealogist,* Dec. 1992, No.12, 161–70.
4. Milton Rubicam, "Pitfalls in Genealogy." *Connecticut Nutmegger*, Dec. 1973, Vol. 6, no. 3, 332.
5. Willam O. Wheeler, *Ogden Family*, 12.
6. Ibid.

1. Coming to the New World

1. William Arthur, *Etymological Dictionary*, 210.
2. Patricia Hanks and Flavia Hodges, *Dictionary of Surnames*, "Ogden."
3. Elsdon Smith, *American Surnames,* 215.
4. Richard McKinley, *Surnames of Lancashire*, 109, 407.
5. John K. Walton, *Lancashire: Social History*, 20–30.
6. Kay Priestley, unpublished letter in the author's possession, Apr. 4, 2005.
7. *Lancashire Life,* "Is Your Name Ogden?" Mar. 1984, 53.
8. Oliver Mason, ed., *Bartholomew's Gazetteer.*
9. "International Genealogical Index: British Isles-England-Lancashire County, 1607–1611." *FamilySearch.org.* [http://www.familysearch.org/Eng/Search/frameset_search.asp?PAGE = igi/search_IGI.asp&clear_form = true] (accessed April 1, 2005.)
10. Charles Banks, *Planters of Commonwealth*, 134–35.
11. George Denton, ed. "Denton Family Genealogy." *Denton Dispatch Newsletter*, Vol. 1, no. 1, 3–4. [http://www.dentongenealogy.org/dispatch1.htm] (accessed April 15, 2005.)
12. Anthony Hewitson, *History of Preston*, 305–6.
13. Christopher Herbert, *The English: A Social History*, 231–32.
14. Frank Smith, *English Ancestors,* 20.
15. John K. Walton, *Lancashire: Social History*, 56.
16. Ibid., 8.
17. Charles Burr Ogden, *Quaker Ogdens in America.*
18. Edwin Butterworth, *History of Oldham*, 111.
19. Ralph Dutton, *Hampshire,* 76.

20. Kay Priestley, unpublished letter in the author's possession, May 23, 2005.

21. William Berry, *Genealogies, County of Hants*: *"Okeden."*

22. Bernard Burke, *Heraldic History*, 538; John Hutchens, *History of Dorset*, 469.

23. Sumner Powell, *Puritan Village*, xv–xvi.

24. Frank Lewis, *Essex and Sugar*, n.p.

25. Charles Banks, *Topographical Dictionary*, 43.

26. John Smith, *Description of New England,* 38.

27. David Cressy, *Coming Over*, 51–57.

28. Virginia Anderson, *New England Generation,* 53.

29. Charles Warner, "Captain John Smith," 5.

30. John Josselyn, *Account of Two Voyages,* 6.

31. Ibid., 7.

32. Ibid., 6.

33. Ibid., 14–15.

34. Ibid., 9.

35. Virginia Anderson, *New England Generations*, 77.

36. John Josselyn, *Account of Two Voyages,* 10.

37. Ibid., 13. (NOTE: There are no specific page number references for the remainder of the voyage portion of this chapter, but all the historical information is taken from the following books and Internet sites:)

Caffrey, Kate, *The Mayflower.* New York: Stein & Day, 1974.

Thomas Langford, ed., *English-America: the Voyages, Vessels, People & Places.* [http://www.english-america.com] (accessed November 15, 2004.)

Heaton, Vernon, *The Mayflower,* New York: Mayflower Books, 1980.

Josselyn, John. *An Account of Two Voyages to New England Made During the Years 1638 and 1663.* 1675. Microfilm of Rep., Boston: Veazie, 1865.

Maddocks, Melvin and the Editors of Time-Life Books. "The Seafarers." *The Atlantic Crossing.* Chicago: Time-Life Books, 1981.

Scholastic Publishing. "The First Thanksgiving: Voyage of the Mayflower." *English-America: the Voyages, Vessels, People & Places.* [http://teacher.scholastic.com/thanksgiving/mayflower/index.htm] (accessed Nov. 15, 2004).

Ancestry.com. *Through the Looking Glass: Mayflower Families.* [http://www.mayflowerfamilies.com] (accessed Nov. 15, 2004.)

2. A NEW HOME IN THE WILDERNESS

1. In the seventeenth century, the term "plantation" did not have the same meaning as we ascribe to it today. At that time the English thought of the process as "planting" people in an uncivilized wilderness. The people involved were either "adventurers" who risked their own money relocating to the New World, or "planters" who were sent over by private companies or the Crown. Thus, these groups of people were called a plantation. The terms "plantation" and "settlement" were often used interchangeably, and these terms would apply as long as the settlement remained outside the recognized territorial limits of another town or township, or gained recognition in its own right as a town, which

required that it had a church in it. A Colony, on the other hand, was made up of a number of scattered settlements or towns, similar to today's states.

2. E. B. Huntington, *History of Stamford,* 14–15.

3. Isabel Calder, *New Haven Colony,* 61–62.

4. Charles Hoadley, ed., *Records of New Haven,* 45.

5. *Stamford Town Meeting Records,* 5.

6. Sherman Adams, *History of Wethersfield,* 142.

7. Jeanne Majdalany, *Early Settlement of Stamford,* 2–4.

8. *Stamford Town Meeting Records,* 6. Wheeler, in his book, credits John Ogden of Rye, with a number of the achievements that later historians credit to John Ogden, the Pilgrim. This includes the building of the mill-dam in Stamford, and the 1675 signing of the Connecticut Colony charter.

9. Sherman Adams and Henry Stiles, *History of Wethersfield,* 145.

10. Ibid., 27.

11. Ibid., 145.

12. E. B. Huntington, *History of Stamford,* 22.

13. R. C. Richardson, ed., *Town and Countryside in the English Revolution,* 2–3.

14. *Stamford Town Meeting Records,* 6.

15. Jeanne Majdalany, *Early Settlement of Stamford,* 70; E. B. Huntington, *History of Stamford,* 39.

16. Sherman Adams and Henry Stiles, *History of Wethersfield, 29.*

17. *Stamford Town Meeting Records,* 8.

18. Jeanne Majdalany, *Early Settlement of Stamford,* 8.

19. *Stamford Town Meeting Records,* 8.

20. Ibid., 6.

21. Bernice Marshall, *Colonial Hempstead,* 5–6.

22. John Winthrop, *Winthrop Journal: History of New England,* 19–20.

23. Ibid., 57.

24. Ibid., 91–92.

25. Sumner Powell, *Puritan Village,* 140–44.

26. Ibid., 182–83. Most early historians agree with the forgoing opinions of historian Powell that a "new American" was born in New England. However, many later historians have begun to challenge these opinions. Among them is David Grayson Allen in his book, *In English Ways.* Allen and others of a like mind argue that most New World agricultural practices, government institutions and elected leaders were in reality an attempt to mimic the practices and institutions these men had known in the old country. Whatever differences we might see from settlement to settlement in the New World were simply the regional differences the people had known back home.

27. Robert Towne, "Introduction: The Grand List." *Stamford Grand Lists: Taxation, 1641–1821.*

28. Alfred Walton, *Stamford Historical Sketches,* 9–12.

29. Herbert Sherwood, *Story of Stamford,* 53–57.

30. Jeanne Majdalany, *Early Settlement of Stamford,* 6–7.

31. Charles Hoadley, ed., *Records of New Haven,* Feb. 6, 1642.

3. THE STONE CHURCH IN THE FORT

1. Martha Lamb and Mrs. Burton Harrison, *History of New York,* 55.
2. Ibid., 71.
3. E. B. O'Callaghan, *History of New Netherland,* 259–60.
4. Franklin Jameson, ed. "Novum Belgium," *Narratives of New Netherland,* 259.
5. Thomas Wertenbaker, *Founding American Civilization,* 40.
6. Russell Shorto, *Island at the Center,* 107.
7. Franklin Jameson, ed. "Novum Belgium," *Narratives of New Netherland,* 259.
8. Ibid., "David De Vries' Notes," 212.
9. Charles Corwin, *Manual of Reformed Church,* 12
10. Franklin Jameson, ed. "Representation of New Netherland," *Narratives of New Netherland,* 326.
11. Ibid., 213–14.
12. Ibid., 326.
13. Ibid., 212.
14. Ibid., 213.
15. Ibid., "David De Vries' Notes," 213.
16. Martha Lamb and Mrs. Burton Harrison, *History of New York,* 72, 105.
17. Charles Corwin, *Manual of Reformed Church,* 13.
18. Dr. E. B. O'Callaghan's translation, from the "Records of New Netherland" Vol. II:18 (N.Y. State Library) states the width to be fifty-four feet.
19. I. N. Stokes, *Iconography of Manhattan Island,* 1:15.
20. Charles Corwin, *Manual of Reformed Church,* 15.
21. I. N. Phelps Stokes, *Iconography of Manhattan,* 96.
22. Russell Shorto, *Island at the Center,* 179.
23. I.N. Phelps Stokes, *Iconography of Manhattan,* 96.
24. Charles Corwin, *Manual of Reformed Church,* 15.
25. Charles Corwin, *Manual of Reformed Church,* 15.
26. W. Seton Gordon, *New York Evening Post,* April 5, 1913, no page number.

4. THE GREAT PLAINS ON LONG ISLAND

1. Thomas Wertenbaker, *Founding American Civilization,* 125.
2. Bernice Marshall, *Colonial Hempstead,* 8–9.
3. George Combes, "The Early Ministers of Hempstead." *Nassau County Historical Journal,* summer 1956, 17, No. 3:1–7. Some historical scholars do not believe that Denton was the first minister at Hempstead, awarding that right to Rev. Robert Fordham. This is probably accurate. Denton's name does not appear on the first lists of settlers, while Fordham's does. Denton and Fordham were also apparently friends, so they could have traveled together from further back in time, just as they would eventually travel together to Southampton in 1649.

4. Bernice Marshall, *Colonial Hempstead*, 10.

5. Ibid.,11.

6. William O. Wheeler, *Ogden Family*, 15–16.

7. Daniel Denton, *Brief Description New York*, 49.

8. Russell Shorto. "Virtual Tour of New Netherland: Long Island, Heemstede." *New Netherland Project.*

9. John Bakeless, *America, First Explorers*, 229–30.

10. George Combes, "Early Hempstead, 1643–44." *Nassau County Historical Journal,* winter 1960, 21, No. 1:23–24.

11. Silas Wood, *First Settlement*, 4.

12. George Combes, "The Fifty Original Proprietors of Hempstead." *Nassau County Historical Journal*, summer 1957, 18, No. 3:15.

13. Ibid.

14. Abigail Halsey, *In Old Southampton*, 18–19.

15. *Records of North, South Hempstead*, Feb. 27, 1656, 435–36.

16. Donald Lines Jacobus, *Old Fairfield*, 447–48.

5. Southampton Calls

1. John Winthrop, *Journal of Winthrop*, James Savage and Laetitia Yeandle eds., 326.

2. George Howell, *Early History of Southampton*, 16–17.

3. John Winthrop, *Journal of Winthrop*, James Savage and Laetitia Yeandle, eds., 326–27.

4. George Howell, *Early History of Southampton*, 14.

5. Ibid., 22.

6. Daniel Denton, *Description of New York*, 43.

7. George Howell, *Early History of Southampton*, 24–25.

8. Russell Shorto, *Island at the Center*, 51.

9. George Howell, Early *History of Southampton*, 16.

10. Ibid., 26.

11. Ibid., 29.

12. Malcolm Freiber, ed., *Winthrop Papers*, 32.

13. Henry Parsons, William Pelletreau, and Edward Foster, eds., *Southampton Town Records*, February 3, 1650.

14. Franklin Jameson, ed., "Representations of New Netherland." *Narratives of New Netherland,* 311.

15. Russell Shorto, *Island at the Center,* 237–38.

16. Henry Hedges, William Pelletreau and Edward Foster, eds., "Book of Records, Southampton," Jan. 30, 1650. Vol. 1, 70–71.

17. Alexander Starbuck, *History of American Whale Fishery*. Repub. as part of "The Plough Boy Anthology" [http://du.edu/~tyler/ploughboy/starbuck .htm#sectionb] (accessed Apr. 18, 2005).

18. Alexander Flick, ed., *History of the State of New York*, 279.

19. Daniel Denton, *Description of New York*, 48.

20. Michael P. Dyer, American whaling historian and the librarian at the

New Bedford Whaling Museum in Massachusetts, disputes that pre-European Eastern Woodland Indians practiced off-shore whaling.

"The lore of American whaling history is replete with the stories of Eastern Woodland native peoples hunting great whales. The actual sources for this lore are extremely limited, however, and there is no physical evidence to support these stories. There are no harpoons, no lances, no floats, drags or any of the other materials commonly associated with native North American whaling peoples such as Northwest Coast native peoples and the various Eskimo peoples of the Eastern and Western Arctic. Strong evidence exists for Eastern Woodland peoples having utilized drift whales that washed up dead on the beaches or whales that stranded themselves, but for the systematic and traditional hunt of great whales there is nothing conclusive." Personal letter in author's possession.

21. George Finckenor, *Sag Harbor History*, 1.
22. George Howell, *Early History of Southampton*, 70.
23. Abigail Halsey, *In Old Southampton*, 103.
24. Henry Parsons, William Pelletreau, and Edward Foster, eds., *Southampton Town Records*, March 7, 1644.
25. Henry Hedges, William Pelletreau, and Edward Foster, eds., *Book of Records, Southampton*, Aug. 21,1654. Vol 1, 71.
26. Lillian Mowrer, *Indomitable John Scott*, 405.
27. Ruth Barker, *Quogue Through Centuries*, 1.
28. Lillian Mowrer, *Indomitable John Scott*, 405.
29. Henry Hedges, William Pelletreau, and Edward Foster eds., *Book of Records, Southampton*, June 10, 1658. Vol. 1, 170–71.
30. George Howell, *Early History of Southampton*, 168.
31. Ruth Barker, *Quogue Through Centuries*, 3.
32. Henry Hedges, William Pelletreau, and Edward Foster, eds., *Book of Records, Southampton*. Aug.16, 1666. Vol 1, 158.
33. Ibid., Vol. I, 38.
34. Ibid., March 14, 1663. Vol. 2, 39–40.
35. Henry Parsons, William Pelletreau, and Edward Foster, eds., *Southampton Town Records*, Nov. 2, 1667.
John Scott, to whom Ogden sold much of his Quogue land, is a paradoxical figure in Long Island history. Considered a scoundrel by some historians, a genius by others, all agree he was a very shrewd man. His land dealings, however, got him into trouble, and he eventually left Long Island for New England, where he lived until his death.
36. Ruth Barker, *Quogue Through Centuries*, 1–4.
37. Edwin Hatfield, *History of Elizabeth*, 65.
38. Daniel Denton, *Description of New York*, 37.
39. Russell Shorto, *Island at the Center*, 265–66.
40. George Howell, *Early History of Southampton*, 178–79.
41. Ruth Barker, *Quogue Through Centuries*, 5.
42. Henry Hedges, William Pelletreau, and Edward Foster, eds., *Book of Records, Southampton*. May 10, 1651, Vol. 1, 84.
43. Daniel Denton, *Description of New York*, 47.
44. Henry Hedges, William Pelletreau, and Edward Foster, eds., *Book of Records, Southampton*. Vol. 1, Jan. 8, 1650, 18.

45. George Howell, *Early History of Southampton*, 88–89.

46. Henry Parsons, William Pelletreau and Edward Foster, eds., *Southampton Town Records*, Oct. 7, 1650 and Oct. 6, 1651.

47. J. Hammond Trumbull, ed. *Public Records, Connecticut*, Vol. 1, 280, 297, 314, 334, 347, 384; Vol. 2, 4.

48. Henry Hedges, William Pelletreaue, and Edward Foster, eds., *Book of Records, Southampton*, Jan. 2, 1641. Vol. 1, 25.

49. Ibid.,Vol. 1. Apr. 14, 1653, 89.

50. Ibid., Vol. 1, Aug. 16, 1653, 94.

51. George Howell, *Early History of Southampton*, 165.

52. James Adams, *History of Town of Southampton*, 79.

53. Henry Hedges, William Pelletreau, and Edward Foster, eds., *Book of Records, Southampton*, April 30, 1657. Vol. 1, 154.

54. Ibid., May 4, 1657, Vol. 1, 153.

55. J. Hammond Trumbull, ed. *Public Records, Colony of Connecticut*, 295–96.

56. Henry Hedges, William Pelletreau, and Edward Foster, eds., *Book of Records, Southampton*. April 30, 1657. Vol. 1, 111.

57. Ibid., Vol. 2, 206.

58. R. R. Hinman, *First Puritan Settlers*, 18.

59. Charles Andrews and Albert Bates, *Charter of Connecticut*, 1–4.

60. Sherman Adams and Henry R. Stiles, *Wethersfield*, 174–84.

61. Henry Hedges, William Pelletreau, and Edward Foster, eds., *Book of Records, Southampton*. Vol. 1, Jun.2, 1657, 127.

6. Nova Caesarea: The Land West of "Hudsons River"

1. Franklin Jameson, ed., "The Third Voyage of Henry Hudson," *Narrative, of New Netherland*, 8.

2. Jeremiah Johnson, trans. Adriaen Van der Donck, *Description of New Netherlands*, 22.

3. John Pomfret, *Colonial New Jersey*, 4–5

4. William Whitehead, *East Jersey, Proprietors*, 23

5. Franklin Jameson, ed., "Letters of the Dutch Ministers," *Narratives of New Netherland*, 414–15.

6. William Whitehead, ed., *New Jersey Archives*, 1:14.

7. Ibid., I:17.
Wampum was the chief medium of barter and exchange when dealing with the Indians. There were two kinds: black and white. The black (or purple) wampum was worth about fifty percent more, and was made from the inside of the clam or muscle, while the white was made from the inside of a conch. The shells would be broken and ground down to a smooth, uniform size, a hole drilled through each piece, then strung together on strings or sinew. The value of goods or services would be measured by the length of a piece of wampum, usually measured in fathoms, and its color. A fathom of wampum was six feet long. The name wampum came from the Indian name for the muscle.

8. Edwin Hatfield, *History of Elizabeth*, 37.

9. William Whitehead, ed., *New Jersey Archives*, 1:17–18.

10. Aaron Leaming and Jacob Spicer, *Grants and Concessions*, 667–68.

11. William Whitehead, ed., *New Jersey Archives*, 1: 9.

12. Brendan McConville, *Daring Disturbers*, 12.

13. Herbert Osgood, *American Colonies*, Vol. 2: 169–70.

14. Theodore Thayer, *As We Were*, 11.

15. Daniel Denton, *Description of New York*, 69.

16. Theodore Thayer, *As We Were*, 13.

17. E. B. O'Callaghan, ed., *Colonial Documents*, 3: 38–39.

18. Elizabethtown Book B, 2–3.

19. John Cunningham, *The East of Jersey*, 26.

20. William Whitehead, ed. *New Jersey Archives*, 1:108.

21. Historians disagree on how many families were settled in Elizabethtown when Gov. Carteret arrived. Some say four, while others—with whom I agree—say the number was higher.

22. Samuel Smith, *History of Nova Caesaria*, 512–21.

23. *Records of Newark, New Jersey*, 11.

24. Edwin Hatfield, *History of Elizabeth*, 515.

25. According to William Whitehead, *East Jersey Under Proprietors*, pg. 36, the settlers denied in court that the name was taken to honor Sir George Carteret's wife. They claimed it was named after "the renowned Queen Elizabeth."

26. William Whitehead, ed., *New Jersey Archives*, I:50.

27. Edwin Hatfield, *History of Elizabeth*, 113.

28. Theodore Thayer, *As We Were*, 20–21.

29. Ibid., 23.

30. Newsday.com. "Harnessing Water and Wind," George DeWan. http://www.newsday.com/community/guide/lihistory/ny-history-ns333a,0,6371263.story Accessed Aug. 22, 2005.

31. Edwin Hatfield, *History of Elizabeth*, 66.

32. Ibid., 277.

33. Federal Writers' Project, U.S. Works Progress Administration for State of New Jersey, *Stories of New Jersey*, 320–22.

34. James Connolly, "Whale Industry in New Jersey," *N.J. Hist. Soc.*, 419.

35. Theodore Thayer, *As We Were*, 84.

36. Ibid., 84, 114–15.

37. Jonathan Belcher, *Belcher House*, 1.

7. Seeds of Revolution

1. William O. Wheeler, *Ogden Family*, 25–26.

2. Aaron Leaming and Jacob Spicer, *Grants and Concessions*, 688–92.

3. *Records of Newark New Jersey*, 10.

4. Aaron Leaming and Jacob Spicer, *Grants and Concessions*, 5.

5. Ibid., 77.

6. Ibid., 78–80.

7. Ibid., 86–88.

8. Ibid., 90–91.

9. Edwin Hatfield, *History of Elizabeth,* 129.
10. E. B. O'Callaghan, ed., *Colonial Documents,* 3:185.
11. Edwin Hatfield, *History of Elizabeth,* 138.
12. William Whitehead, ed., *New Jersey Archives,* 1:83–87.
13. Ibid., 82–87.
14. *Records of Newark, New Jersey,* 43.
15. Edwin Hatfield, *History of Elizabeth,* 145.
16. Ibid., 147–148.
17. Ibid., 152.
18. E. B. O'Callaghan, ed., *Colonial Documents,* 2, 571 and 582.
19. Ibid., 595.
20. Ibid., 620–22.
21. William Whitehead, ed., *New Jersey Archives,* 133.
22. E. B. O'Callaghan, ed., *Colonial Documents,* 2, 607.
23. Ibid., 633.
24. William Whitehead, ed., *New Jersey Archives,* 141.
25. E. B. O'Callaghan, ed., *Colonial Documents,* 2, 658.
26. Edwin Hatfield, *History of Elizabeth*, 179–80.
27. Ibid., 182–84.
28. Thomas Wertenbaker, *Founding of American Civilization*, 348–49.

8. A VIGOROUS PLANTATION IN EAST NEW JERSEY

1. Thomas Wertenbaker, *Founding of American Civilization,* 138.
2. Aaron Leaming and Jacob Spicer, *Grants and Concessions,* 133.
3. Franklin Jameson, ed., Narratives of New Netherland, "Of the American or Natives, their Appearance, Occupations and Means of Support," 300–301.
4. Daniel Denton, *Description of New York*, 62. Denton (p. 57) also describes the strange language custom of the Algonquians that made it so difficult to communicate with them. Tribe members had names relative to their place in the community, a significant event that occurred around the time of their birth, or some description of natural surroundings, i.e.: Red Bear, Rising Moon, or Bucks Horn. When an Indian died, his or her name died with them, and the words could never be spoken again. The idea was that speaking the words showed disrespect to friends or relatives of the deceased by reminding them of his passage. So each time these words were eliminated from the language, new words had to be substituted, making the language very difficult to master.
5. George Scot, "Model of Government." Rep. Published as an Appendix in Whitehead's *East Jersey Proprietors,* 271–77.
6. Peter Christoph and Florence R. Christoph, eds., *Andros Papers,* 256.
7. Aaron Leaming and Jacob Spicer, *Grants and Concessions,* 677–78.
8. Jasper Danckaerts, *Journal of a Voyage,* 347–52.
9. Aaron Leaming and Jacob Spicer, *Grants and Concessions*, 681–82.
10. Ibid., 685.
11. Lisa Wilson, *Ye Heart of a Man,* 35.
12. Ibid.,171.
13. Edwin Hatfield, *History of Elizabeth*, 196–97.

14. Ibid., 200.

15. William Whitehead, *East Jersey Proprietors,* 103, 207–13.

16. Elizabethtown Book B, 6 (or, Hatfield 309)

17. Elizabethtown Book B, 1–2.

18. Hatfield, 310–311 (or Elizabethtown Book B)

19. Charles Shallcross, Letter.

20. Nicholas Murray, *Notes Concerning Elizabethtown,* 12–13.

21. Julian Niemcewicz, *Under Their Vine and Fig Tree,* 19.

9. OGDEN FAMILY NOTES

1. William O. Wheeler, *Ogden Family,* 253.

2. Ibid., 39.

3. Frank Ogden, *Ogden Pedigree.*

4. William O. Wheeler, *Ogden Family,* 39.

5. Ibid., 33.

6. Ibid., 40.

7. Edward Salisbury, *Family Histories, Ogden,* 235.

8. William O. Wheeler, *Ogden Family,* 40.

9. William O. Wheeler, *Inscriptions,* 58.

10. Charles C. Gardner, "Ogden Family File." *Collection of New Jersey Families.*

11. Edward Salisbury, *Family Histories,* 235.

12. Frank Ogden, *Ogden Pedigree.*

13. Ibid.

14. William O. Wheeler, *Ogden Family,* 40.

15. Ibid.

16. Edward Salisbury, *Family Histories,* 236.

17. Frank Ogden, *Ogden Pedigree.*

18. Gardner, "Ogden Family File." *New Jersey Families.*

19. William O. Wheeler, *Inscriptions,* 59.

20. Henry Parsons, William Pelletreau, and Edward Foster, eds., *Southampton Town Records,* Vol 2, Sep. 7, 1665, 236.

21. James Thompson, "The Wife of Stephen Crane of Elizabeth, New Jersey." *Genealogies, New Jersey Families,* Joseph Klett. Ed. Vol. 1, 182–83.

22. Edwin Hatfield, *History of Elizabeth,* 196–97.

23. William O. Wheeler, *Ogden Family,* 76

24. Edwin Hatfield, *History of Elizabeth,* 70.

25. Mrs. Daniel Price, *Genealogies of Robert Bond.*

26. Charles Baird, *Rye N.Y.,* 430.

27. William O. Wheeler, *Ogden Family,* 202–12.

28. Ibid., 323–26.

Works Cited

Adams, James Truslow. *History of the Town of Southampton*. Bridgehampton, N.Y.: Hampton Press, 1918.

Adams, Sherman W., and Henry R. Stiles. *The History of Ancient Wethersfield*. 2 vols., 1904. Fac. ed. Somersworth: New Hampshire Publishing, 1974.

Allen, David Grayson. *In English Ways: The Movement of Societies and the Transferal of English Local Law and Custom to Massachusetts Bay in the Seventeenth Century*. New York: W.W. Norton, 1982.

Ancestry.com. *Through the Looking Glass: Mayflower Families*. http://www.mayflowerfamilies.com Accessed Oct. 4, 2004

Anderson, Virginia DeJohn. *New England Generation: the Great Migration and the Formation of Society and Culture in the Seventeenth Century*. Cambridge, UK: Cambridge University Press, 1991.

Andrews, Charles M., and Albert C. Bates. *The Charter of Connecticut, 1662*. Published for the Connecticut Tercenteneary Commission. New Haven: Yale University Press, 1933.

Arthur, William. *An Etymological Dictionary of Family and Christian Names*. New York: Blakeman, 1857.

Baird, Charles W. *History of Rye, Westchester County, New York, 1660–1870, Including Harrison and the White Plains Till 1788*. New York: Anson Randolph, 1871.

Bakeless, John. *America as Seen by its First Explorers*. Rpt. of *The Eyes of Discovery*, 1950. New York: Dover Publications, 1961.

Banks, Charles E. *The Planters of the Commonwealth: A Study of the Emigrants and Emigration in Colonial Times*. 1930. Rep. Baltimore: Genealogical Pub., 1975.

———. *Topographical Dictionary of 2885 English Emigrants to New England, 1620–1650*. Rep. Baltimore: Southern Book, 1957.

Barker, Ruth Fournier. *Quogue Through the Centuries: a Brief Historical Sketch Describing the Development of the Village of Quogue, Long Island, New York, During the Past Three Hundred Years*. Long Island: Weisberg, 1955.

Belcher, Jonathan. *The Belcher House*. N.p., 198? Available through library at Family History Center, Church of Jesus Christ of Latter-Day Saints, Salt Lake City, Utah.

Berry, William. *County Genealogies: Pedigrees of the Families in the County of Hants: Collected from Heraldic Visitations, 1634*. London: Sherwood/Gilbert/Piper, 1833.

Brown, Richard D., and Jack Tager. *Massachusetts, a Concise History*. Amherst Mass.: University Mass. Press, 2000.

Burke, Bernard. *Burke's Genealogical and Heraldic History of Landed Gentry*. Eighteenth edition. London: Burke's Peerage, 1965.

Burrows, Edwin G., and Mike Wallace. *Gotham: a History of New York City to 1898*. New York: Oxford University Press, 1999.

Butterworth, Edwin. *History of Oldham*. n.p.: c. 1845.

Caffrey, Kate. *The Mayflower*. New York: Stein & Day, 1974.

Calder, Isabel MacBeath. *The New Haven Colony*, 1934. Rep. New Haven: Yale University Press, 1970.

Christoph, Peter R., and Florence R. Christoph, eds. *The Andros Papers, 1679–1680: Files Of the Provincial Secretary of New York During the Administration of Governor Edmund Andros, 1674–1680*. Charles T. Gehring, Trans. Syracuse: Syracuse University Press, 1991.

Clayton, W. Woodford, ed. *History of Union and Middlesex Counties, New Jersey, with Biographical Sketches of Many of Their Pioneers and Prominent Men*. Philadelphia: Everts & Peck, 1882.

Combes, George. *Nassau County Historical Journal*. Vols. 17, 18, 21. Garden City N.Y.: Nassau County Historical Soc.

Connolly, James. "Whale Industry in New Jersey." *Proceedings of the New Jersey Historical Society*, New Series, Vol. 13, 1928.

Corwin, Charles E. *Manual of the Reformed Church in America, 1618–1922*. 5th ed., rev., New York: Board of Publications & Bible-School Work, Reformed Church of America, 1922.

Cressy, David. *Coming Over: Migration and Communication Between England and New England in the Seventeenth Century*. Cambridge, Eng.: Cambridge University Press, 1987.

Cunningham, John T. *The East of Jersey: A History of the General Board of Proprietors of the Eastern Division of New Jersey*. Newark: N.J. Historical Soc., 1992.

Danckaerts, Jasper. *Journal of a Voyage to New York*. Trans. Henry C. Murphy, 1867. Readex Microprint of original. Salt Lake City: LDS Church, 1996.

Denton, Daniel. *A Brief Description of New-York Formerly Called New-Netherland, With Places Thereunto Adjoyning*. London: 1670. Rep, Seattle: Westvaco, 1973.

Denton, George, ed. "Denton Family Genealogy." *Denton Dispatch Newsletter*, Jan. 1986, Vol. 1, no. 1. Fiche. Salt Lake City: Genealogical Soc. Of Utah. 1992.

Doyle, J. A. *The Middle Colonies*. 1907. Rep. Bowie, Md.: Heritage, 1998.

Dutton, Ralph. *Hampshire*. London: Batsford, 1970.

Elizabethtown Book B: Narrative of the Records of the Original Surveys of East New Jersey, Signed by all Parties in Interest, 1729, to Replace the Original Records Destroyed at that Time. Copied by the Princeton University Library, Princeton: 1965.

Federal Writers' Project. *Stories of New Jersey*. U. S. Works Progress Administration for the State of New Jersey. New York: M. Barrows, 1938.

Finckenor, George A. *Sag Harbor History*. Sag Harbor N.Y.: Sag Harbor Pub., 1977.

Flick, Alexander, ed. *History of the State of New York: Under Duke and King*. Vol. 2. Port Washington, N.Y.: Friedman, 1962.

Follet, Ken. *The Pillars of the Earth*. New York: Morrow, 1989.

Freiber, Malcolm, ed. *Winthrop Papers*. Vol. 6: 1650–1654. Boston: Massachusetts Historical Society, 1992.

Gardner, Charles C. *Collection of New Jersey Families, 1600–1900: Family Records Taken from Civil, Court, Land and Probate Records*. Microfilm of handwritten notes, New Brunswick, N.J.: Rutgers University Press, 1970.

Gordon, W. Seton. *New York Evening Post*, April 5, 1913.

Halsey, Abigail Fithian. *In Old Southampton*. New York: Columbia University Press, 1940.

Hanks, Patricia, and Flavia Hodges. *A Dictionary of Surnames*. Oxford: Oxford University Press, 1988.

Harrison, Henry. *Surnames of the United Kingdom*. London:1958.

Hatfield, Edwin F. *History of Elizabeth, New Jersey, Including the Early History of Union County*. 1868. Rep. Salem, Mass.: Higginson, 2004.

Heaton, Vernon. *The Mayflower*. New York: Mayflower Books, 1980.

Hedges, Henry, William Pelletreau, and Edward Foster, eds. "The First Book of Records of the Town of Southampton With Other Ancient Documents of Historic Value." Vols. 1–3. 1874. CD-ROM, *Genealogy and History of the Town of Southampton, New York*. Coram, N.Y.: GenealogyCDs.com, 2003. http://genalogycds.com

Herbert, Christopher. *The English: A Social History 1066–1945*. New York: Norton, 1987.

Hewitson, Anthony. *History (From A. D. 705 to 1883) of Preston in the County of Lancashire*. Preston, Lancashire, Eng.: Chronicle, 1883.

Hinman, R. R. *Index to the First Puritan Settlers of the Colony of Connecticut*. Rep. Conroe, Tex.: n.p., 1992.

History of Antiquities of the County of Dorset. London: n.p., 1868.

Hitching, F. K., and S. Hitching. *References to English Surnames in 1601 and 1602*. London: Walton-on-Thames, 1910.

Hoadley, Charles J., ed. *Records of the Colony and Plantation of New Haven from 1638 to 1649*. 1857. Microfilm, New Haven Research Publications, 197?.

Howell, George Rogers. *The Early History of Southampton L. I., New York*. 1887. CD-ROM. "New York Volume 1." New York: Heritage Books Archives, 1999.

Huntington, E. B. *History of Stamford Connecticut, 1641–1868, Including Darien Until 1820*. 1868. Rep. Harrison, N.Y.: Harbor Hill, 1979.

Hutchens, John. *The History of Antiquities of the County of Dorset*. "The Pedigree of Okeden." Vol. 3. Warcham, Dorset, Eng: 1868.

"International Genealogical Index." *Familysearch.org*. Salt Lake City: Church of Jesus Christ of Latter Day Saints. http://www.familysearch.org

Jacobus, Donald Lines, ed. *History and Genealogy of the Families of Old Fairfield*. Vol. 1. Fairfield: DAR, 1930.

Jameson, Franklin, ed. *Narratives of New Netherland, 1609–1664*. 1909. CD-ROM. "New York Volume 1." New York: Heritage Books Archives, 1999.

Johnson, Claudia Durst. *Daily Life in Colonial New England*. Westport Conn.: Greenwood, 2002.

Josselyn, John. *An Account of Two Voyages to New England Made During the Years 1638 and 1663*. London: 1675. Microfilm of 1865 rep. Washington: Library of Congress, 1988.

Klett, Joseph, ed. *Genealogies of New Jersey Families: From the Genealogical Magazine Of New Jersey*. 2 Vols. Baltimore: Genealogical Pub., 1996.

Lamb, Martha J., and Mrs. Burton Harrison. *History of the City of New York: Its Origin, Rise and Progress*. Vol. 1. New York: Barnes, 1877.

Lancashire Life Magazine. "Is Your Name Ogden?" Mar. 1984. 3 Tustin Ct., Port Way, Preston, Co. Lancashire, Eng.

Langford, Thomas, ed. *English-America: The Voyages, Vessels, People & Places*. http://www.english-america.com/ships/index.html#top

Leaming, Aaron, and Jacob Spicer. *The Grants, Concessions and Original Constitutions of the Province of New-Jersey: the Acts Passed During the Proprietors' Governments, and Other Material Transactions Before the Surrender Thereof to Queen Anne*. Philadelphia: Bradford, 18??.

Lewis, Frank. *Essex and Sugar: Historic and Other Connections*. London: Phillimore, 1976.

Maddocks, Melvin, and the Editors of Time-Life Books. *The Atlantic Crossing*. "The Seafarers." Chicago: Time-Life Books, 1981.

Majdalany, Jeanne. *The Early Settlement of Stamford, Connecticut: 1641–1700*. Rep., Bowie, Md.: Heritage Books, 1991.

Magie, William J. *New Light on Famous Controversy in the History of Elizabeth-town*. 1917. Microfilm. Ann Arbor: Michigan University Press, 1985.

Marshall, Bernice Schultz. *Colonial Hempstead*. Rep. Salem, Mass.: Higginson, 1997.

Mason, Oliver, ed. *Bartholomew's Gazatteer of Britian*. Edinburgh, Eng: n.p., 1977.

McConville, Brendan. *These Daring Disturbers of the Public Peace: The Struggle for Property and Power in Early New Jersey*. Ithica: Cornell University Press, 1999.

McKinley, Richard. *Surnames of Lancashire*. London: Leopard's Head, 1981.

Mead, Spencer P. *Ye Historie of Ye Town of Greenwich, County of Fairfield and State of Connecticut*. New York: Knickerbocker, 1911.

Mowrer, Lillian T. *The Indomitable John Scott, Citizen of Long Island, 1632–1704*. New York: Farrar, Straus & Cudahy, 1960.

Murray, Nicholas. *Notes, Historical and Biographical, Concerning Elizabeth-*

town, Its Eminent Men, Churches and Ministers. Elizabeth, N.J.: E. Sanderson, 1844.

New Jersey Historical Records Survey. "Historical Sketches of the Presbytery of Elizabeth." *Inventory of the Church Archives of New Jersey Presbyterians.* U. S. Works Project Administration, New Jersey State Planning Board, 1940. Fiche of original, from typewritten copy. Sanford, N.C.: Microfilming Corp., 1983.

Newsday.com. "Long Island, Our Story," Ch. 3, The Colonial Period. http://www.newsday.com/community/guide/lihistory Accessed 05/23/05.

Niemcewicz, Julian Ursyn. *Under Their Vine and Fig Tree; Travels Through America in 1797–1799, 1805, with some Further Account of Life in New Jersey.* Elizabeth: Grassman, 1965.

O'Callaghan, E. B., ed. *Documents Relative to the Colonial History of the State of New York; Procured in Holland, England and France.* Vol. 1. Albany: Weed, Parsons, 1856.

———. *History of New Netherland, or New York Under the Dutch.* New York: D. Appleton, 1846.

Ogden, Charles Burr. *The Quaker Ogdens in America: David Ogden of Ye Goode Ship "Welcome" and his Descendants, 1682–1897.* Philadelphia: Lippincott, 1898.

Ogden, Frank Barber. *Descendents of John Ogden, Pedigree Chart.* 1890. Rep. on microfilm, Genealogical Society of Utah, 1991. Available at the Family History Center, Salt Lake City.

Ogden, Henry, ed. *Ogden Newsletter.* Vol. 1, no. 1, Vol. 12, no. 4, Jan. 1979, Oct. 1990. Wichita Falls Tex.: by the editor.

Osgood, Herbert L. *The American Colonies in the Seventeenth Century.* 2 vols. New York: Columbia University Press, 1904.

Parsons, Henry, and William Smith Pelletreau, and Edward H. Foster. *Second Book of Records of the Town of Southampton, Long Island, New York, with Other Ancient Documents of Historic Value.* 1877. Facsim. ed., combined with the first book of records, 2001. Salt Lake City: Genealogical Society of Utah, 2003.

Pepys, Samuel, *Diary of Samuel Pepys,* rep. New York: Modern Library, 2001.

Pomfret, John E. *Colonial New Jersey, a History.* New York: Scribner, 1973.

Pomfret, John E. *The New Jersey Proprietors and Their Lands: 1664–1776.* Princeton: Van Nostrand, 1964.

Post, Richard H. *Notes on Quogue, 1659–1959.* The Quogue Tercentenary Committee. East Hampton, L. I., N.Y.: East Hampton Star, 1959.

Powell, Sumner Chilton. *Puritan Village: the Formation of a New England Town.* Middleton, Conn.: Wesleyan University Press, 1963.

Price, Mrs. Daniel. *Family Record or Genealogies of Robert Bond; Also the Descendents Of Jacob Price.* 1872. Fac. rep., Salem, Mass.: Higginson Books, 199?.

Priestley, Kay. Unpublished letters in possession of the author. Apr. 4, 2005 and May 23, 2005.

Reaney, Percy Hide. *Dictionary of British Surnames*. London: Routledge & Kegan, 1958.

Records of the Town of Newark New Jersey from its Settlement in 1666 to its Incorporation as a City in 1836. Newark: New Jersey Historical Soc., 1864.

Records of the Towns of North and South Hempstead, Long Island, N. Y. Jamaica, N.Y.: L. I. Farmers Print., 1896.

Remington, Gordon L. "Gustave Anjou—Forger of American Genealogies." *Swedish American Genealogist*, 12, Dec. 1992: 161–72.

Richardson, R. C., ed. *Town and Countryside in the English Revolution*. Manchester, Eng.: Manchester University Press, 1992.

Rotuli, Hundredorum, Special Collections (SP5) of the Hundred Rolls, Vol. 1. Located at British National Archives, Kew, Richmond, County of Surrey. 1812 & 1818.

Rubicam, Milton. "Pitfalls in Genealogy." *The Connecticut Nutmegger*, Dec. 1973, Vol. 6, No. 3, Connecticut Society of Genealogists, E. Hartford, Conn.

Salisbury, Edward. *Family Histories and Genealogies: A Series of Genealogical and Biographical Monographs on the Families of . . . Ogden . . . Bond . . . Others*. Vol. 2. Private Printing, 1892.

Scholastic Publishing. "The First Thanksgiving: Voyage on the Mayflower." http://teacher.scholastic.com/thanksgiving/mayflower

Scot, George. "The Model of the Government of the Province of East New Jersey in America." 1685. Rep., published as an Appendix in Whitehead, *East Jersey Under the Proprietary Governments*. New York: N.J. Hist. Soc., 1845.

Shallcross, Charles. Letter in author's possession from Elizabeth N.J. city historian, Apr. 26, 2005.

Sherwood, Herbert F. *The Story of Stamford*. Sectional History Series. New York: States History Co., 1930.

Shorto, Russell. *The Island at the Center of the World: The Epic Story of Dutch Manhattan & the Forgotten Colony that Shaped America*. New York: Doubleday, 2004.

——— "Virtual Tour of New Netherland: Long Island, Heemstead." *New Netherland Project*. Charles Gehring, ed. http://www.nnp.org/newvtour/regions/LongIsland/Hempstead.html (accessed Nov. 28, 2004).

Smith, Elsdon C. *American Surnames*. Baltimore: Genealogical Publishing, 1986.

Smith, Frank. *The Lives and Times of our English Ancestors*. Logan, Utah: Everton, 1980.

Smith, John. *A Description of New England, or, Observations and Discoveries of Captain John Smith in the North of America in the Year of our Lord 1614: with the Success of Six Ships that Went the Next Year,1615, and the Accidents that Befell Him Among the French Men of Warre*. 1616. Microfilm Rep. Boston: W. Veazie, 1865.

Smith, Samuel. *The History of the Colony of Nova-Caesaea, or New Jersey*. 1720. Rep. New York: Arno, 1972.

Stamford Town Meeting Records, Books 1 and 2, 1630–1806. Transcribed from original, 1886. Connecticut State Library, Hartford, Microfilm reel no. 4244.

Starbuck, Alexander. *History of American Whale Fishery from its Inception to the Year 1876.* 1878. Repub. As part of "Plough Boy Anthology." Denver: University of Denver. http://du.edu/~ttyler/ploughboy /starbuck.htm#sectionb

Stokes, I. N. Phelps. *The Icongraphy of Manhattan Island 1498–1909.* Vol. I. New York: Arno Press, 1967.

Taylor, Alan. *American Colonies.* New York: Viking Penguin, 2001.

Thayer, Theodore. *As We Were: The Story of Old Elizabethtown.* Elizabeth, N.J.: Grassman Publishing, 1964.

Thompson, Benjamim F. *History of Long Island from its Discovery and Settlement to the Present Time.* Vol. 3. New York: Dodd, 1918.

Town of Stamford Town Records, Vol. I, 1630–1723 (original book, in the Stamford Town Clerk's office).

Towne, Robert D. *Stamford Grand Lists: Taxation in Stamford, CT from 1641 to the Code of 1821.* Research Library, Record Group RG-13. Stamford, Conn.: Stamford Historical Society, 1994.

Trumbull, J. Hammond, ed. *The Public Records of the Colony of Connecticut Prior to the Union with New Haven Colony, May, 1665.* Vol 1 & 2. Hartford: Brown & Parsons, 1850.

University of California, Berkeley, Sims School of Information Management and Systems. http://www.sims.berkeley.edu/academics/courses/is182/s01/ first0.html

Van der Donck, Adriaen. *Description of New Netherlands.* 1655. Trans. Jeremiah Johnson. Rep. Syracuse, N.Y.: Syracuse University Press, 1968.

Vaughan, Alden T. *New England Frontier: Puritans and Indians, 1620–1675.* Boston: Little, Brown, 1965.

Walton, Alfred Grant. *Stamford Historical Sketches.* Stamford, Conn.: Cunningham, 1922.

Walton, John K. *Lancashire: A Social History, 1558–1939.* Manchester, Eng.: Manchester University Press, 1987.

Warner, Charles Dudley. "Captain John Smith, a Fiction." Chapter 15, http:// www.readbooksonline.net/read/194/6246 (accessed Jan. 4, 2005).

Weinstein, Allen, and David Rubel. *The Story of America: Freedom and Crisis from Settlement to Superpower.* New York: D.K. Publishing, 2002.

Wertenbaker, Thomas Jefferson. *The Founding of American Civilization: The Middle Colonies.* New York: Cooper Square, 1963.

Wheeler, William Ogden. *The Ogden Family in America, Elizabethtown Branch, and Their English Ancestry: John Ogden, the Pilgrim and His Descendants 1640–1906, Their History, Biography & Genealogy.* Philadelphia: Lippincott, 1907. Facsim. ed., Pawtucket, R.I.: Quintin Publications, 2003.

Wheeler, William Ogden, and Edmund D. Halsey, *Inscriptions on Tombstones & Monuments in the Burying Grounds of the First Presbyterian Church & St. John's Church at Elizabeth, New Jersey, 1664–1892.* 1892. Rep. Family Line Publishers, 1997.

Whitehead, William A., *East Jersey Under the Proprietary Governments: A narrative of Events Connected with the Settlement and Progress of the Province until the Surrender of the Government to the Crown in 1702.* New York: N.J. Hist. Soc., 1846.

Whitehead, William, ed. *New Jersey Archives: Documents Relating to the Colonial History of the State of New Jersey.* Vol. 1, 1631–1687. Newark, N.J.: Daily Journal, 1880.

Wilson, Lisa. *Ye Heart of a Man: the Domestic Life of Men in Colonial New England.* New Haven, Yale University Press, 1999.

Winthrop, John. *The Journal of John Winthrop, 1630–1649.* James Savage and Laetitia Yeandle, eds. Cambridge: Belknap Press, 1996.

——— *Winthrop Journal: History of New England, 1630–1649.* Vol. 2. James Kendall Hosmer, ed. New York: Barnes & Noble, 1953.

Wood, Silas. *A Sketch of the First Settlement of the Several Towns on Long Island, With Their Political Condition, to the End of the American Revolution.* 1828. Microfilm, Genealogical Society of Utah, 1990.

Index

About the Author

Jack Harpster is a 10th-generation descendant of John Odgen, the Pilgrim. Jack was born in Burlington, Vermont, raised in Memphis, Tennessee, and earned his degree in journalism from the University of Wisconsin. He spent the next forty-two years on the business side of the newspaper industry, first in Torrance, California, and later in Las Vegas, Nevada. Now retired in Reno, Nevada he spends his time researching and writing history and biography books on important but little known people and institutions. Harpster currently has eight books published, with a ninth book coming out in mid- to late-2016.

Harpster's third book, a biography on his first cousin four times removed, William B. Ogden, was published in 2009 by Southern Illinois University Press. It is the biography of another Ogden family member, a very influential man in 19th century American history, but today all but forgotten. Ogden was one of Chicago's founders, its first mayor, one of the nation's earliest railroad builders, and a major force in the country's western expansion.

Harpster can be reached at www.JackHarpster.com

www.ingramcontent.com/pod-product-compliance
Lightning Source LLC
Chambersburg PA
CBHW021357090426
42742CB00009B/888